The Book of Kin

Anastasia herself has stated that this book consists of words and phrases in combinations *which have a beneficial effect on the reader.* This has been attested by the letters received to date from tens of thousands of readers all over the world.

If you wish to gain as full an appreciation as possible of the ideas, thoughts and images set forth here, as well as experience the benefits that come with this appreciation, we recommend you find a quiet place for your reading where there is the least possible interference from artificial noises (motor traffic, radio, TV, household appliances etc.). *Natural sounds,* on the other hand — the singing of birds, for example, or the patter of rain, or the rustle of leaves on nearby trees — may be a welcome accompaniment to the reading process.

Disclaimer: The USA Food and Drug Administration has not evaluated any of the information and advice contained in this book. This book is for informational purposes only and is not provided or intended to diagnose, treat, prevent or cure any disease, nor does the Publisher make any claim as to the accuracy or appropriateness of any particular course of action described.

Accounts, views and opinions expressed by the author in this book do not necessarily reflect the views of the Publisher, Editor or Translator.

Ringing Cedars Press is not affiliated with, does not endorse, and assumes no responsibility for any individuals, entities or groups who claim to be manufacturing or marketing products or services referred to in this book, or who otherwise claim to be acting in accordance with any of the information or philosophies set forth herein.

THE RINGING CEDARS SERIES • BOOK SIX

6

The Book of Kin

Vladimir Megré

Translated from the Russian by **John Woodsworth**
Edited by **Dr Leonid Sharashkin**

KAHULUI • HAWAII • USA

Cover design by Bill Greaves, Concept West

Printed on 100% post-consumer recycled paper

Publisher's Cataloging-In-Publication Data

Megre, V. (Vladimir), 1950-
[Rodova´i`a kniga. English.]
The book of kin / Vladimir Megré ; translated from the Russian by John Woodsworth ; edited by Leonid Sharashkin. — 2nd ed., rev.

p. ; cm. — (The ringing cedars series ; bk. 6)

ISBN: 978-0-9801812-5-8

1. Spirituality. 2. Nature—Religious aspects. 3. Human ecology. I. Woodsworth, John, 1944- II. Sharashkin, Leonid. III. Title. IV. Title: Rodova´i`a kniga. English. V. Series: Megre, V. (Vladimir), 1950- Ringing cedars series, bk. 6.

GF80 .M44 2008f
304.2 2008923351

Contents

Chapter One

Who raises our children?

There was a large sign on the office door of the private clinic giving the M.D.'s full name, along with a title indicating an advanced academic degree, and identifying him as a specialist in child psychology. He had been recommended to me as one of the best scientific minds on the subject of parent-child relationships. I had put my name down for his last appointment of the day, as I didn't want to limit the length of our consultation — if it proved useful, I was prepared to pay him extra to continue as I was in such desperate need of advice. I opened the door and walked in.

Behind the desk was seated a gentleman of retirement age with a drawn face, listlessly stuffing sheets of scribbled paper into a file. After inviting me to take a seat, the doctor placed a clean sheet of paper before him and said:

"So? How can I help you?"

To avoid getting into a long, extended story about everything that had happened after meeting with Anastasia, I did my best to put the essence of my question in a nutshell:

"Alexander Sergeevich,[1] I need to learn how to get along with my child — my son — who will soon be five years old."

"So, you believe you have lost contact with your son?" the psychologist asked blandly and dispiritedly.

"There has been practically no meaningful contact as such to date. The way it's turned out, since his birth I've hardly

[1] *Alexander Sergeevich* — first name and patronymic, the usual polite form of address in Russian among adults.

had any communication with him at all. I did see him one time while he was still an infant, but after that... I haven't talked with him even once. So, I have to say, he's started learning about life without me. We've been living quite apart from each other.

"But now I'm going to have a chance to meet with my five-year-old son and actually talk with him. Maybe there are some ways to help make him favourably disposed toward me? Like when a man marries a woman who already has a child, and wants to get along with him, to become his father and friend."

"There are ways, certainly," Alexander Sergeevich observed, "but none which are guaranteed to be effective in all cases. There's so much in parent-child relationships that depends on individual nature and character."

"I realise that, but still, I'd like to become familiar with whatever specific hints you may have."

"Specific... Hmm... When you make your appearance in the family — and you have to remember that even a single mother with a child constitutes a family — try to interfere as little as possible with the way of life they have already established. It will take some time before you become anything beyond an outsider to your son, and that's something you've got to accept. At the beginning stages you will have to spend some time sizing up the whole situation AND... give them a chance to size *you* up.

"You could try tying in your appearance with the fulfilment of some dream or desire the child has had but which has been impossible to fulfil. You could find out from his mother some kind of toy he's had his eye on which she hasn't been able to buy for him. But don't buy it yourself in advance. Start talking with him about your own childhood and the toys you had, and tell him how you dreamt of getting this one in particular. If he picks up on that and mentions about how he wants the same thing, then you can suggest the two of you go to the store together and get it. What's important here is the actual conversational process, and the outing itself. The boy should get to the point of trusting you with his dream, allowing you to have a hand in making it come true."

"The toy example really won't work in my case. My son has never seen store-bought toys."

"Strange... So, that won't work, eh?... Well, my friend, you've got to be frank with me. If you want to hear some useful advice, then you'll have to give more details about your relationship with your child's mother. Who is she? Where does she work? Where does she live? What's her family's financial situation? What do you think led to the break-up?"

It was dawning on me, finally. If I wanted to get more specific advice out of the psychologist, I would have to go into my relations with Anastasia, which I still hadn't fully fathomed myself, so how was I going to explain them to a psychologist?

Without mentioning her name, I began describing the situation as follows:

"She lives in a very remote area, in Siberia. I happened to make her acquaintance while I was on a trade expedition. I've been doing business there since the beginning of *perestroika* — on a ship which took me to some isolated settlements along the Ob River, selling various manufactured goods and bringing back fish, furs and wild mushrooms, berries and nuts."

"I see. So, like Paratov,[2] this tradesman makes everyone jealous with his romantic exploits along a Siberian river?"

"No romance, just work. Haven't you heard? Entrepreneurs work like dogs!"

[2]*Sergei Paratov* — a cynical, hard-nosed character in Alexander Ostrovsky's drama *The dowerless bride* (*Bespridannitsa*), who betrays the affections of a poor girl named Larissa in a small town on the Volga River.

"Well, let's say they do, but... entrepreneurs also find time to have fun, do they not?"

"Believe me, with this woman it wasn't a question of having fun at all. I wanted to have a child by her. I'd been wanting a son for a long time, but then I seemed to forget about that particular dream. The years went by... But as soon as I saw her — how wholesome, young and beautiful she was... It seems just about every woman today is sick or sickly, but she — well, she was simply beaming with energy, the picture of health! So I figured her child would turn out healthy and good-looking too.

"She bore me a son. I went to see them when he was still quite little, before he could walk or talk. I held him in my arms. But since then I've had no contact with him."

"And why is that?"

How on earth was I to explain to this gentleman during our brief conversation everything that it had taken me several books to describe? How could I tell him that Anastasia had refused to leave her taiga glade and move with our son into town, while I on the other hand was not adapted to life in the taiga? Or that she was the one who would not let me even communicate with him, let alone give him traditional toys?

Every summer I had gone back to Siberia, to the very glade where Anastasia and my son made their home, but I never managed to see my son again after that one time. Each time he would be somewhere else — with her grandfather and great-grandfather, who lived not far away, in the wilds of the endless Siberian forest. Anastasia refused to take me to visit them, and further insisted each time that I should first prepare myself for conversation with my son.

In attempting to find out more about child-raising, I would put a single question to many of my friends and acquaintances, which was invariably greeted with misunderstanding and astonishment, even though it was quite a simple question:

"Have you ever had a serious conversation with your child?"

It would always turn out that the topics of conversation were pretty much the same: "Come to the table... Time for bed... Stop fooling around... Pick up your toys... Got your homework done?..."

The child gets older, goes to school, but talking about the meaning of life, Man's destiny or even just about what his future path in life will be — well, most of them don't have time for that, or even think it anything worth discussing. Maybe they feel the time isn't right yet, that they'll still have a chance to... But they never do. The child grows up...

But if we ourselves never even try having a serious conversation with our children, who then is raising them?

Why has Anastasia not allowed me to communicate with my very own son all these years? I have no idea what she's been afraid of or trying to ward off.

Anyway, the day came when she all at once asked me whether I felt I was ready to meet and talk with my son. I replied that I did want to meet with him, but I still couldn't quite bring myself to say I was 'ready'.

All these years I had been reading anything I could lay my hands on concerning parent-child relationships. I kept writing my books, giving talks at conferences in various countries, but wrote and said almost nothing about the most important thing that interested me during all this time — the raising of children and how older generations should interact with them.

I kept thinking about all the different words of advice I had encountered in child-raising literature, but each time I would find myself coming back to what Anastasia said: "*Raising children means also raising yourself.*"[3] It took me a long time to comprehend the meaning of that saying, but I finally managed to reach a definite conclusion:

Our children are not raised by parental admonition, nor by kindergartens, schools and colleges. Our children are raised by the way people live — the way we ourselves live and the way society in general lives. And no matter what kids hear from their parents or teachers in school or any other institution of learning, no matter what clever systems of education are adopted, children will follow the lifestyle practised by the majority of people around them.

That means that the raising of children depends entirely on your own understanding of the world, on how you live your own life, how your parents live and how society in general lives. A sick and unhappy society can only give birth to sick and unhappy children.

"If you don't tell me in detail about your relationship with the mother of your son, I'll have a hard time finding any real advice to give you!" said the psychologist, interrupting a rather lengthy pause.

"That's a rather long story," I mused. "To put it briefly, the way things turned out, I've had no communication with my son for several years, and that's all there is to it."

"Okay, then tell me, in all these years have you given any financial support to your child's mother? I think, for an entrepreneur, financial support would be the simplest way to show your interest in the family."

"No, I haven't. She believes she is fully provided for."

"So, she's a wealthy woman, then?"

"Let's just say she has everything she needs."

Alexander Sergeevich rose sharply from behind his desk and blurted out:

[3]See Book 4, Chapter 30: "In His image and likeness".

"She lives in the Siberian taiga. She lives the life of a recluse. Her name is Anastasia, your son's name is Volodya,[4] and you are Vladimir Nikolaevich Megré. I recognise you. I've read your books — more than once, in fact."

"Yes..."

Alexander Sergeevich started pacing the room excitedly. Then he began talking again:

"Well, well, well! I was right, eh? I guessed it! So, would you please answer me one thing. I need an answer! It's very important to me. To science... But no, don't answer. I'll say it myself. I'm beginning to understand... I'm sure that all these years since you first met Anastasia you've been doing intensive studies in psychology and philosophy. You've been constantly thinking about child-raising. Am I right?"

"Yes."

"But the conclusions you reached after reading these 'scholarly' books and articles did not satisfy you. And so you started looking for answers within yourself, or in other words, you started reflecting on the rising generation, on child-raising?"

"More or less. But most of all about my son."

"That's an inseparable part of it. You came to see me in desperation, and without too much hope for answers to the questions you've come up with. And if you don't get them from me, you'll go on searching on your own."

"Probably."

"So... Amazing! I'm going to mention the name of someone who is immeasurably stronger and wiser than me in all this."

"Who is that person and how can I arrange an appointment?"

"That person is none other than your Anastasia, Vladimir Nikolaevich!"

[4] *Volodya* — an endearing form of the name *Vladimir.*

"Anastasia? But she's hardly said anything about child-raising lately. And she's the one who wouldn't let me communicate with my son."

"That's just it — she's the one. And up to this moment I haven't been able to find any logical explanation for this decision on her part. Such strange behaviour! A loving woman suddenly announces to the father-to-be that he shouldn't communicate with his own son. A most irregular situation — never come across it before. But the result!... The result is simply amazing! You see, she's succeeded in making you... No, that word isn't applicable here. Anastasia's succeeded in attracting... And who? If you will pardon me, she's made a not-very-well-educated entrepreneur get interested in psychology, philosophy and the problems of child-raising. You've been thinking about that through the years — I can tell as much just by the simple fact that you came to see me. She's been raising your son all these years by herself, but at the same time she's also been educating you! She's been preparing you for this meeting of father and son."

"Yes, she actually has been raising our son alone. As for educating me, I don't think so. We don't get together all that often. And only for a brief time."

"But that information she gives you, even during those 'brief' moments, as you say, you're still having to sort out even today. The information is truly amazing. You, Vladimir Nikolaevich, say that Anastasia rarely talks about child-raising, but that isn't so."

Alexander Sergeevich quickly went over to his desk and pulled a thick grey notebook out of one of the drawers. Tenderly stroking it in his hands, he continued:

"I took all Anastasia's sayings in your books about the birth and raising of children and wrote them out in order, leaving out the details of the plot. Maybe, though, it wasn't right to take these quotations out of context. After all, there's no doubt the plot makes them a lot easier to comprehend.

"These sayings of Anastasia's are fraught with great meaning — a great philosophical meaning, I would say, and wisdom from an ancient culture. I'm inclined to suppose — and I'm not alone here — that these principles are set forth in some kind of ancient book, maybe millions of years old. What Anastasia says has the kind of depth to it and the accuracy of expression that one associates with what I think are the most important thoughts set forth in ancient manuscripts, as well as modern scholarly works.

"After I had written out everything I could find concerning the birth and raising of children, what I had before me amounted to a treatise with no equal anywhere in the world. I am sure it will be used as the basis for a great number of dissertations and awardings of academic degrees, along with amazing discoveries. But even more importantly, it will give rise to a new race on the Earth known as *Man*!"

"But Man[5] already exists right now."

"I think, when people look back from the future, the fact of Man's existence may be in some doubt."

"How can that be? You and I exist. How can our existence ever be placed in doubt?"

"Our bodies exist, and we call them *people*. But in the future the content, or mental makeup of the human individual will be vastly different from yours and mine today, and so to underline the difference, the name will have to be changed. Possibly today's people will be called 'Such-and-such-a-period Man', or else they'll find a new name for those who are born in the future."

[5]*Man* — Throughout the Ringing Cedars Series, the word *Man* with a capital *M* is used to refer to a human being of either gender. For details on the word's usage and the important distinction between *Man* and *human being* please see the Translator's Preface to Book 1.

"Is it really that bad?"

"It is — no question about it. You've gone and read a lot of books about child-raising — books written by scholars. Now tell me, at what point does child-raising begin?"

"Some writers think it should begin when the child's a year old."

"Precisely. At best, starting at a year old. But Anastasia showed how Man is formed even before... I know you're thinking 'in the mother's womb'. But she showed that parents can form their future offspring even before the sperm and the egg get together. And this is explainable scientifically. Anastasia stands head and shoulders above all other psychologists who exist or have ever existed on the Earth. Her sayings are potent, they cover all stages of the development and the raising of the child — the pre-conceptual, the conceptual, the fœtal stage and so forth.

"She covers topics which neither wise men of the past nor contemporary scholars have been able to grasp hold of. She has specifically highlighted what is absolutely essential to bearing and raising a fully fledged Man."

"But that's not something *I* remember. I never wrote about developmental stages."

"The books you wrote just documented the events you witnessed. Anastasia realised that that is just how you would be writing. Her next move was that she herself began giving specific form to these events, effectively clothing a great scientific work in an entertaining narrative form. She created your book with her very life, using it to bring invaluable knowledge to people.

"Most readers feel this intuitively. Many are ecstatic over the books, but they are unable to fully make sense of the cause of their excitement. They are absorbing information they never knew about before, on a subconscious level. But it can be taken in consciously too. I'll prove it to you.

"Look, here before you is a transcript of Anastasia's sayings about the birth of a Man. My colleague and I have gone over them very carefully and noted down our comments. He is a sexopathologist with a post-graduate degree in medicine, and has the office next to mine. We conducted experiments and analysed the situation."

Alexander Sergeevich opened his notebook and began speaking excitedly, almost exultantly:

"So, we have the beginning... The *pre-conceptual stage*. This is hardly ever looked upon as an aspect of child-raising, either in the present time or in the past as we know it. But it is quite clear today that at some point on the Earth, or somewhere in the limitless expanses of the Universe, there existed or still exists a culture in which the relationships between men and women were immeasurably more perfected than our own. And that the pre-conceptual stage was an important component — perhaps the basic component — in the upbringing of Man.

"Following the cultural traditions of a civilisation hitherto unknown to us, Anastasia carries out specific preparatory steps before conceiving a child. First, she dulls your sexual appetite. This is quite evident to me as a psychologist from the events described in your first book. Let me remind you of the order in which these events take place.

"During a rest stop on your trek through the taiga, you drink some cognac and have a bite to eat, but Anastasia does not respond to your offer of food and alcohol. She takes off her outer clothing and lies down on the grass. You are awed by her natural beauty, and you are aroused by a natural desire to possess this beautiful womanly body. Driven by a sexual impulse, you attempt to penetrate her, you touch her body and then... you lose consciousness.

"We shan't go into the details of just how she manages to make you lose consciousness. The important thing as that as a result of this you no longer look upon Anastasia as a sexual object. And you yourself mention this — I wrote down your words: 'I had no thought of wanting to possess her.'"[6]

"Yes. You're right — after the incident at the rest stop I had no further sexual desires in regard to Anastasia."

"Now to the *second event — conception* — you tell about the proper way to conceive a child.

"Night-time in a cosy dug-out, with the fragrance of sweet grass and flowers. But you are not accustomed to spending the night alone in the taiga, and you ask Anastasia to lie down beside you. You already realise that if she is with you nothing bad will happen. She lies down beside you.

"So it turns out that in this intimate situation you find this most beautiful young womanly body right next to yours — a body which has the added attraction of being radiant with health. Unlike most women's bodies you have known before, this one actually luxuriates in health. You sense the fragrance of Anastasia's breath, yet at the same time you feel no sexual inclination. It has been expelled from you. The space it occupied has been cleansed to make way for another mental state — an aspiration to ensure the continuation of the family line. You are thinking about a son! A son that doesn't yet exist. This is what you wrote in your book:

"'It would be good if my son could be borne by Anastasia! She is so healthy. That means my son will be healthy and good-looking too.'[7]

"You involuntarily place your hand on Anastasia's breast and start caressing it, but not with the same caresses as before. This time they are not sexual. It is as though you are caressing your son. Then you write about the touch of the lips, about Anastasia's gentle breathing, and then — a complete

[6]Quoted from Book 1, Chapter 9: "Who lights a new star?".

[7]Quoted (with slight variations) from Book 1, Chapter 9.

lack of any kind of details. Then you jump to describing the following morning, your excellent mood, and the feeling that an extraordinary feat has been performed.

"I wouldn't be surprised if your publishers tried to persuade you to describe that night in greater detail, to increase the book's popularity."

"Yes, they actually did try to do this, several times."

"But still, you did not describe that night in any of the subsequent editions of your book — why?"

"Because—"

"Stop! Please, don't go on. I want to see if my own conclusions are correct. You did not describe the sexual details of that night because you simply didn't remember anything after touching Anastasia's lips."

"You're right, to this day I can't remember anything about it. Except for that unusual sensation the following morning."

"What I'm going to say to you now you may find incredible. On that marvellous night you spent with Anastasia, absolutely no sex took place."

"No sex? But what about my son? I saw my son with my own eyes."

"What you experienced that night was indeed physical intimacy. There was sperm involved — in fact, everything that accompanies the conception of children, but there was no sex. My colleagues and I kept going over and over what happened with you. Just like me, they too concluded that you did not have sex with Anastasia.

"You see, the word *sex* in our time implies the satisfaction of fleshly needs, the aspiration for the pleasure of fleshly gratification. But in the context of the events of that night in the taiga, that particular motivation was lacking — in other words, you were not aiming to achieve sexual satisfaction. This time your aim was quite different — namely, a child.

Consequently, even the name of that event must be different. It's not just a question of terminology here — we are talking about a fundamentally different way of giving birth to Man.

"I'll say it again: *this is a fundamentally different way of giving birth to Man.* This is not an abstract statement — it is easily provable by means of scientific comparisons. Judge for yourself: no psychologist or physiologist today would deny the influence of external mental factors on the formation of the fœtus in the mother's womb. Among other factors a major one (and frequently the dominant one) is the man's attitude toward the mother-to-be. Similarly, we cannot deny that a man's thoughts about a woman at the moment of their sexual intimacy has an unmistakable influence on the formation of the future individual. In one instance he is thinking of her as an object of sexual gratification. In the other he looks upon her as a co-creator. The result will naturally be different. It is possible that the child born under such circumstances will be just as strikingly different intellectually from contemporary Man as contemporary Man is different from the ape.

"Sex and the pleasure associated with it during the moment of co-creation is not an end in itself, but merely a means to an end. Other mental energies will govern the couple's bodies, and the child's psyche will be formed quite differently.

"Here is the first rule following from what I have said: a female desiring to bear a fully fledged Man and create a solid and happy family must be able to capture the moment at which the male wishes to join with her for the purpose of giving birth to a Man, cherishes the image of their child-to-be and desires its birth.

"Under these conditions the man and the woman achieve a mental state which allows them to obtain the highest possible satisfaction from their intimacy. And the child-to-be obtains a kind of energy which is absent in those who are born in the traditional manner — i.e., haphazardly."

"But how does the woman feel this moment? How is she to know about the man's thoughts? Thoughts, after all, are not something you can see."

"Caresses! That's how she can tell. The mental state is always expressing itself through outward signs. Joy is shown in smiles and laughter, sorrow in a telltale expression of the eyes, position of the body etc. In this particular case, I think, it is not too hard to distinguish purely sexual caresses from the way he would touch his future child. Only with this kind of touch a certain 'something' happens that Man alone, of all the creatures living on the Earth, can experience. Nobody will ever be able to describe or scientifically explain this 'something'. At the moment when it occurs any kind of analysis is impossible.

"As a psychologist, I can only assume that what is paramount in such an event is not the coming together of two physical bodies, but something immeasurably greater: the merging of two thoughts into one. More specifically: the merging of two complexes of feelings into one. The pleasure and bliss experienced through this are significantly superior to mere sexual gratification. Its continuity is not fleeting as with ordinary sex. The inexplicable pleasant feeling that it brings can last for months and even years. This is what makes a strong and loving family. This is what Anastasia is talking about.

"This also means that once the man has experienced it, he cannot bring himself to exchange the new sensation for mere sexual gratification. He will not be able to, or even desire to, betray his wife — his beloved. That is the moment that marks the beginning of the formation of the family. A happy family!

"There is a saying that 'marriages are made in heaven'. The saying is quite true in respect to this particular case. Judge for yourself. What is generally considered today to attest to a heavenly marriage? A scrap of paper issued by the Civil

Records Office, or all sorts of church rituals. Funny, isn't it? Funny, yet at the same time sad.

"Anastasia is quite right when she says that a marriage made in heaven can only be affirmed by the couple's extraordinarily splendid mental state, which leads to the birth of a new and fully fledged Man.

"And I might add that the majority of children born today are born out of wedlock... And now... Now I'd like to read to you some comments made by my colleague, the sexopathologist:

> *The mutual sexual relations between a man and a woman as described in the book* Anastasia, *bring out a whole new meaning of* sex. *All currently existing textbooks on the subject, beginning with those of Ancient India and Greece right up to our contemporary treatises, may be seen as naïve and ridiculous in comparison to the significance of what Anastasia has to say. All the research described in all known works on sex, both ancient and modern, is focused solely on discovering various body positions, caressing techniques and sexual aids. But people have different physiological and psychological abilities and capabilities.*
>
> *For any given individual there may be just a single most effective and acceptable position and just one particular sex aid that will match his character and temperament.*
>
> *One would be hard put to find anywhere in the world a specialist capable of pinpointing with any degree of accuracy the most appropriate technique (out of the thousands of possibilities) in the case of a particular individual.*
>
> *To carry out such a task the specialist would need to know the thousands of existing techniques with all their nuances, and study the physical and mental abilities of the individual in question, and that is patently impossible.*
>
> *Evidence that the questions raised in regard to men and women's sexual relations have not been solved by modern science may*

be seen in the ever-increasing loss of potency on the part of the majority of men and women in today's society. There is a growing number of sexually dissatisfied family couples. But this joyless picture can be changed.

Anastasia has shown that there exists in Nature some kind of mechanism, some kind of higher power capable of solving a seemingly insoluble problem in an instant. Through a couple's — a man and a woman's — specific mental state, this mechanism or power will help them find the conditions and techniques of sexual intercourse appropriate solely to them.

Undoubtedly, the pleasure experienced in this particular case will achieve the highest level attainable. It is quite possible that the man and woman who have experienced such satisfaction will maintain their conjugal fidelity for ever, quite independently of the dictates of laws and rituals.

"Conjugal fidelity! Conjugal infidelity. Betrayal."

Alexander Sergeevich got up from behind his desk and continued to talk while standing.

"Anastasia was the first to show the nature of this phenomenon. I remember by heart not only isolated phrases, but whole monologues. Listen to what she says:[8]

They try all sorts of tricks to persuade people that satisfaction is something you can easily obtain, thinking only of carnal desire. And at the same time they separate Man from truth. The poor deceived women who are ignorant of this spend their lives accepting nothing but suffering and searching for the grace they have lost. But they are searching for it in the wrong places. No woman can restrain a man from fornication if she allows herself to submit to him merely to satisfy his carnal needs.

[8]This and subsequent quotations (unless otherwise indicated) are taken from Book 1, Chapter 9: "Who lights a new star?".

"And again... I'll have it in a moment... Yes, here it is:

> *They will strive to possess body after body, or make paltry and fateful use of their own bodies, realising only intuitively that they are drifting farther and farther away from the true happiness of a true union!*

"Here is an absolutely accurate explanation of the cause of conjugal infidelity. I can also explain it as a psychologist. It's all quite logical: a man and a woman — the so-called husband and wife — engage in sex just for the sake of sex. When they intuitively feel they are not getting sufficient satisfaction, they turn to a specialist and read supplementary literature on the subject. They are advised to try various positions and ways of caressing each other — in other words, to engage in a search for greater satisfaction through switching sexual techniques.

"Note what I said — 'engage in a search'. They may not say this explicitly, but if they themselves, as Anastasia has correctly pointed out, have an intuition about the existence of a higher happiness, they will engage in a search. But... where are the limits of this search? Is it just limited to a change of positions? The logical next step is a change of bodies.

"'Aha!' society cries. 'That's conjugal betrayal!' But there's no betrayal going on here. There's no betrayal, because there is no married couple!

"A marriage dependent on a scrap of paper is not a marital union. It is nothing but a convention thought up by society.

"A marital union should be established by a man and a woman through their attainment of the highest mental state Anastasia describes. She not only talked about it, she showed how to achieve it. This is an entirely new culture in male-female relationships."

"Does that mean, Alexander Sergeevich, that you are recommending young people engage in intimate relations before a marriage is officially recognised?"

"Most people today are doing just that. Only we're ashamed to talk about it openly. But what I am proposing is to *refrain from engaging in sex just for the sake of sex, either before or after the marriage is registered.*

"We consider ourselves a free society. We have the possibility of freely engaging in debauchery. And oh, how we engage in it!

"Debauchery has become a whole industry. Look at the cinema and the endless stream of all kinds of pornography, look at prostitution or the rubberised dolls you can buy at sex-shops. What more evidence do you need?!

"In the face of this whole sexual orgy, which only attests to the failure of modern science to understand the nature and function of the mechanisms involved in the union of two people, Anastasia's words come as a discovery — literally a revelation!

"As a psychologist I have been able to appreciate the grandness of Anastasia's discovery. She has brought to light a whole new culture in male-female relationships.

"The primary role in them is taken on by the woman. Anastasia has succeeded in bringing you, too, to the understanding of this culture. She has been able to do this, using — intuitively, perhaps — the knowledge of some kind of ancient civilisation. But... we — or rather, my colleague — he has proved it in practice. He has proved that even a man can...

"He's a sexopathologist. He and I have worked together to analyse Anastasia's sayings. He was the first to talk about the new culture in relationships that has been unknown up to now. He was especially struck by this saying — you should remember it — she said:

...who — what individual — would want to come into the world as a result of carnal pleasures alone? We would all like to be created under a great impulsion of love, the aspiration to creation itself, and not simply come into the world as a result of someone's carnal pleasure.

But that is precisely how our children have come into the world — as the result of carnal pleasure. My wife and I wanted a child, so we had sex. I don't even know which day it was my wife conceived. It wasn't until after she became pregnant that we started thinking more specifically about the child. But Anastasia says that a particular mental state and aspiration is required right at the very moment preceding intimacy. Anyway, my colleague, no doubt, got more out of those sayings of hers than I. Or he felt more. He wanted to experience this mental state. He wanted them to have a child — a son.

"My colleague is already past forty, and his wife is two years younger than he. They have two children. He himself admitted that they have rarely had any sex these past few years. But he began talking with his wife about a child.

"At first she was quite surprised at his desire. She said it was too late for her to bear children. But her attitude toward her husband took a turn for the better. He gave her the book with Anastasia's sayings to read. And now the woman herself would start a conversation — no, not about her desire to have a child, but about how true the sayings in the book were.

"And then one night my colleague began caressing his wife — only not thinking about sex, but about their future son. He probably managed to do the same thing you did. The only difference is that you were led to that point by Anastasia, while he achieved it all on his own. Whether it just happened that way or not, it's hard to say, but he managed to achieve, in all probability, precisely the mental state you experienced. His wife responded with the same kind of caresses.

"These are not young people, and naturally they were not feeling the same strong sexual inclinations as in their youth. Their thoughts about their future child, no doubt, pushed any concerns about sexual techniques into the background.

"As a result... as a result, that 'something' happened. Neither my colleague nor his wife could remember any of the details of their intimacy. Just like you, they don't remember anything. But, as you did, they talk about the unforgettable, marvellous sensations they experienced the next morning. My colleague tells me that he has never felt anything like it in all his life, from intimacy either with his wife or with any other women — and, believe me, there were quite a few of those.

"His forty-year-old wife is now pregnant, in her seventh month. But that's not the main thing. The main thing is that his wife has fallen in love."

"With whom?"

"With her husband, my dear Vladimir Nikolaevich! Just imagine, here's this woman who used to be rather irritable and nagging, now coming to our clinic and waiting for her husband to finish work. She sits in the reception room and waits like a young girl newly in love. I have often caught the expression on her face out of the corner of my eye. It too has changed, and a barely noticeable hidden smile is now evident.

"I've known this family quite some time. About eight years. This plump, depressed woman has suddenly become ten years younger. And she is beautiful, in spite of her all-too-obvious pregnancy."

"What about your colleague's attitude toward his wife — has it changed too, or has it remained the same?"

"He's changed too. He's completely given up drinking, even though he didn't really have a serious problem with it before. He's stopped smoking. He and his wife have a new favourite pastime — painting."

"Painting? What do they paint?"

"They paint their future family domain, the kind Anastasia talks about. They want to get a piece of land and build on it — wrong word: not to build a house, but to lay the foundation for a future corner of Paradise for their children-to-be."

"You said, *children-to-be*?"

"Exactly. His wife's only regret is that the conception took place in an apartment, and not in their own domain, as Anastasia recommends — in the Space of Love built with their own hands, where the woman should stay during the whole period of her pregnancy and where the birth should take place.

"My colleague's wife is convinced she can have still another child beyond this one. And my colleague thinks so too.

"I am convinced that the instinct one finds among animals to perpetuate the species differs from the human condition in the fact that the animals' mating is governed only by the call of nature. When Man engages in so-called sex, he is merely imitating the animals. A child brought into the world as the result of this process is half-man, half-animal.

"A true Man can be born only when the energies and feelings inherent in Man alone are involved — i.e., love, a vision of the future, an awareness of what is being created. In fact, the word *sex* isn't really applicable at all. It only trivialises the event taking place. The term *co-creation* is much more accurate here.

"When a man and a woman achieve the mental state where co-creation takes place, it is at that point that they enter into a marriage made in heaven. This is not a union sealed by a scrap of paper or a ritual, but by something immeasurably greater and more meaningful, and hence it will be solid and happy.

"And you mustn't think that only young people can enter into a union like this. The example of my colleague shows that it is available to people of all ages. Such a union is possible only on the condition that they themselves are able to comprehend the significance of what Anastasia has set forth."

"So what does all this mean?" I asked. "Does it mean that all the people whose passport[9] is stamped with a marriage registration aren't married after all?"

"A passport stamp is nothing but a convention thought up by society. The pieces of paper and all the rituals practised by different peoples in different historical periods may be outwardly different, but in essence they all amount to the same thing — an attempt to impress the mind and artificially create at least an appearance of union among two people. As Anastasia correctly points out:

> *A false union is a frightening thing.*
>
> *Children! Do you see, Vladimir? Children! They sense the artificiality, the falsity of such a union. And this makes them sceptical about everything their parents tell them. Children sub-consciously sense the lie even during their conception. And that has a bad effect on them.*

"It turns out that in Nature there is not an artificial, but a natural, Divine union. And Anastasia has shown people living today how it can be achieved."

"So what you're saying is that even people who are married — even the ones with a stamp to that effect in their passport — should really be marrying their spouse a second time?"

"Not the *second* time, but *for the first time in actual fact,* it would be more accurate to say," observed Alexander Sergeevich.

"That's going to be a hard one for most people to understand. In every country of the world sex is held up as the

[9]*passport* — in this case, an internal document issued by the Russian government as proof of one's identity, which includes a record of marriage where applicable.

highest form of pleasure, and every last individual engages in it for the sake of pleasure."

"All a lie, Vladimir Nikolaevich! Ninety percent of men are incapable of satisfying a woman.

"The myth that the majority of people derive supreme delight from sex is nothing but a psychological suggestion. Human beings' appetite for sex is the basis of a whole commercial industry. The flood of legal and underground porno-magazines is a veritable gold-mine. And they know how to pull the wool over people's eyes. Films where all sorts of supermen freely satisfy their partners — that's all business too.

"The simple fact is: we are too timid and too afraid to admit to each other that we don't have the right partner. But the fact remains — an indisputable fact — that sixty percent of marriages do not last. And the other forty percent are far from perfect, as is evidenced by continual spousal betrayals and the tremendous increase in prostitution.

"The gratification we derive from sexual experiences today is hardly satisfying. It is no more than an infinitesimal part of the satisfaction Man experiences from the genuine co-creation appointed by God, in partnership with Him — something we search in vain for all our lives.

"*We're 'searching for it in the wrong places'!* The truth of this saying is indisputably borne out in our very lives.

"Anastasia represents a culture of some kind of ancient civilisation which our historians probably haven't the faintest concept of. She completely destroys prevailing stereotypes. Just how perfect this culture was can be seen by considering how it dealt with pregnant women, who upon conception were expected to stay in the same place for nine months, and give birth there. How important is this?

"The advantage of this policy can be corroborated by information from modern science and comparative analysis. The place where the mother conceives and carries her child-to-be is termed a *domain*. In this domain a man and a woman have established a garden with their own hands, a garden containing all sorts of plants. Physiologists recognise the importance of proper nourishment for pregnant women — this has been written up in dozens of scientific and popular publications. But what of it? Is it necessary for every pregnant woman to study these? Just forget about everything else and set about studying the literature on the subject? That would be rather hard to swallow!

"Even if every single pregnant woman took to studying these scientific treatises, she would inevitably be faced with another insoluble problem: where could she obtain the products recommended?

"Let's suppose a couple had unlimited funds at their disposal and could buy whatever they liked. *An illusion!* No money will or even can buy what a pregnant woman desires, and right at the very moment she desires it. I'm thinking, for example, of an apple of the quality a woman can pick in her own garden and eat on the spot.

"Then there are the psychological considerations, which are no less important than the physiological. Let's take and compare two situations.

"The first is a standard scenario, which happens with the vast majority of people. Let's take a young family with an average or slightly-above-average income. A pregnant woman lives with her husband in a flat. Is she able to feed herself with the proper quality of food? No! Modern supermarkets, even those with upscale prices, are unable to offer us good-quality food. Tinned or frozen foods are *not* something natural for Man.

"Well, what about the farmers' markets, then? Even there the quality is doubtful, to put it mildly. Private farmers too have learnt to use all sorts of chemical additives in raising their crops. When they're growing things for themselves, that's one thing, but when they're growing to sell, that's when their desire to make money pushes them to use all sorts of stimulating devices. Everyone knows about it, and so there is naturally a feeling of concern and alarm over using food from unknown sources.

"*A feeling of alarm!* A feeling that has become modern Man's bosom companion!

"Pregnant women today are overwhelmed by an endless flood of information about constant social cataclysms and ecological disasters. Both her consciousness and sub-conscious become home to an ever-increasing fear over the future of her child-to-be. Where can we possibly find anything positive to counteract it? There are no positive aspects — indeed, under the monstrous circumstances of contemporary life we have doomed ourselves to, there cannot be.

"Even in a comfortably appointed apartment we get used to our surroundings and they cease to delight our eye with anything new. We also get used to everything in the apartment ageing and breaking, even as we are accustomed to our tap water being undrinkable.

"All this all of a sudden starts to weigh upon a pregnant woman's acute sensibilities. All she can do is to hope for a miracle. Under the constant pressure of hopelessness, this is the most she can count on.

"In the second scenario, the woman is surrounded by a Space of Love, as Anastasia terms it, where in addition to the satisfaction of her physiological needs she is also given a powerful psychological boost.

"Modern science is capable of explaining and demonstrating the truth of practically every one of Anastasia's sayings. They are altogether simple and logical. The only wonder is that in spite of all our studied speeches on the subject we have never given them much heed.

"But Anastasia also talks about mysterious phenomena that modern science cannot explain:[10]

Parents should impart to their co-creation the three most important points, the three primary planes of being.

"She further says that for all three planes of being to merge into one in one spot, namely, in one's family domain, the following must occur:

The thoughts of two in love will merge into one... Here is the first point — it is called parental thought... *The* second point, *or rather, yet another human plane, will be born and light a new star in the heavens when two bodies merge into one — merge in love and with thoughts of a splendid creation... And a* third point, *a new plane of being should come about in that space. Right there on the spot where the conception occurred the birth should take place. And the father should stay close around. And the great all-loving Father will raise over the three of them a crown.*

"I am certain that physiologists and psychologists will be able to explain the advantages of conceiving, carrying and giving birth to a child all in the same spot — in a splendid kin's domain. But Anastasia talks about something even greater. She says that in such a case the individual who is born experiences a complete connection with the Universe. Why? How does it happen? How important is this approach to a child's birth for his future as a Man? Scholars today can only guess.

"I tried juxtaposing what Anastasia said with the prognostications of the horoscopes that are popular today. The question naturally arose, which of the three points Anastasia

[10]These passages are quoted (with a slight variation) from Book 4, Chapter 30: "In His image and likeness".

mentions is the most important constituent of a Man's birth — the thought, the physiological conception or the emerging of the infant from the mother's womb?

"It is generally accepted today that one's birthdate is defined by the moment of emergence from the mother's womb. This is what horoscopes are based on. But science has already determined that the fœtus, even before it has emerged from the womb, is alive, it has feelings. And if that is so, then the Man already exists. He is already born. He can move — the mother can feel the push of his little legs and arms. Perhaps, then, it would be more accurate to calculate a Man's birthdate from the moment the sperm fertilises the egg? Certainly from the physiological point of view, this could be considered the most accurate defining moment of somebody's 'birth'. But...

"The meeting of the sperm and the egg is still not a cause — it is an effect. It is preceded by the couple's thoughts. Could it be that *these thoughts* define one's birthdate? Of the three moments we have mentioned, it is generally accepted today that one's birthdate is the moment of emergence into the world. Tomorrow, though, the calculation could be different.

"According to Anastasia's theory, Man's birthdate is the point where these three moments merge into one. And here may be seen her irrefutable logic. But we (and here I am referring to religious teachings as well as modern science) are afraid even to mention this."

"What is there to be afraid of?" I queried.

"There *is* something, actually... You see, Vladimir Nikolaevich, if we accept the irrefutability of Anastasia's statements, then we are obliged to admit that by comparison with the people of the culture she represents, we are not fully fledged people. Most of us today are lacking one or two of the components inherent in a fully fledged Man. So that's why we're afraid not just to talk about it, but even to think about it. And yet we should be thinking about it..."

"But perhaps we don't think or talk about these statements because they're too controversial?"

"On the contrary! They are too *un*controversial — they are incontrovertible!

"*First,* think about this: who will deny that a situation where thought rather than debauchery precedes the birth of a child — the meeting of the sperm and the egg — is more moral and more psychologically fulfilling?

"*Second:* it is also absolutely indisputable that a pregnant woman should receive a wholesome variety of nourishment and avoid stress. One's own family domain, as Anastasia describes it, is ideal for this.

"*Third:* giving birth in familiar surroundings, in a setting one is accustomed to, will create a much more favourable condition for the birthing mother and, more importantly, for the newborn. This is also an irrefutable fact in both psychology and physiology. Now, are you in agreement with these three points so far?"

"Of course I am."

"You see, they are indeed irrefutable, and not only for scholars. Consequently, we cannot deny the positive influence produced by the union of these three positive components into a single whole.

"As a psychologist, I can conjecture that in such a union, a psychic reaction takes place in space. The whole Space of the Universe reacts to it — accepting the newborn and establishing an information link with him."

"Possibly. But what is the significance here of establishing an exact birthdate for Man?"

"A tremendous significance! A global significance! This is what determines the level at which we perceive the world. If we give priority to the emergence of the fœtus into the world, that means *matter* is primary in our worldview.

"If on the other hand we give priority to the moment at which the man's and woman's thoughts merge together, then *consciousness* takes precedence in our world-view.

"The upshot is that we are dealing with the formation of two different cultures which determine our way of life. In the first instance *matter* takes predominance, in the second, it is *spirituality*. This conflict has been going on for ages, either openly or below the surface. But now I am beginning to see the absurdity of such a conflict. Anastasia talks about the merging not only of these two concepts, but of a third as well, into a single whole. On the basis of her statements one can postulate not only a *theory* of the birth of a fully fledged Man, but also the possibility of its realisation in practice. It comes right down to something that is available to everyone. But why do we not take advantage of the opportunities we have? Why is there chaos in our consciousness, and why does life evaporate into vanity? — there's the question!"

"I still think," I said, "you should use the date and hour when the infant emerges into the world from the mother's womb as one's birthdate. Only phrase it more accurately: 'the moment of emergence into the world'."

"Possibly. Quite possibly! But as to the moment of the birth itself, I still think you'd better ask Anastasia."

"I shall indeed ask her. I'll be interested to know myself exactly when I was born, and when my son was born."

"Oh, your son! You came to me asking for advice, and here I've been rambling on about my own — Sorry, I got talking too much. It's something that's been nagging at me. You see, I hold consultation three times a week. People come to me with their problems.

"They all ask the same kinds of questions: *How to raise a child? How do I establish contact with my son or daughter?* And the child may be already five, or ten or even fifteen years old.

"If I tell someone: 'Well, old chap, it's too late to think about raising them now!', then I'm killing his last hope. So my real task is basically one of comforting."

"Well, my son too will soon be five years old. Does that mean it's too late for me too?"

"You, Vladimir Nikolaevich, are in quite a different situation. Your son's got Anastasia watching out for him. It's just as well she prevented you from tossing your child out into the routine of our world. She's raising him in the context of a totally different culture."

"Does that mean my son and I are of different cultures, and so we'll never be able to understand each other?"

"Parents and children always represent what seem to be different cultures, different world-views. Each generation has its own priorities. Granted, the distinction is generally not so sharp as in your case. My advice to you is this: before attempting to communicate with your son, have a talk with Anastasia about how best to approach it. Pay careful attention to whatever she says. After all, you've been reading a lot and thinking a lot about the raising of children. Now it'll be easier for you to understand her."

"Understanding her doesn't always work out," I countered, "even after a long time goes by. Some of her sayings still provoke doubts in me. They are mystical and not the kind you can prove. In fact, I've deliberately refrained from publishing a lot of her sayings — a lot of them sound more like fantasy and—"

Alexander Sergeevich suddenly banged the palm of his hand down on the table and sharply — even somewhat rudely — interrupted me:

"You've no right to do that. If your mind won't allow you to make sense of something, at least give others the opportunity."

I did not appreciate the psychologist's sharp tone of voice or his message. This wasn't the first time I had heard or read such accusations directed at me. They would reduce me to some kind of half-wit and say that my role was no more than transcribing as accurately as possible everything this Siberian recluse had said. But in making such statements these smart alecs weren't taking the whole picture into account. I decided to put this suddenly aggressive psychologist in his place:

"Naturally you count yourself among those — those others, who are able to understand everything she says. I may not be a psychologist with an academic degree, but there is one simple truth even I can comprehend: if I were to publish all her mystical sayings without back-up evidence, people would be inclined to treat everything written in the books as a fairy tale. And all the practical stuff that can be put into practice today would get lost. By not publishing some of her mystical sayings, it is quite possible that I have saved the practical message she has for people."

"Can you tell me specifically what kind of 'mystical sayings' you're talking about?"

"Well, here's a good example. She said that she's taken the best combination of sounds in the Universe and hidden them in the text of the book and they will have a beneficial influence on the readers."[11]

"Yes, I remember that. I remember it very well. It's written right in the first book. It also says there that the effect is increased if the reader listens to natural sounds while reading."

"You remember that, eh? And the fact that these words can be found not only in the text itself, but right at the front of the book. Remember? The publishers suggested I put them there, to intrigue the readers. And I did..."

"And rightly so."

[11]See Book 1, Chapter 27: "Across the dark forces' window of time".

"You think so? But you know, that particular saying right up front turned a lot of people off the book. Many saw it as just an advertising gimmick, and said so in the media. I removed it in some of the editions. Many people consider it mystical, or just something made up."

"Idiots! Don't tell me... Don't tell me the mind of society can atrophy to that extent! Or has mental laziness switched off any logical thinking on the part of the masses?"

"What's mental laziness got to do with it? If the saying is impossible to prove?"

"*Prove?* What is there to prove? This saying is nothing if not a psychological test ingenious in its simplicity and effectiveness. It has the power to identify at a single glance complete dullards with atrophied mental capacities. If they go ahead and mention this in the media, it'll be as though they're saying: *Look at what utter klutzes we are!* A most ingenious test, indeed."

"What's this about a test? The saying in question is simply not provable."

"Not provable, you say? Well, it's not a matter of proving anything. What Anastasia says here is an axiom. Judge for yourself. The text of any book — and I mean *any* book, any letter, any oral speech — consists precisely of combinations of sounds. Does that make sense? Do you agree?"

"Well, yes, in general, I agree. It's true that the texts of all books are made up of combinations..."

"You see how simple it all is? It is this very simplicity that people who are too lazy to think logically have stumbled over."

"Possibly... But, after all, she did say she had found and collected the best combinations from the expanses of the Universe and that they would exercise a beneficial effect on the readers."

"But there is absolutely nothing 'mystical' in that. Judge for yourself: when you read any kind of book, or newspaper or magazine article, doesn't it have an effect on you? The reading can leave you indifferent, provoke irritation, satisfaction, anger or joy. Well? Get it? D'you agree?"

"Yes."

"Okay. As for the beneficial effect of Anastasia's texts, it's clearly evident in the reaction of the readers. I'm not talking about published reviews, which are sometimes paid for. The fact of beneficial influence is confirmed in the creative urges shown by the readers. It is evident in the multitude of poems and songs your readers have composed. I myself have bought five audiocassettes of songs dedicated to Anastasia. They have been written by people who are very simple, or maybe just the opposite — quite possibly they're not so simple after all. I bought these cassettes and listened to them. What Anastasia said has been confirmed by life itself. After all, the poetry came about under the influence of the reading. And you call it 'mystical'. You have no right to censor Anastasia."

"Okay. That's it — I'm leaving. Thanks for the advice."

I had already taken hold of the doorknob and was about to walk out, when I heard the doctor say:

"Hold on a moment, please, Vladimir Nikolaevich. I can see you've taken offence at what I said. I'm sorry if I sounded a bit sharp. I don't want us to part with bad feelings."

Alexander Sergeevich was standing in the centre of the room. A little bit pudgy around the middle, getting along in years. He neatly buttoned up his jacket and went on:

"You should understand that you have a duty to publish everything Anastasia says. Don't worry if not everything she says is clear to you, or to me or to someone else. Don't worry about that. It's important for *them* to understand."

"And who's *they*?"

"Young women still capable of bearing healthy children. If they get it, that means everything will change... Anyway, look at how little we've talked about your son, and that is the whole reason you came to see me!"

"Of course it is."

"There's no concrete advice I can really give you. Your situation's too irregular. Maybe you could take some picture-books to Siberia for him. History books, for example. You might also try dressing up. Maybe this all sounds silly, but I just want to make sure you don't paint too harsh a picture of our reality for him."

"What picture would you like me to paint? All prettied up and glossed over?"

"That's not what I'm talking about. Remember, you'll be introducing yourself to your son as a representative of our reality, and this may mean you'll be compromising yourself in his eyes."

"And why should I alone be expected to answer for all the perversions of our society?"

"If you show your son that you are incapable of changing anything in our society for the better, you'll simply be demonstrating how powerless you are. You'll be compromising yourself in your son's eyes. I have a feeling he has been raised in such a way that he will not understand how anything *im*possible can exist for Man."

"I guess you're right, Alexander Sergeevich. Thanks for the practical advice. Really, it's *not* a bad idea to put a good face on our life as far as the child is concerned. Yes, definitely it's worth it, or else he'll think..."

We shook hands and, as far as I could tell, parted friends.

Chapter Two

Conversation with my son

Having trekked from the river the whole way to Anastasia's glade all on my own, I felt right at home as I approached the familiar places. This time nobody was there to greet me. It even gave me a good feeling to walk through the taiga all on my own, without a guide.

I wasn't about to cry out, or call Anastasia's name. Perhaps she was occupied with her own affairs. When she was free, she would feel my presence and come to me on her own.

Spying my favourite spot on the lakeshore where Anastasia and I were wont to spend time together, I decided I would change my clothes first before sitting down and relaxing after my trip.

I took out of my backpack a dark grey wrinkle-resistant suit, a thin white sweater and a new pair of comfortable shoes. In getting ready for my trip I had also thought of taking along a white shirt and tie, but then decided that the shirt would only get wrinkled, and there would be no place to iron it in the taiga. But I had the suit packed in the store so it wouldn't wrinkle.

I decided I should present myself to my son in a solemn, elegant manner, and so I spent a great deal of time and effort in thinking about my outward appearance.

I had brought along a battery-powered razor and a mirror. Resting the mirror on a tree-branch, I proceeded to shave and comb my hair. Then I sat down on a small hillock, took out a notepad and pen to round out my plan for meeting my son with some thoughts that had come to me along the way.

My son will soon be five years old. Of course he can talk already. The last time I saw him he was still very little, he wasn't talking yet, but by now there must be a lot of things he can understand. He probably natters on with Anastasia and his grandfathers for days on end. I had it all set in my mind that just as soon as I saw Anastasia I would let her know how I had planned out my meeting with our son and what I would say to him.

For the past five years I had been diligently studying all the various systems of child-raising, taking from them what I considered the best and easiest to understand. After talking with educational experts and child psychologists I had arrived at the conclusions I needed for myself. Now, before meeting with my son, I wanted to talk with Anastasia about these conclusions, along with the plan I had worked out — to think through everything once again in detail, this time with her. Perhaps Anastasia could suggest what first words I should say to him, and what pose to adopt while saying them. I had decided the pose was important, too, since a father should appear to his son as a significant person. But first Anastasia had to introduce me to him.

The first point on my notepad read: *Anastasia presents me to my son.*

All she had to do was introduce me with some simple words, such as: "Here, son, here before you is your birth father."

But she had to say them quite solemnly, so that our son would be able to feel from her tone of voice his father's significance, and subsequently treat him with respect.

All at once I felt everything around become quiet, as though put on alert. The sudden onset of silence didn't frighten me. This always happened every time I met Anastasia in the taiga. The taiga and all its residents literally froze, listening, watching and deciding whether the newcomer might have brought their mistress any kind of unpleasantness. Then, if no aggression were detected, everything would calm down.

I surmised from the ensuing silence that Anastasia had quietly approached me from behind. It wasn't a difficult thing to sense her presence, especially since I always experienced something like a warming sensation in my back — something only Anastasia was capable of producing with her look. I didn't turn around right away, but continued sitting there for some time, luxuriating in the pleasant and cheering warmth. Finally I turned, and lo and behold...

There before me was standing my little son, his bare feet planted firmly on the ground. He had grown. His straw-blond hair was already falling in curls down to his shoulders. He was dressed in a collarless shirt woven from nettle fibres. His features resembled those of Anastasia's — perhaps mine too, though this was not obvious at first glance.

Turning to face him, my hands pressed against the ground, I found myself standing on all fours, watching him intently, oblivious to everything else in the world. He in turn kept his eye silently trained on me, watching me with Anastasia's kind gaze. Perhaps the unexpectedness of it all would have continued to prevent me from saying anything for a long time, but he was the first to speak.

"Greetings to your bright thoughts, my dear Papa!"

"Eh?... And greetings, of course, to you as well," I responded.

"Forgive me, Papa."

"Forgive you for what?"

"For interrupting your important reflections. I have been standing at a distance, so as not to interfere, but I wanted to come and be close to you. Please, Papa, let me sit beside you quietly until you have completed your reflections."

"Eh? Okay. Sure, have a seat."

He quickly approached, sat down a half-metre away and didn't move a muscle. I continued kneeling distractedly on all fours. As he was settling in, I managed to think: *I must adopt a deep-thought pose while I finish my 'reflections', as he put it. I need to think of what to do next.*

I took up what I thought was a dignified pose, and for a while we just sat there side by side without saying a word. Then I turned to my little son and asked him:

"Well, how are things going with you?"

Upon hearing my voice he gave a joyful start, turned to me and looked me straight in the eye. His look told me he felt tense, not knowing how to answer my simple question. But he finally responded:

"I cannot, Papa, give you an answer to your question. I do not know how things are going. Here, Papa, life is going on. It is something very good, life is."

Somehow I've got to carry on the conversation, I thought. *I can't afford to lose the momentum.* And so I asked him another traditional question:

"Well, how are you doing here? You minding your Mama?"

This time he replied at once:

"I am always happy to mind my Mama when she speaks. And when my Grandfathers speak, it is interesting to listen to them too. I talk to them as well, and they listen to me. But Mama Anastasia thinks that I talk too much — I ought to think more, says Mama Anastasia. But my thoughts come very quickly and I want to talk differently."

"What do you mean, differently?"

"Like my Grandfathers, I want to arrange my words one after another, like Mama does, like you do, Papa."

"And how do you know how I arrange my words?"

"Mama showed me. I get very interested when Mama starts talking with your words."

"Really? Wow!... Well... and what do you want to be?"

Again this very ordinary question, which adults frequently ask children, was apparently beyond his understanding. After a brief pause he replied:

"But I already *am*, Papa."

"I know that you are, but I meant: what do you want to become? When you grow up, what are you going to do?"

"I shall be you, Papa, when I grow up. I shall carry on what you do now."

"How do you know what I do?"

"Mama Anastasia told me."

"And what all has she been telling you about me?"

"A whole lot. Mama Anastasia tells me that you are such a... What is the word? Oh yes, I remember — that you are such a *hero,* my dear Papa!"

"A hero?"

"Yes. It is hard for you. Mama wants life to be easier for you. She wants you to be able to rest in normal conditions for Man, but you go to a place where many people find it very hard to live. That is why you go away, to do good to people there. I was very sad to learn that there are people who do not have their own glade and they are always being frightened and made to live in a way they themselves do not want. They cannot pick their own food. They have to... well, *work,* I think it is called. They have to do not what they want themselves but what somebody tells them to do. And for this they are given paper — money — and they then exchange this money for food. They have simply forgotten a bit how it is possible to live otherwise and enjoy life. And you, Papa, you go to that place where it is hard for people to live, to bring good to the people there."

"Eh? Yes, I do go there... There should be good everywhere. But how do you plan to carry on with the good? — how are you preparing for it right now? You need to study, to learn."

"I am learning, Papa. I like learning very much, and I try my best."

"What are you learning, what subject?"

Again, he didn't understand the question right off, but then replied:

"I learn the whole subject. Just as soon as I chase it up to the speed Mama Anastasia has, I shall immediately understand the whole subject, or all the subjects. Yes, it is better to say: *all the subjects.*"

"What do you chase up to the speed your Mama has?"

"My thought. But for the time being I cannot chase it up as quickly. Mama's thought runs more quickly. Her thought is quicker than my Grandfathers' — quicker than a ray of sunshine. She is so quick that only He thinks faster."

"Who? Who's *He*?"

"God — our Father."

"Oh yes, of course. Still, you have to try. Yes, you must try your best, my son."

"Fine, Papa, I shall try even harder."

In an effort to continue the conversation about learning without saying something stupid and meaningless, I reached into my backpack and pulled out a book at random — one of the books I had brought with me. It turned out to be a Grade 5 textbook called *A history of the ancient world.* I explained to my son:

"You see, Volodya, this is one of the many books people are writing today. This book tells children about how life began on the Earth, how Man and society developed. It's got a lot of colour illustrations along with a printed text. This book outlines the history of mankind. Scholars — they're such smart people, well, smarter than others, or so people say — have described in this book the life of primordial people on the Earth. When you learn to read, you'll be able to learn a lot of interesting stuff from books like this."

"I know how to read, Papa."

"Eh? Really? Your Mama's teaching you to read?"

"Mama Anastasia once drew the letters for me in the sand and said their names aloud to me."

"D'you mean to tell me you memorised all the letters right off?"

"I did. There are very few of them. I was sad to learn there are so few."

I didn't pay any attention at first to his remark about the fewness of the letters in the alphabet. I was interested in hearing whether or not my son could actually read a printed text. I opened the book to the first page, handed it to him and said:

"Here, try to read this."

A distorted view of history

He took the open book, in his left hand for some reason, and spent a few moments silently looking at the printed text, before starting to read:

> *The earliest people lived in hot climates, where there were no frosts or cold winters. People did not live by themselves, but in groups, which scholars call human flocks. Everybody in the flock, from the littlest to the greatest, collected food. They would spend whole days searching for edible roots, wild-growing fruit and berries, and birds' eggs.*

After reading this text aloud, he raised his head from the book and began looking me straight in the eye, enquiringly. I said nothing, not understanding his query. His voice betrayed concern as he began talking.

"I do not have any concept from this."

"What kind of 'concept' do you mean?"

"No concept at all comes to me. Either it is broken, or it cannot present a concept of what is written in this book. When Mama Anastasia or my Grandfathers speak, I have a clear concept of everything they say. When I read His book, the whole concept is even clearer. But from this book I have only a distorted kind of concept. Or it is somehow broken within me."

"What do you need this 'concept' for? Why waste time on a concept?"

"The concepts come all by themselves, when there is truth being told... but here, it is not happening — that means... One moment... I shall try to check. Perhaps the people written about in this book had no eyes, if they had to search all day long for food? Why did they spend days searching for food if it was always right with them?"

Then something inexplicable began happening with the child. He suddenly shut his eyes tight and began feeling the grass around him with one hand. Upon finding something, he picked and ate it. Then he got to his feet, and said without opening his eyes:

"Perhaps they did not have noses either."

He pinched his nose tight together with his fingers and began walking away from me. After proceeding about fifteen metres, he lay down on the grass, his hand still covering his nose, and uttered a sound something like *a-a-a.*

At that point it seemed as though everything around sprung into motion. Several squirrels jumped down together out of the trees, spreading their paws and fluffing out their tails like a parachute. Running up to the child lying on the grass, they would put something down beside his head, then dash back up into the trees and again parachute down to the ground.

Three wolves standing some distance away also came running up to the boy lying on the grass and began hovering anxiously around him.

With a noisy crunch of branches a young bear appeared, toddling quickly along, then a second bear, a little smaller but more agile.

The first bear sniffed the child's head and licked his hand, which was still holding on to his nose. Various other creatures of the taiga, big and small, kept popping out of the bushes. They all began to hover anxiously around the little fellow lying on the grass, completely oblivious to each other's presence. It was quite evident they didn't understand what was happening to him.

I too could not understand at first my son's strange actions. Then I figured it out. He was portraying a helpless person deprived of sight and smell. The little *a-a-a* sounds he kept making from time to time were to signal to those around him that he was hungry.

The squirrels kept arriving and departing as before, bringing cedar cones, dry mushrooms and something else besides, and piling them up on the grass beside the child.

One squirrel stood up on its hind legs, its front paws holding a cedar cone. With its sharp teeth it quickly began extracting the nuts inside. Another squirrel bit the nuts open and made a pile of the freshly shelled kernels.

But the boy did not take the food. He continued lying there with closed eyes, his hand holding his nose, and uttering his *a-a-a* with growing insistence.

At this point a sable came running headlong out of the bushes. A beautiful fluffy creature with a luxuriant coat of fur. It ran two circles around the boy, paying no attention to the gathering cluster of animals. And the creatures, whose attention had been totally focused on the unusual behaviour of the child, didn't seem to take any notice of the sable at all. But when it suddenly pulled up sharply and stopped at the pile of cedar nuts the squirrels had shelled and began eating them, the creatures reacted.

The first ones to bare their teeth and have their hair stand on end were the wolves. The bear, which had been swaying back and forth, shifting its weight from one paw to another, first froze still, his gaze trained on the glutton, then he gave it a slap with his paw. The sable flew off to one side and flipped over, but immediately jumped up again and made a nimble dash for the child, putting its front paws up on his chest. Directly the little one tried making his usual demanding *a-a-a,* the sable brought its muzzle right up to the boy's open mouth and deposited therein the food it had just chewed.

At long last Volodya sat up on the grass, opened his eyes and let go of his nose. He surveyed all the creatures around him, who were still showing signs of concern. Then he got to his feet and began calming them down.

Then each creature in its turn, according to a hierarchy known only to them, approached the boy. Each one received a reward. The wolves got a friendly clap on the mane. With one of the bears Volodya took its muzzle in both hands and gave it a shaking, then for some reason rubbed the second bear's nose. He used his leg to press the sable squirming at his feet to the ground, and when it flipped over onto its back, he proceeded to tickle its tummy.

After receiving their due reward, each creature in turn respectfully withdrew.

Volodya picked up a handful of shelled cedar nuts from the ground and made a sign to the squirrels which by all appearances was intended to let them know that they need not bring any more gifts. Even though the child had been calming the creatures down, up to this point the squirrels had been continuing to feed him, but stopped immediately upon Volodya's signal.

My little boy came over to me, handed me a fistful of nuts and said:

"In the concept I have within me, Papa, when the first people began to live on the Earth, they did not need to spend entire days searching for and gathering food. They did not need to think about food at all. Forgive my concept, Papa — it is not at all like what the intelligent scholars wrote in the book which you brought me."

"Yes. I realise it is quite different."

I sat down again on the hillock. Volodya immediately followed suit, and asked:

"But why are they different — my concept and the one in the book?"

I'm sure my own thought must have been working faster than ever before. Indeed, why did this book, a textbook for children, contain such hocus-pocus? Even an adult unfamiliar with the wilds of nature must grasp the fact that in a warm climate, especially a tropical climate, there would be all sorts of food in abundance. So much so that even the huge creatures — mammoths and elephants — had no trouble in finding enough to eat. And the smaller animals didn't go hungry either. And yet here was Man, the most intellectually developed creature among them, having difficulty feeding himself! Really, a virtually impossible scenario!

It turns out that the majority of people who study history simply do not think about the implications of what is written in history textbooks. They do not evaluate what they read against the criterion of the most elementary logic, but simply accept the historical past in whatever form it happens to be served up to them.

Try telling a dachnik,[1] for example — a dachnik with just six hundred square metres of land — that his neighbour spends his day walking among the food growing there and can't find anything to eat. The dachnik would get the impression that his neighbour must be sick, to put it mildly.

By the same token, how could a child who has grown up in the taiga and tasted all the various fruits and growing plants, imagine any need for searching for them if they are always at hand? Especially when the creatures around him are ready at any moment to serve him, to spare him the necessity of climbing trees to fetch nuts and even the task of shelling them?

Earlier I had observed still another phenomenon. All the female creatures living on Anastasia's family territory accepted the child born to her as their own.[2] And I am not the only one to have described this phenomenon. There are many instances recorded where animals have nourished human children. And many people, no doubt, have observed a dog feeding a kitten or a mother cat feeding a young puppy. But animals have a special relationship to Man.

Creatures in the taiga always mark out their territory. It is on such a territory that Anastasia's family lives, and hence their special relationship to her too. How is it that all the creatures are so drawn to Man and ready to serve him with heartfelt desire? How is it that Man's loving attitude is so essential to them? Just like household pets in a modern apartment — a cat, a dog or a parrot, for example — each and every one tries to get at least some kind of attention from Man, and treats any indication of love as the ultimate reward. They are even jealous when a Man shows attention to some pets more than others.

---

[1] *dachnik* — one who has a *dacha* — something like a country cottage but always with a garden where enough fruits and vegetables are grown to feed the family right through the winter (for further details, see the Translator's Preface to Book 1: *Anastasia*).

[2] See Book 3, Chapter 14: "A father's role".

While this is something we easily take for granted with pets, it may seem a little unusual here in the taiga, and yet fundamentally it is the same amazing phenomenon — all animals aspire to feel the invisible light of grace (or feelings, or some other kind of radiance) emanating from Man. The specific term may vary, but the fact is incontestable. The important thing is that this is a real natural phenomenon, and we need to understand its specific purpose.

Did this phenomenon exist right from the very beginning, or has Man trained the animals over the centuries? It is quite possible that every single one of them has been trained. After all, look at how many different animals and birds on all continents serve Man today! They know who their master is. In India we are talking about elephants and monkeys, in Central Asia — camels and donkeys. And almost everywhere this applies to dogs, cats, cows, horses, chickens, geese, hawks and dolphins — so many kinds of creatures, it is hard to name them all. The important thing is that they are in service to Man — a fact practically everyone is aware of. But when did it begin — three thousand years ago? Five, ten thousand years ago? Or possibly this was part of the Creator's thought right when He created Nature? Most likely the latter.

It says in the Bible: "To determine the purpose of every creature."[3] And if all this was planned and implemented right from the beginning, then Man could not possibly have had any problems finding food.

Why then do our history books — those written for adults as well as children — say exactly the opposite? This happens

[3]The reference here is apparently to Genesis 2: 15, 18–20. In Anastasia's (and Megré's) interpretation, based on what they understand to be the logic of the biblical text, Adam's *naming* actually refers to an *assignment of function* to each creature in respect to the task of tending the Paradise garden and its human resident.

not just in our country, but such absurdities are inculcated in people the world over. A mistake? Probably not! Whatever's behind this is more significant than a mere mistake. Design! If so, that means it's important to someone. To whom? Why? What would happen if history were written differently? If the truth were written? What if textbooks all over the world stated something like this:

> *The first people living on our Earth did not have any problems finding food. They were surrounded by a great variety of high-quality and nourishing food.*

But then... Then the question would arise in the vast majority of minds: *What happened to this great variety and abundance? Why is Man today forced to work as a slave for someone just to earn a piece of bread?* And perhaps the most important question of all: *How flawless is the course of human society's development today?*

How was I now to answer my son as to why this 'intelligent' book — a textbook — was spouting such absurdities? People in the tropics spending whole days searching for food? To one brought up in the taiga surrounded by faithful creatures, these sayings of so-called 'intelligent people' were patently absurd.

I remembered Anastasia's words: *To perceive what is really going on in the Universe one need only look into one's self.*[4] In an attempt to extricate myself from the situation, I tried explaining to my son:

"This is not a simple book. You should examine everything written here against your own concept. Why write about something that you have such a clear concept of already? Here everything is presented upside-down. You need to use your own concepts to verify whether something you read is

[4]Quoted from Book 2, Chapter 6: "The cherry tree".

the truth, or whether it's turned upside-down. You need to be more attentive to that. Do you understand me, Volodya?"

"I shall try to understand, Papa, why people write what is not true. At the moment I do not understand. I know that some creatures use their tails to wipe out their tracks. Others build fake burrows, and there are those that even construct traps. Only why do human beings need to be so deceptive?"

"I told you, it's for their self-development."

"But can they not develop themselves through the truth?"

"They could do that too... But it would be different."

"Where you live, Papa, do they develop themselves through the truth or through lies?"

"They try all sorts of things — sometimes truth, sometimes lies — whatever will get them ahead most effectively... Anyway, Volodya, do you often read books?"

"Every day."

"What kind of books do you read? Who gives them to you?"

"Mama Anastasia has given me all the books to read that you wrote, Papa. I read them very quickly. But every day I read other books. Books that have lots of different happy letters of the alphabet."

At first I didn't pay any attention to his words about some kind of strange books with 'lots of different happy letters'.

"You loved Mama, but did not recognise it"

A fearful conjecture flashed through my mind: *If my son has read all my books, then he is well aware of my relationship to*

Anastasia during those first few days after I met her. He knows how I insulted her and even wanted to hit her with a stick. What child who loves his mother can forgive such shameful treatment? There can be no question that every time my son remembers this, he will think evil of me. Why did she give him my books to read? It would have been better if he hadn't learnt to read at all. Or maybe she remembered to tear out the pages describing my despicable behaviour?

Grasping at this latter hope, I carefully asked Volodya:

"So, Volodya, you've read all the books I wrote, eh?"

"Yes, Papa, I have."

"And did you understand everything in them?"

"Not everything, but Mama Anastasia explained to me how to figure out what I could not understand, and then I understood."

"What did she explain to you? Could you give me at least an example of something you didn't understand?"

"Yes, I can. I did not understand at first why you got angry at Mama Anastasia and wanted to hit her. She is very good, kind and beautiful. She loves you. And if you got angry at her, that must mean you did not love her. But then Mama explained everything to me."

"What? What did she tell you?"

"Mama Anastasia explained how you loved her very much but did not recognise it. But all the same, even with your love that you did not recognise, when you returned to the place where people find it hard to live, you began doing what Mama asked you to. She says that you, Papa, did everything your own way, the way you thought best. But when you remembered Mama, you wrote a book which people liked. People started writing poems and songs. People started thinking about how to do good. Now there are more and more of them — people thinking about what is good. That means that good shall prevail on the Earth.

"Yet people both criticised you and envied you over the book. But then, Papa, you wrote another book, and then another and another. Some people got even more angry at you. But others clapped their hands when you went to meet with them, they understood what you wrote in the books. They felt the energy of Love — which you still did not recognise — helping you write those books. And I was born, because you very much wanted to see me, and so did Love. You wrote the books, Papa, because you wanted to make the world better for my birth. Only you were not able to make it completely better by the time I was born. Because the world is very, very big.

"Mama Anastasia told me I must be worthy of you and the world. I need to grow up and understand everything. And Mama told me too that she has never been offended at you. She recognised at once the energy of Love. Then Mama Anastasia read you a book written with letters of the alphabet that are not sad. She did not read you the whole book. But what she read, you were able to write with letters which people could understand. And you got almost all of it right."

"What book? What do you mean, Mama read you a book? What's it called?"

"It is called *Co-creation*."

"*Co-creation*?"

A book of pristine origins

"Yes, *Co-creation*. And I love to read it every day. Only not with your letters, Papa. Mama taught me to read this book with different alphabetical letters. I love all sorts of happy letters. This is a book I can read my whole life. It tells about everything. And soon a new book will appear on the Earth. And you, my dear Papa, will write about this new book."

"I don't think you said that right, Volodya. You should have said: 'will *write* this new book'."

"But your ninth book, Papa, will not be one *you* will write. It will be co-created by many people — grown-ups and children. It will be a living book. It will consist of a whole lot of splendid chapters — paradise domains. People will write this book on the Earth with their Father's happy letters. It will be eternal. Mama taught me to read these living and eternal letters, to make words from them."

"Wait," I interrupted my son. "I have to think about that one."

He meekly fell silent at once.

Incredible, I thought. *That means, somewhere here in the taiga Anastasia has an ancient book written in letters nobody else knows.* She *knows these letters, and she has taught our son to make words out of them and read them. She read me chapters from this book for my* Co-creation. *The chapters about how God created the Earth and Man, and I wrote them down. That's how it worked out, according to my son. But I never saw Anastasia with any kind of book in her hands. And yet my son tells me that she translated the letters of this book for me. I shall have to find out everything through my son.*

And I asked him:

"Volodya, you know that in the world there are a whole lot of different languages — for example, English, German, Russian, French and many others?"

"Yes, I know."

"What language was it written in — the book Mama can read, and you too?"

"It is written in its own language, but its letters can speak in any language. And they can be translated into the language you speak, Papa. Only not *all* the words can be translated, because in your language, Papa, there are so few letters."

"Can you bring this book to me — the one with 'all sorts of happy letters', as you put it?"

"I cannot bring you the *whole* book, Papa. I could bring you some of the little letters. Only why carry them around — it is better for them to stay where they are. If you wish, Papa, I can read you the letters right from here. Only I cannot read as fast as Mama."

"Well, read it as best you can."

Volodya rose to his feet, and pointing his finger out into space, began 'reading' sentences from the chapters of *Co-creation*:[5]

> *The Universe itself is a thought, a thought from which was born a dream, which is partially visible as matter. ... My son, you are infinite, you are eternal, within you are your dreams of creation.*

He read syllable by syllable. I followed the expression on his face as it slightly changed with each syllable — now showing wonder, now attentiveness, now joy. But when I looked in the direction his finger was pointing, there were no letters, let alone syllables, to be seen out there in space, and so I interrupted this strange reading:

"Hold on a moment, Volodya. Does this mean you see some kind of letters out there in space? Why can't I see them?"

He gave me a quizzical look. He thought for some time before saying hesitantly:

"Do you not see, Papa? Do you not see that birch tree over there, the pine, the cedar, the rowan-tree?"

"Sure I see them, but where are the letters?"

[5]Quoted from Book 4, Chapter 8: "Birth".

"Those *are* the letters, the ones our Creator writes with!"

He began to read further, his finger pointing to each plant or tree in turn. And at last I grasped this incredible phenomenon. The whole area of the taiga surrounding the lake where my son and I were sitting (and where I had sat many times with Anastasia) was filled with growing things. The name of each tree or plant began with a particular letter, and some were known by different names. Name by name, letter by letter — and out came a syllable, then a word, and a sentence.

It was much later that I learnt that the trees, bushes and herbs throughout the whole area of the taiga around the glade were not just arranged randomly, but that they actually formed living, growing letters. It was an incredible book that, it seemed, one could read *ad infinitum*. It turned out that the very same plant names made up one set of words and sentences if read from north to south, but a whole different set if read from west to east. A third set resulted if one read strictly around the perimeter. And the names of the plants made up yet another series of words, sentences and images if one followed the movement of the Sun's rays, which acted literally as a pointer.

I understood why Volodya called these letters "happy". In traditional books all the printed letters are pretty much uniform. But in this situation, the living letters, even those associated with the same species, were always different. Under different angles of the Sun's illumination, they greeted Man with their rustling leaves. Indeed, one could go on 'reading' them indefinitely.

But who *wrote* this amazing book and when, and how many centuries did it take to write? Generations of Anastasia's forebears? Or...? Later I heard from Anastasia this brief, laconic answer: *For thousands of years generations of my forebears preserved the letters of this book in their original order.*

I looked at my son and feverishly tried to find a topic of conversation on which we could reach a complete mutual understanding.

One plus one equals three

Arithmetic! Mathematics! Of course, there will be no disagreements over an exact science like that. If Anastasia has taught our son to count, then a conversation on that subject cannot include any contradictions or superiorities. Two times two is always four, in any language at any time. Encouraged by my 'discovery', I asked hopefully:

"Volodya, has your Mama been teaching you how to count, add and multiply?"

"Yes, she has, Papa."

"Good. Where I live there is a science known as mathematics. It is very significant. A lot of things are based on calculations and computations. People have invented a good many devices to make it easier to add, subtract and multiply, and it would be difficult to get along without them today. I brought you one of them — it's called a calculator."

I took out a solar-powered Japanese pocket calculator which I had brought, switched it on and showed it to my son.

"You see, Volodya, this little device can do a great deal. You know, for instance, what you get when you multiply two by two?"

"You want me to say 'four', do you not, Papa?"

"That's right, four. But the fact that I want you to say it is not important. That's just what it is. Two times two is always four. And this little device too can count. Look at the little screen. When I press the '2' button, the screen lights up with the figure '2'. Now I press the multiplication sign and then the '2' again. Then I press the 'equals' sign to find out what the result will be, and the figure '4' lights up on the screen.

"But this is a very simple arithmetical calculation. This device can count in a way impossible for human beings. For example, 136 times 1,136. I only have to press the 'equals' sign and we can find out how much it is."

"154,496," Volodya blurted out, ahead of the calculator.

After that I began to multiply and divide four-, five- and six-digit numbers, but each time my son beat the electronic calculator. He named the correct figure immediately and without any trace of tension. The competition with the calculator resembled a game, but my son showed no sign of any real interest. He simply named the figures, all the while evidently thinking about something else.

"How do you do that, Volodya?" I asked in amazement. "Who taught you to compute so quickly in your head?"

"I'm not computing, Papa."

"What d'you mean, you're not computing? You're telling me the result, you're answering the questions."

"I am simply naming the figures because they are always invariable in a dead dimension."[6]

"Don't you mean 'exact dimension'?"

"You may call it that, but it amounts to the same thing. Figures always come out invariable if you picture time and space as frozen. But time and space are always in motion,

[6]The Russian word for *dimension* (*izmerenie*) can also be taken in the sense of *measurement* (which is how the author interprets it); hence in Russian the phrase 'exact dimension' in fact can also mean 'exact measurement'.

and their movement changes figures, and then calculations become more interesting."

Volodya went on to name some incredible formulas or arithmetical operations which turned out to be way beyond my comprehension. I only remember that the formula was extremely long — in fact, it really didn't have an ending. He quite animatedly told me the results of some arithmetical operations, but they invariably turned out to be transitional. Each time after naming a figure, Volodya would add excitedly:

"When interacting with time, this number produces..."

"Hold on there, Volodya," I interrupted my son. "I don't understand this 'dimension' of yours. One plus one is always two. Look, I'm taking here... one twig."

I picked up a small twig off the ground and placed it before my son. Then I found another twig, put it beside the first and asked:

"How many twigs?"

"Two," Volodya replied.

"Exactly — two, and it can't be anything else, not in anybody's 'dimension'."

"But in the *living* dimension the calculation is completely different, Papa. I have seen it."

"What d'you mean, you've seen it? The calculation with this other 'dimension' — is that something you can show me on your fingers?"

"Yes, I can, Papa."

He raised his little hand in front of me with his fingers compressed into a fist and began to demonstrate. First he unfolded one finger and said: "Mama". Then a second finger with the words: "Add — Papa — equals..." and, finally, out came a third finger: "— Me."

"You see, three fingers. In order for there to be only two, I would have to take one away. But I do not want to take away any of these fingers. I want them to be even more, and in a living dimension that is possible."

Neither did *I* want any one of the three fingers to be taken away. So long live this other 'dimension' — this *'living dimension',* as he puts it. And may the calculation increase. Oh, wow! One plus one equals three! Most extraordinary! Still, the most incomprehensible thing for me remains the book of the taiga with its living letters.

"I shall make a Universe Girl happy"

I looked at my little son, who could read and had revealed to me the most extraordinary and probably the 'livingest' book in the world. I realised it would take a very long time to read it in its entirety. Besides, I would need to know the names of all the plants. But for some reason I had a good feeling in my heart just from the fact that it existed — this book with "all sorts of happy letters" (the way my son expressed it). And he will read it.

But what then? What will happen when he grows up? He said he would be like me. That means he'll go into *our* world. Into a world full of wars, drugs, violent crime and poisoned water. Why should he go there? And yet he's got himself ready for it. He's ready to go into our world when he grows up and do something good in it. *I wonder what?* I asked him:

"Volodya, when you grow up, what kind of task or job do you think will be the most important for you?"

"Mama Anastasia told me. First and most important when I grow up is... I need to make a particular Universe Girl happy."

"Who? What kind of Universe or Girl?"

"Every girl living on the Earth is the likeness of the Universe. At first I did not understand this. Then I read, I read the book, and understood. Every girl is like the Universe. Each girl has within her all the diverse energies of the Universe. Universe Girls should be happy. And I must be sure to make one of them happy."

"And how do you intend to carry out your project when you grow up?"

"I shall go where many people are living and find her."

"Who?"

"A girl."

"She will, of course, be extraordinarily beautiful?"

"Probably. But perhaps she will be a bit sad, and not everybody will think she is beautiful. Perhaps she will be someone who is ill. Where you live, Papa, many people are ill from 'anti-living' conditions."

"And just why would you pick a girl who is *not* the healthiest and most beautiful?"

"I am the one, Papa, who will make her the happiest, healthiest and most beautiful Universe Girl."

"But how? Though by that time, when you're grown up, you'll probably have *learnt* how to make another person — your girl — happy. But, Volodya, you don't know everything there is to know about the world in which I live. It could be... it could turn out, after all, that the girl you pick may not even want to talk with you.

"You know who today's girls notice? You don't know. I'll tell you. The pretty ones and the not-so-pretty, the sick and the healthy — they notice first and foremost men who have heaps of money, and a *car* — men who dress smartly and have a good social position. Not all of them, of course, but the majority are that way. And where are you going to get heaps of money?"

"'Heaps' — how much is that, Papa?"

"Well, for example, let's say at least a million. Better still, a million dollars. You know about currency units?"

"Mama Anastasia told me about the scraps of paper and coins which people love. She said people give out clothes, food and all sorts of things in exchange for them."

"They do. But where do they get the money, d'you know? To get this money, you have to work somewhere. No, just working isn't enough, if you want a lot... You have to get into business or invent something. For example, Volodya, could you really invent something people need, something they're really missing?"

"And what kind of invention are people missing the most, Papa?"

"What kind? Well, all sorts. A lot of regions are being hit by an energy crisis, for example. There's not enough electric power. People don't want to build nuclear power plants — they're dangerous, they can explode. But they can't get along without them."

"Nuclear? Where radiation from them can kill people and growing things?"

"You know about radiation?"

"Yes, it is everywhere. It is energy. It is good. Needful. Only it should not be collected in a large quantity in one place. Grandfather taught me how to control radiation. Only it must not be talked about openly — some people turn good radiation into weapons to kill other people."

"Yes. Better not to talk openly about it. I should think you would really be able to invent something and earn a good deal of money for your girl."

"Probably I shall be able to. But money does not make people happy."

"What do you think makes people happy?"

"The Space they make for themselves."

I pictured to myself my son becoming a young man. Maybe knowing a lot of unusual things, all sorts of phenomena, albeit naïve. Capable of coping even with radiation, but still naïve in respect to the intricacies permeating our lives... and there he'll be, off to look for his girl to make her happy.

He'll try not to stand out amidst other people. That was always Anastasia's strategy when she left the taiga and went out among people. He will try not to stand out, yet all the same, he will never be able to completely blend in. He's preparing himself, he's acquiring a colossal amount of knowledge, he's trying to become physically fit and all for the sake of one lonely girl!

I thought Anastasia would prepare our son for great deeds and to this end would share her own knowledge and abilities with him. And now it turns out that he sees a man's main goal in life as simply making just one woman happy. My son's convinced that every woman is the likeness of the whole Universe. Could it really be like that? An extraordinary philosophy, but in any case the point is: my son is convinced of it and one of his chief aims in life will be to make just one girl happy — a girl he doesn't even know. Maybe she hasn't even been born yet. Maybe she can crawl already, or she's just taking her first steps. Or — maybe no girl will want to, or rather, maybe no girl is capable of loving him.

Initially, when he fulfils her wishes and brings her money, she may pretend to love him. Oh, how many women there are like that in our world! They're even ready to jump into marrying some oldster for the sake of his money. They've learnt how to feign love.

My son will grow up and meet some girl like that, he'll keep fulfilling her wishes, she'll keep telling him she loves him, but what will happen when he starts talking about the need to create a Space of Love and plant a garden? Will she laugh at him? Will she call him crazy, or will she understand? Maybe she'll understand. But maybe... No, it's better to prepare him for the worst.

"You see, Volodya, when you find this girl and you manage to make her healthy and very beautiful — absolutely the most beautiful, as you say — something might still happen that you know nothing about. The prettiest girls in our world aspire to become models and actresses and go into show-business. They like it when all the men around them pay them compliments. So, just imagine she wants to dazzle the public like a queen, and here you start proposing to create a Space of Love. Maybe she'll hear you out, but that'll be it. She'll leave you and go off somewhere where there's lots of bright lights, compliments and applause, and she could even — God forbid! — leave you holding a baby! What'll you do then?"

Volodya replied unhesitatingly:

"Then I shall build a Space all on my own. First on my own, and then with the child she leaves me — and together we shall preserve Love in this Space."

"Preserve it for whom?"

"For myself, Papa, and for the girl, who, as you say, will go off into the world of artificial lights."

"Then why preserve a Space of Love specifically for her? Don't you see how naïve you are in such matters? You'll have to look for another girl. And be more careful the next time."

"If I look for another, then who will make the girl who left happy?"

"Let anyone who wants to try to, do that. It's not worth breaking your neck over. She's gone, and that's it."

"She will come back. And she will see the marvellous forest and garden. I shall make it so all the creatures serve and obey her. Every one and every thing in this Space will sincerely love her.

"She will probably come back all tired out. She will wash herself in pure water and have a good rest. She will become even more beautiful and will never want to leave her Space of Love ever again. Our Space. She will be happy. And the stars above her will shine brighter and happier than anywhere else. But if you, Papa, had not thought all this up, if you had not brought about such a situation with your thought about her leaving, she would not have left."

"I? I brought it about?"

"Yes, Papa. After all, you are the one that spoke about it. It was your thought. Man creates all kinds of situations with his thought, and this is what you have created."

"But you, your thought — can't it change the situation? Can't it counteract mine? You did say it was quick, almost as quick as Anastasia's."

"It could counteract it."

"So go ahead, counteract it."

"I do not want my thought to run counter to yours, Papa. I shall seek out another way."

How to bridge the gap?

I could not talk with my son any longer. Everything I said he automatically checked against his 'concept', with which he easily distinguishes between truth and falsehood. He even discredited the conclusions of the historians outlined in the textbook. There was no question here of a father's superiority over his son. The conversation did not endow me with any more authority and probably erased the authority I had before thanks to Anastasia. Moreover, his unusual confidence in the power of thought frightened me and put a gap between us. We were so different. There was no father-son contact with the child. I could not feel in him my own birth son. On the whole he seemed like another being to me.

We didn't say a word to each other. And then I remembered Anastasia's words: *With children one must be absolutely sincere and truthful.* I even felt anger over the hopelessness of the situation. So, I'm supposed to be sincere? I'm supposed to be truthful? I tried to be that way, but what came of it? Indeed, if I were to be completely sincere and truthful, then in the present situation I'd have to resort to some pretty bad language. So I said, spilling it all out on one breath:

"Volodya, if everything is to be said absolutely sincerely, you and I cannot hope to have a father-son conversation. We are different, you and me. We have different concepts, information and knowledge. I do not feel as though you are my son. I'm even afraid to touch you. In our world a father can show affection to his son pure and simple, and even punish him or strike him for insubordination. But doing anything like that with you is something I can't even imagine. There's an unbridgeable gap between us."

My outburst at an end, I sat silently, not knowing what to say next or how. I sat and looked at my little son, who seemed to be lost in thought — and what strange thoughts he has!

At last he turned his curly little head in my direction, and reinitiated the conversation, but this time I could feel a note of sadness in his voice:

"Is there some kind of gap between you and me, Papa? You say it is hard for you to accept me as your own birth son? You spend a long time in that other world, where things are not exactly the same as here. I know, Papa, that parents there sometimes beat their children... Everything is a bit different there. I have been thinking, Papa... Just a moment...

He quickly got up and ran off a little ways. He returned carrying a branch with dry needles and handed it to me.

"Take this branch, Papa, and beat me with it. The way parents beat their children in that other world which you spend so much time in."

"Beat you? Why? What have you thought up now?"

"I know, Papa, that over there, in the world you have to spend so much time in, parents beat only their own birth children. I am your birth son, Papa. You can beat me so you can feel yourself to be my birth father. Perhaps it will be easier for you that way. Only do not strike this arm or this leg — this arm will not feel pain and this leg will not feel at all — they are still a little numb. But all the rest of my body will feel pain. Only I probably shall not be able to cry the way children do. I have never cried in my life."

"Nonsense! Sheer nonsense! Nobody ever beats their children, not even in that 'other' world — as you call it — without a reason. Sometimes, yes, they punish them, and give them a light slap. But only when children do not obey their parents, when the kids don't do as they're supposed to."

"Yes, of course, Papa. When parents decide that their children have behaved improperly."

"Exactly."

"So, Papa, I want you to consider something in my behaviour improper!"

"What d'you mean, you want me to 'consider'? When behaviour's improper, it's clear to everyone that it's improper — it's not up to the parent to 'consider' it proper or improper. Everyone should understand that it is improper."

"And the children who are beaten should understand?"

"The children too. That is why they beat them, to make them realise that they were wrong."

"And cannot they understand this before being beaten?"

"They can't, obviously."

"Even when parents explain it to them, they cannot understand?"

"They cannot, and that's why they're at fault."

"And the one who did not explain it to them understandably is not at fault?"

"Well... no... that is... Now see how you've thrown me off completely with your misunderstanding!"

"Good! Now that I cannot understand, that means you can beat me. And there will be no more gap between us."

"Oh, why can't you understand? Punishment comes when, for example... Well, for example... Let's say Mama tells you in no uncertain terms: 'Volodya, don't do that.' And in spite of her telling you not to, you go ahead and do what she told you not to. D'you understand now?"

"I do."

"Have you ever done something Mama told you not to?"

"Yes, I have. Twice. And I will do it again, no matter how many times Mama Anastasia tells me not to do it."

My conversation with my son continued to unfold quite differently from the way I had planned. There was no way I could present modern civilised society — and, consequently, myself — to him in a favourable light. I got so upset over my son's latest arguments that I banged my fist on a tree-trunk. I spelled out to him — or perhaps more to myself:

"Not all parents, even in our world, punish their children by beating them. On the contrary, many of them look for a better system of child-raising. I tried to find one, but it didn't work out. The last time I saw you here, you were still quite little. I wanted to hug you and squeeze you. But Anastasia said I shouldn't interrupt a child's thoughts even to give him a pat on the head. She said a child's thought-process was an extremely important matter. And so I just watched you, and you were always busy with something. And now I've come to the point where I don't know how to talk with you."

"And today, Papa, you no longer want to give me a hug?"

"I want to, but I can't — my head has been turned upside down with all these systems of child-raising."

"Then may I do it, may I give you a hug, Papa? After all, our thoughts are the same now."

"You? You want to hug me too?"

"Yes, Papa!"

He took a step toward me. I gradually lowered myself to my knees — it felt as though my whole body was sinking to the ground. He grasped me firmly around the neck with one arm and pressed his head to my shoulder. I could hear his heart beating. My own heart was beating fast and irregularly. I started finding difficulty in breathing. It must have been just a few seconds, though — a minute at the most — before my heartbeat began to even itself out, as though tuning in to the rhythm of another heart. My breathing became natural and gentle. In fact, my whole feeling of well-being suddenly changed. I wanted to say or cry out: *How wonderful everything is around! How splendid Man's life is! Thank you to whoever thought up this world!* And I felt like saying a whole lot of other good things. But the words came together only inside me. I stroked my son's hair and asked him, for some reason in a whisper:

"Well, tell me, son. What could you possibly have done that your Mama told you not to? And that you would still do even now?"

"It was once when I saw Mama Anastasia..." he replied, also in a whisper to start with, without raising his head from my shoulder. "It was when I saw..."

And at this point he detached himself from me, sat down on the ground and stroked the blades of grass with his little hand. "The grass is always green when it feels good."

For a while he didn't say a word. Then he raised his head and continued talking.

"I shall save my Mama"

"One time I did not see Mama for a long while," Volodya began. "I wondered where she was, and decided Mama must have gone to the neighbouring glade, the one next to ours. It is similar to ours, but it is not as nice there. I walked over to the neighbouring glade. There I saw Mama. She was lying on the ground without moving, and was all white. And the grass around her was all white too.

"At first I stood there wondering why this had happened — Mama's face and the grass around should not be all white like that. Then I decided to touch Mama. She managed to open her eyes, only just, but she did not stir. Then I took her by the hand and began to drag her out of the white circle. She helped me with her other hand, and we got ourselves out of the white circle.

"When Mama got back to her normal self, she told me never to touch her if this should happen again. She said she herself could cope with it, but that I could not. After being in the white circle and dragging Mama out, my arm and leg grew numb and are taking a long time to recover. Mama gets better very quickly, but my arm and leg have still not fully recovered.

"When I saw Mama once again in the same circle... When I saw her lying there all white, I was not going to touch her myself. I cried out, I called the strong she-bear to help, the one I slept on when I was little. I told the bear to drag Mama out of the circle. The bear stepped onto the white part of the grass, and fell down, and now she is no more. Only her children remain.

"The bear died at once, as soon as she stepped on the white grass. Everything dies on the white grass.

"Then once again I entered the white circle and began to drag Mama Anastasia out. The two of us pulled ourselves away from the dead grass. This time my arm and my leg did not grow as numb as before, only my whole body was trembling a little. Now it does not tremble any more. You see, Papa? My body does not tremble, it obeys me. And I shall soon be able to raise my arm when I want to. I can already lift it a little. Before I could not raise it at all."

I listened to my son's story in astonishment. I remembered how once I had seen Anastasia in a similar situation — I too had instinctively tried to pull her out of the white circle. I remembered the elderly philosopher Nikolai Fiodorovich talking about it.[7]

But why does she put herself in that kind of danger? Even risking her own son? Can it be so important to her — burning within herself some sort of invisible energy directed at her?

A number of times on TV there have been reports on unusual circles with perfect geometrical shapes. They have appeared in various countries — usually in grain fields. Right in the middle of ordinary grain crops people have discovered circles with the stalks trampled to the ground. Not just trampled at random but with all the stalks pointing in the same direction and forming perfect geometric figures. Scientists are

[7]See Book 1, Chapter 28: "Strong people" and Book 5, Chapter 18: "The philosophy of life".

studying these mysterious phenomena, but so far haven't been able to come up with any explanation for them. In Anastasia's case the grass has also been trampled down in a circle, but in contrast to what's been shown on TV, the grass here has gone all white besides, as though it hadn't got enough sunlight.

Anastasia says that this is human-generated negative energy. Maybe it is, but why has it been focused so strongly on Anastasia? What kind of people are aiming it at her? Forgetting myself, I said aloud:

"Why does she struggle with it? Whom does the struggle benefit? Who is made better by it?"

"Everybody benefits a little," I heard my son's voice say. "Mama says that if the energy of evil lessens — if she is able to reduce it by burning it up inside her so that it is not reflected back into space — there will be less of it. And those who produce it will mellow somewhat themselves."

"Show me, how many of these white circles are there? And *where* are they?"

"Next to our glade there is a very small glade. The white circles are always appearing there. Afterward the grass becomes green again, but it has not yet greened over completely, and you can still see the circles. If you wish, come with me and I can show them to you, Papa."

"Let's go."

I quickly rose to my feet and took my son's hand. The child trotted quickly along on his little legs, though I noticed that he was limping slightly, and so I endeavoured to walk a little more slowly.

From time to time Volodya tried to look into my eyes. He chatted away the whole time, telling me about something as we walked. But all I could think about were the strange white circles and Anastasia's inexplicable behaviour, and the reasoning behind her actions, about this whole unusual phenomenon.

To somehow keep the conversation going with my son I asked him:

"Volodya, why do you sometimes call her Mama, and sometimes Mama Anastasia?"

"I know a lot of Mamas who lived earlier on the Earth. Mama Anastasia told me about them. I can call them grandmothers, or great-grandmothers, but I can also call them mamas. My grandmothers gave birth to Mama. I can also call them mamas. When I hear them being talked about, I can feel them, and see them, and picture them, and sometimes I picture them all on my own. But so as not to get confused, I sometimes call my mama Mama Anastasia. All mamas are good, but for me Mama Anastasia is the closest and the best, and she is more beautiful than the flowers and the clouds. She is very interesting, and cheerful. I hope she is for ever. As soon as I chase my thought up to speed, I shall always be able to bring her back."

I wasn't listening carefully enough to grasp what he was trying to say. By this time we had arrived at another little glade, and I saw four whitish circles on the grass. The circles were about five or six metres in diameter. They were barely noticeable, but one of them was whiter than the rest — it had probably been made quite recently.

Now I realised why Anastasia had not come to meet me and why she wasn't with me at the moment. It meant that she was lying helpless somewhere. And she didn't want us to take pity on her, or become upset by her appearance.

I looked at the white circles, and my thoughts kept racing and intertwining. Of course, a lot of people can turn pale from troubles which befall them unexpectedly. Almost all people turn pale when anger is unexpectedly directed at them. But here? Can it be possible to feel it just like that, at such a great distance away? Can such a huge amount of hateful human energy be concentrated into a single stream?

So huge that not only Man, but all the growth around him turns pale?

Apparently so. There they are — the traces of the most wicked attempts... And once again I remembered her words, which I cited in the fourth book:

> *All anger on Earth, leave your deeds and make haste to me, join fray with me, try your utmost. ... I stand alone before you. Try to defeat me. To defeat me, all of you come meet me together. The fight will be fightless...*[8]

I thought these were just words. But everything she says comes true. The books, just like she said, and the bards' songs, and the poems... She's not just whistling in the wind. But why did she say: "The fight will be fightless"? The upshot is that she tries to simply burn up the anger inside of her. And she tries to do this alone! As far as I'm concerned, I think one should fight them out and out! Smash their rotten mugs in! But she's all alone. *No! You shall not be alone, Anastasia! I can at least try... I can at least take a little of this filth upon myself. And I shall fight it. Oh, if I could only speak the way she does... I'd tell them!...* I probably got a little too carried away and blurted out:

"Hey you, malice-mongers, come'n try to get me, and I'll burn at least a few of you!"

Little Volodya all at once let go of my hand and ran on ahead, then looked me intently in the eye with amazement. Then he stamped his little foot and, grasping hold of his injured arm with his healthy one, he raised both arms above his head and cried out, imitating my tone of voice:

"Hey, come'n try to get me too, you malice-mongers. You see, my arm is getting better. Mama Anastasia is not alone. I

[8] Quoted from Book 3, Chapter 24: "Who are you, Anastasia?".

am here too, and my thought will be racing faster and faster. Hurry and come on, you malice-mongers, leave what you are doing and hurry over to me. Look at how I am growing!"

And he got up on his tiptoes in an attempt to raise his arms even higher.

"So, my fine warriors, my dashing young braves! Who are you about to make war on today, my gallant knights?" came Anastasia's quiet voice.

I turned around and caught sight of Anastasia, sitting under a cedar tree. She was evidently very tired — her head was even resting against the tree-trunk. And her shoulders and arms were sinking, and her hands were resting on the ground. Her face was pale, and her eyelids slightly lowered.

"Papa and I were standing up against malice, Mama!" Volodya responded on my behalf.

"But to fight against malice, you have to know where to find it, what forms it takes. It is essential to know everything about your enemy," Anastasia said quietly, and with difficulty.

"Mamochka, you rest here while Papa and I try to do that. If we do not do it properly, you can tell us later."

"Papa has had a long journey, little one. He should have a rest first."

"I've had a rest, Anastasia. In any case, I'm not all that tired... Hello there, Anastasia! How are you?"

For some reason I was overwhelmed by the sight of her helplessness and couldn't move. I started talking disconnectedly, not knowing what to say or do next. Volodya came over to me, took me by the hand, and went on talking to his mother.

"I shall give Papa some refreshment after his journey and bathe with him in the pure water in the lake. And I shall collect some cleansing herbs. You, Mamochka, just rest here in the meantime. Do not waste your energies on conversation. I shall take care of everything myself. Then Papa and I shall come to you. I want you to recuperate your strength as quickly as possible..."

"I shall go bathing with you too," Anastasia declared. "Wait, and I shall go with you."

Supporting herself with her hands against the cedar trunk, Anastasia tried to get up. She managed to raise herself a little, but again sank back down to the ground, her hands slipping against the trunk. Her whisper was barely audible:

"Oh, how could I have failed so badly?! I am unable even to rise to greet my son and my love?!"

Once more, leaning against the cedar trunk, she began the challenging task of raising herself off the ground. She probably would not have made it this time either. But all at once something incredible happened. The huge cedar tree Anastasia was leaning against suddenly began to extend the needles of its lower branches out toward her. The needles began emitting a barely noticeable pale-bluish glow. Slowly, almost imperceptibly, the glow enveloped Anastasia. Then I heard a crackling sound coming from above, not unlike the kind one hears when standing under high-voltage transmission lines.

I looked up and saw that the needles of all the surrounding cedar trees had also started glowing with the same faint bluish light. But that wasn't all. They were all pointing in the direction of Anastasia's tree. This tree's upper branches were receiving the light emanating from the neighbouring cedars. And the glow of its lower needles kept increasing in intensity.

This phenomenon lasted approximately two minutes. Then there was a pale blue flash, and the light coming from the needles was extinguished. The needles looked to me as though they had become slightly withered.

Anastasia was scarcely visible in the bluish radiance still enveloping her. After it had dispersed, or gone into her — I could not tell — I saw...

There beneath the cedar tree, back to her normal self, full of life, stood Anastasia, looking unusually beautiful, smiling at me and our son. Looking up, she quietly said "Thank you!" Then... Can you imagine a grown woman showing off this way?

Anastasia sprang into action, making a dash over to the largest of the white circles. Upon reaching its edge, she made another leap in the air, this time quite high. A triple somersault landed her in the very centre of the circle. Another leap, and this time she did a leg-split just like a ballerina. With a trill of her alluring laughter, she twirled in a dance over the white circles.

All around, the forest seemed to come to life and echo her joyful excitement. Squirrels leapt from branch to branch around the perimeter of the glade. Through the bushes some kind of creatures' eyes gleamed like precious stones. Two great eagles flew down one after the other from the sky and circled over the glade, rising and descending by turns.

Anastasia continued laughing and dancing like an acrobat and a ballerina. And gradually the grass beneath her feet began to turn green. And even the whitest circle became barely noticeable. My heart kept feeling lighter and lighter from her dancing, her laughter and everything around. And then all at once...

All at once my little son ran out and did a double body roll across what remained of the white circle. Then, quickly regaining his feet, he leapt in the air and spun around, trying to imitate his mother's dance. Even I couldn't refrain myself, and joined in the fun, dancing or just jumping up and down for joy alongside my son.

"Let's go! To the water! Who can catch up to me?" exclaimed Anastasia as she made a headlong dash for the lake, with Volodya and me in hot pursuit.

Slightly panting from all the jumping, I began to lag a little behind. But I saw how Anastasia leapt and somersaulted in the air before plunging into the lake. A few moments later Volodya took a flying leap from the shore and his bottom hit the water with a loud smack.

I began taking my clothes off on the run, tossing them on the ground along the way. I plunged into the water still wearing my undershirt, trousers and boots. As I surfaced, I caught Anastasia's shrill trill of laughter. Our son was laughing, too, with a surfeit of emotion, slapping the water with his hand.

I was the first to come out of the water. I began to peel off my wet clothes and wring them out. Upon reaching the shore Anastasia immediately put on her light dress right over her wet body. Then she helped me spread out my trousers over a bush so that they would dry more quickly in the breeze.

I fetched a track suit from my backpack and put it on. Anastasia stood beside me, and her dress was already dry. I wanted to give her a hug, but for some reason could not bring myself to go through with it.

She came up very close to me, and I could feel the warmth emanating from her. I felt as though I wanted to say something nice to her, but nothing came to mind. All I could muster was:

"Thank you, Anastasia!"

She smiled, put her hands on my shoulders, rested her head on my shoulder and responded:

"And thank *you,* Vladimir."

"Great!" Volodya's cheerful voice rang out. "I shall be off now."

"And where are you off to?" Anastasia enquired.

"I shall go and see my elder grandfather. I shall give him permission to bury the body, and I shall help him. So I am off."

Volodya quickly departed, with hardly a limp to be noticed.

Chapter Three

An invitation to the future

"What did he mean when he said he would give his grandfather permission to bury the body?" I asked in some bewilderment.

"You will see for yourself, and understand," replied Anastasia.

A little while later I saw Anastasia's great-grandfather, alive, but no signs of any funeral. That was how he remained in my memory — alive and unfathomable.

Anastasia was the first to sense her grandfathers' approach. We were walking together across the glade at the time. All of a sudden Anastasia stopped, and gestured to me to stop as well. As she turned in the direction of the tallest and mightiest cedars, I followed her gaze, but saw no one. I wanted to ask her what was going on, but could not. She took my hand and gave it a squeeze in a silent plea to refrain from uttering a sound.

It wasn't long before I caught sight of the figure of Anastasia's great-grandfather making his way among the majestic cedars. The majestic elder was wearing a long light-grey shirt which went down below his knees.[1] As he entered the glade at an unhurried but confident pace which betrayed no sign of ageing, I noticed our son — his great-great-grandson, Volodya — trotting along beside him, holding his hand tight. The old man's own son, Anastasia's grandfather, followed at a little distance behind.

[1]This is typical of many Russian peasant-style shirts.

It seemed that everybody, including me, felt some kind of solemnity surrounding the approaching encounter, and only the child accompanying the elder was behaving his natural and unaffected self. Volodya kept chatting away the whole time to his great-great-grandfather. Occasionally he would run slightly ahead and turn to look him in the eye, or suddenly stop, let go the old man's hand and bend down to the grass to inspect something that had captured his attention, whereupon the old fellow would stop too. Then Volodya would take his hand once more and begin telling him animatedly about what he had seen, all the while leading him over to where we were standing.

As they drew near, I couldn't help noticing that the usually severe- and majestic-looking elder was sporting a faint smile. His bright face was radiant with grace and, at the same time, a degree of solemnity. Even as he stopped but a few steps from us, his gaze was still aimed somewhere far off in the distance. We were all speechless — only Volodya's voice was to be heard, speaking at a fairly rapid pace:

"Here, Grandpakins, here right before you are my Papa and Mama. They are good people. Even though your eyes cannot see them, Grandpakins, you can still feel everything. But I can see them with my eyes. You can look at what is good through my eyes, my dear Grandpakins, and that will be good for you too."

Then, turning to us, Volodya all at once announced even more joyfully:

"Mama and Papa, a little while ago, when we were all swimming together, I realised something, and I have allowed the body of Grandfather Moisey[2] to die. We have already found a spot for me to bury the body of my Grandfather Moisey."

[2]*Moisey* (pronounced: *ma-yi-SAY*) — a Russian man's name, the equivalent of *Moses* in the Bible.

Volodya pressed his whole head and body against Grandfather Moisey's leg. The majestic grey-haired elder carefully and tenderly stroked his great-great-grandson's head. The love, tenderness, understanding and joy inherent in their mutual relationship was only too palpable. It made the conversation about burial all the more bewildering to me. In line with the way I was brought up, I felt like stopping my son and telling him his great-great-grandfather looked terrific and still had many years ahead of him. That is what we always say, even to an elderly person who is very ill, and I wanted to say that to him — in fact the words were already on the tip of my tongue — when Anastasia suddenly gave my hand another squeeze, and I stopped myself from speaking my mind.

Grandfather Moisey then turned to Anastasia and said:

"Granddaughter Anastasia, the Space you are creating, how is it being limited by your thought?"

"My thought and my dream have merged into one, without encountering any limitations," replied Anastasia.

Whereupon Grandfather Moisey asked her another question:

"Human souls are accepting the world you are creating... Tell me, what energy is driving your creation?"

"The same energy that grows a tree and unfolds the buds to turn them into the flowers we see."

"What kind of forces might interfere with your dream?"

"When I dream, I do not visualise any interference. All the challenges I can see on my path ahead can be overcome."

"You are free in everything, Granddaughter Anastasia. Order my soul to embody itself as you see fit."

"I cannot permit myself to order anybody's soul. The soul is free — the work of the Creator. But I shall dream, my dear Grandfather, that your soul find a worthy embodiment in the most splendid garden you have ever seen."

A pause ensued. Grandfather Moisey did not ask any new questions, whereupon Volodya once more began talking apace:

"Neither shall *I* order you, Grandpakins. Only I shall urge you most strongly to embody yourself soon once more upon the Earth. You will appear once more, young as before and will be my best friend. Or you will become someone else for me... I am not ordering... I am simply talking... My dear Grandpakins Moisey, let your soul be always within me and beside me."

Upon hearing these words the majestic elder turned to Volodya, and slowly got down on one knee in front of him, then on both knees, bent down his grey head, raised the child's little hand to his lips and kissed it. Volodya put his arms around the elder's neck and started whispering something quickly in his ear.

Then Grandfather Moisey got up from his knees with only one small child helping this very old man. Even now, when remembering this scene for the umpteenth time, I still can't figure out how it happened. They simply held hands, and the great-great-grandfather rose to his feet without leaning on anything.

Upon standing, he took a step in our direction and made a bow. Then, without uttering another word, he turned and held out his hand to Volodya. Off they walked, hand in hand, chatting away to each other. The younger grandfather followed a few paces behind, without interrupting their conversation.

I now realised that Anastasia's great-grandfather was going away for good. He was going away to die.

I could not take my eyes off the receding figures of the child and Grandfather Moisey. Earlier Anastasia had told me about her attitude toward modern cemetery rituals and funerals, and I even wrote about that in my previous books.[3]

She and, of course, all the other members of her family who had either lived or were currently living in the taiga, believe that there should be no cemeteries. Cemeteries are like refuse dumps, places where people toss out the lifeless bodies of the deceased as useless garbage. People are afraid of cemeteries, they believe, because things happen there that go against the laws of nature. They believe that the relatives of the deceased, through their very thoughts about their departed loved ones as gone forever, prevent them from reappearing in a new earthly embodiment.

In going over in my mind the various burials I have witnessed, I'm inclined to agree. There are simply too many falsehoods involved. People practically kill themselves over a deceased family member, but after just a few years... well, you go to a cemetery, and you rarely find a grave of someone who died ten or twenty years ago well tended. In fact at some untended gravesites workers are already digging new pits.

In the meantime the people who are buried are forgotten by everyone. Nothing remains of their brief sojourn on the Earth, and nobody even needs their memory any more. If that is how they end up, why were they born in the first place? Why did they live? Anastasia says the bodies of the deceased should be buried in their own domain with no special headstone to mark the burial place. The grass and flowers, trees and bushes that come up will be the continuation of the life of their bodies. That way the soul upon leaving the body is afforded greater opportunity for splendid reincarnations.

In the kin's domain the thoughts of the deceased before they die will have been creating a Space of Love. Their descendants will stay on to live in this Space, in contact with

---

[3]See Book 4, Chapter 31: "But who is to blame?" and Book 5, Chapter 1: "Two civilisations".

everything growing therein, which means keeping in contact with the thoughts of their parents as they take loving care of what their parents have created. And the Space itself will take care of those living therein, consequently maintaining one's earthly life forever.

But what about people who live in the cities? How are they to get along without cemeteries? Well, perhaps their lifestyle will give them pause to reflect — at least in their old age — on how they shouldn't live a life devoid of thought for the future, for eternity.

And I am in agreement with Anastasia's philosophy. But it is one thing to agree in thought, quite another to witness the departure of a great-great-grandfather in real life. Though in this case he — or, rather, his soul — will not die. It will evidently stay somewhere in the vicinity or very quickly embody itself in a new life — most certainly a good one. After all, neither Anastasia nor our little son, nor her grandfather, nor even Great-Grandfather himself, is projecting any kind of tragedy, even in their thinking. They have an entirely different approach to death from ours. For them it is not a tragedy, but simply a transition to a new and splendid existence.

Stop! Even Great-Grandfather himself showed no sign of grief. Quite the opposite. So that's it! That's the ticket! "When you go to sleep overwhelmed by heavy, dark and unpleasant thoughts, you will most probably have a nightmare. If you go to sleep with bright thoughts, you will have pleasant dreams," says Anastasia. And again: "...death is not a tragedy, it is only a dream — shorter or longer, it makes no difference. Man should enter into any dream contemplating what is beautiful — then his soul will not suffer. Through his thoughts Man can create a Paradise — or anything else — for his soul."

And Great-Grandfather knew this. He did not suffer. But what was it that brought him such obvious joy during those final hours? Something happened. He wouldn't have been smiling like that just for no reason at all. But what *did* happen? I turned to look at Anastasia and saw...

There she was standing a little distance away from me, her arms outstretched to the Sun, and whispering, it seemed, some kind of prayer. The Sun's rays would hide themselves behind a cloud, then shine brightly, reflected in a single tear rolling down Anastasia's cheek. But her face showed no sign of sadness, only peace. After whispering, she listened, as though somebody were answering her. I stood and waited, not daring to approach her or even utter a word. It was only when she turned, caught sight of me and headed over my way that I asked:

"Were you praying for the peace of your great-grandfather's soul, Anastasia?"

"My great-grandfather's soul will rest in great peace, and its earthly life still lies ahead when the soul itself desires it. I was actually asking about our son, asking the Creator to furnish him with greater strength.

"Our son, Vladimir, has been doing works undertaken by few people today. He has now accepted within himself all of Great-Grandfather's strength, which Great-Grandfather imparted to him with his soul. Because he is still in the process of maturing, he will find it difficult to contain the multitude of diverse energies within him as a single whole."

"But why," I asked, "after all this happened, did I not notice any particular change in our son?"

"Our son, Vladimir, uttered some special words before Great-Grandfather knelt in front of him. He uttered words whose meaning is comprehensible only to those who are able to fathom the process of the Creator's work. Possibly the child did not fully understand this, yet he told Great-Grandfather sincerely and confidently that he was capable — through his own self — of helping him and his soul stay on the Earth. I was not able to say the same for myself. I do not feel that kind of strength within me."

"I noticed that after hearing these words Great-Grandfather began simply radiating with joy," I observed.

"Yes, few indeed are those who have heard words like that in their grand old age. You see, Great-Grandfather received from the child's own lips an invitation to the future — an incarnation of the Future."

"It looks as though they had a strong love for one another."

"Our son, Vladimir, had begged Great-Grandfather to keep on living when he could not go on living any longer. And Great-Grandfather did live — he could not refuse the child's request."

"But how is such a thing possible?"

"It is very simple. But not automatically so. After all, doctors, too, are able to bring back people from a state of unconsciousness or oblivion. And not just doctors, but someone close to this person may call or stir them out of a faint or a state of unconsciousness, and they will live. Great-Grandfather's will and his love allowed him to prolong his life at his great-great-grandson's request. Great-Grandfather is the descendant of priests who did tremendous works through the centuries. Once he even stopped a huge explosion through his will, through his gaze, but it made him blind."

"What d'you mean, through his gaze? Is it possible for one's gaze to stop an explosion?"

"It is possible if the gaze is consciously directed with confidence in Man's power and unshakable will. Great-Grandfather knew where the disaster was about to happen and went there. He was just a little late with his foresight and an initial explosion did take place. But then he stood facing the source of life-threatening danger and through his gaze was able to tame the manifestations of the dark forces already whirling through space. Just one explosion happened, and that not at full strength, and two others could have taken place. But if Great-Grandfather had flinched even for a moment...

"You see, Vladimir, he stopped the explosion. Only he went blind."

"But why are you so concerned about our son's abilities which he has inherited from his great-great-grandfather?"

"I thought that the abilities he had inherited from you and me were sufficient. I taught him to conceal his additional abilities so that he would not appear strange to people. I wanted our son to go out and live in the world and not stand apart from others in his appearance. After all, there is a lot one can do without standing out from others.

"But something too extraordinary has happened. Who our son is now, and what his purpose in life is — that is something we must definitely try to decipher. And so I was asking the Creator to give him the strength to remain, at least for just a little longer, a simple child."

"You're concerned about this now, Anastasia. But I think in many respects it is you and your method of upbringing that are at fault here. You talk a lot about the soul, about Man's purpose in life. You have taught the child to read that extraordinary book about co-creation. So he's gone and formulated his own peculiar world-view.

"Why should a child at that age have to know about Soul, about God? You see, he calls me Papa, and at the same time he says he has a father. I realise he's calling God his Father. Even I have a hard time understanding that, but you've gone and given him an information overload. It's the way you've brought him up that's to blame, Anastasia."

"Remember, Vladimir, how I replied to Great-Grandfather that I could not order anyone's soul. And our son heard what I said. And yet some power higher than I has allowed him to act otherwise. But you should not worry. I shall be able to understand what has happened, even though our son may possibly look at me now in a different light. It will not be long before his strength exceeds both of ours combined."

"Well, okay. Every generation should be stronger and smarter than the one before."

"Yes, you are right, of course, Vladimir, but there is an element of sadness when someone is stronger and more insightful than his own generation."

"Eh? I don't understand what kind of sadness you're talking about, Anastasia."

She didn't reply, only hung her head, and her facial expression became sad. She is rarely sorrowful or sad. But this time... I understood... I understood the great tragedy of this Siberian recluse — Anastasia. She is all alone. Incredibly alone. Her world-view, her knowledge, her abilities are so vastly different from those of other people. And the more pronounced they are, the more tragic is her loneliness. She lives in another dimension of conscious awareness. This other dimension may be marvellous, but she is all alone there. Of course she could come down to other people's level, she could be like everyone else. But she has not done this. Why? Because to do that she would have to betray herself and her principles — perhaps even betray God. And then Anastasia decided to do something amazing. She began calling others into this splendid dimension. And there have been those capable of understanding her. And I, it seems, am just beginning to understand her, to really feel... Six years have passed and I am only beginning, just barely, to understand. And she has been patiently waiting all this time, calmly explaining everything without getting angry. Perseverant, unshakable in her hope.

Christ Jesus was probably the same way. Of course he had his disciples and people were constantly coming to hear him. But who could have been a *friend* to him? A friend who could finish his sentences and help him in a pinch. But not a single kindred spirit was at hand. Not one.

God! How do most people perceive Him? As an unreachable, amorphous, feelingless being! All they can say to Him is "Gimme this!" or "Judge that!" But if God is our Father, if He has created the world around us, then, quite naturally, the fundamental desire of our Parent can only be for a meaningful existence for His children, along with their understanding of the essence of creation and the opportunity to co-create together with them. But how can we talk about a meaningful existence when we constantly trample down everything God has created around us — trample on His thoughts — and yet all the while engage in various forms of worship to someone, only not Him?

But He doesn't need to be worshipped. He is waiting for our co-operation. But we... Well, we can't even comprehend such a simple truth as: if you're the son of God and can understand your Father, take just one hectare of land and create a Paradise on it, bringing joy to your Father. But no! All mankind is striving for something like crazy, but what? Who is it that is constantly making idiots of us all? And what does He, our Father, think when He sees all this earthly debauchery? He watches and waits for His earthly sons and daughters to wake up and come to their senses. He watches and causes the Sun to illuminate the whole Earth, so His children can breathe.

How are we to comprehend the essence of being? How are we to make sense of what is really happening to us? Is it mass psychosis? Or the deliberate influence of some kind of forces? What forces? When will we be free from them? Who are they?

Chapter Four

A dormant civilisation

This conversation took place on the second day of my stay.

Anastasia and I were sitting quietly together in our long-time favourite spot by the lake. Evening was coming on, but the cool evening freshness had not yet set in. A barely perceptible breeze fanned our bodies from constantly changing angles, as though designed to delight us with the many and variegated fragrances of the taiga.

With just a trace of a smile on her face, Anastasia contemplated the mirror surface of the lake before us. She seemed to be waiting for me to ask her the questions I wanted answers to. Only somehow I wasn't able to reduce my questions to a brief and concrete formulation. It appeared that what I managed to formulate in my mind did not reflect the main thing I really wanted to know. So I approached it circuitously:

"You see, Anastasia, here I am writing books using many of the words you have given me, even though I don't understand all your words right off, but it's not so much the words but the reaction to them that has me baffled most of all.

"Before I met you I was a simple entrepreneur. I worked and, like everyone else, wanted to make as much money as I could. I could afford to enjoy a drink and have a rousing good time, but nobody laid into me or my company's workers with the kind of criticism that the media is now overwhelming me with.

"Strange as it may seem, back then nobody faulted me for earning money, but as soon as the books came out, some personages began right off publishing articles saying I was nothing but a gold-digger, if not a charlatan and a bigot. It'd be okay if it were just me, but they've also gone and insulted my readers too, calling them bigots and fanatics. And goodness knows what they write about you. Either they argue that you don't exist at all or they say you're the queen of the heathens.

"It's funny how everything's turned out: here in Siberia there are a lot of minority ethnic groups, with different cultures and beliefs, some of them still practise shamanism, and nothing bad is ever said about them — on the contrary, they say these peoples' cultures need to be preserved. And here you are, all alone — well, apart from your grandfather and great-grandfather, and now your son — you live all alone here. You don't ask for anything, and yet the words you say provoke a storm of emotions. Some people absolutely delight in the words you say and get all excited, and start acting on them, while others attack you with unabashed fury and anger. Why is that so?"

"And you, Vladimir, can you not answer this question yourself?"

"Myself?"

"Yes, yourself."

"I've got very strange thoughts running through my head. I get the impression that out there in human society there are some kind of unknown people or forces who will do everything they can to make people suffer. These forces thrive on wars, the drug trade, prostitution and disease. And on their constant increase. How else to explain it? They don't attack books about murders or magazines with half-naked women, but there's something about books on Nature, or books on the soul, that isn't to their liking. And in your case it's even more peculiar. Here you are calling upon people to build their Paradise domains for happy families, and many people are strongly behind you in this endeavour.

"And not just in their words. People are starting to act. I myself have seen people who have taken land and begun working it, as you said, building their own kin's domain. These include young and old, rich and poor, and yet somebody's really uptight about that. And the media's constantly trying to distort what you say. They resort to outright lies, to put it bluntly. I can't understand how the words of a single woman living in the taiga and apparently not bothering anyone can be so powerful.

"And why would anybody try to engage in direct conflict with your words? There's also the claim that behind those words of yours lurks some kind of great power — occultism, maybe."

"And what do *you* think — is there a power behind them or are they just words?"

"I think there must be some kind of occult power in them, yes. That's what some of the esoterics are saying."

"Be careful, Vladimir, and try not to take in what others say. Try listening instead to your own heart and soul."

"I'm trying, only I haven't got enough information."

"What information, specifically?"

"Well, for instance, what ethnic background are you Anastasia? What religion are you and your relatives? Or maybe you don't have any ethnic background?"

"I have," replied Anastasia, rising to her feet. "But if I tell you now, the dark forces will rise up and scream in fright. Then they will try to come down with all their might — not just on me, but to crush you too. You will be able to withstand it once you have got beyond noticing their attempts and give your thought over completely to the marvellous reality. But as long as you consider yourself defenceless in the face of their anger, you should withdraw your question and forget about it until the right time."

Anastasia was now standing in front of me, her arms hanging loose at her side. I gazed up at her from below and couldn't help noticing how proudly, splendidly and unassailably she carried herself. Her tender and enquiring look was awaiting my response. I had no doubt that what she was about to say was indeed capable of provoking some kind of extraordinary reaction. I had no doubt because over the years I have known her I have seen a feverish reaction to her words on the part of many people. And for that reason I didn't doubt the possibility of danger either, but I responded:

"I'm not afraid. Even though I'm sure it's all going to come about just as you say. Maybe I'll be able to hold out myself, but then I'm not the only one... We have a son now. I don't want anything to threaten him."

At this point Volodya suddenly appeared and went over to Anastasia. He must have been quietly standing somewhere nearby and listening to our conversation, without interfering. But now that the topic had turned to him, he probably felt it was time to make himself known.

Volodya took Anastasia's hand in his own little hands, pressed his cheek against it, lifted up his head and said:

"Mamochka Anastasia, go ahead and answer Papa's question. I can take care of myself. History need not continue to be hidden from people on my account."

"Yes, that is true," observed Anastasia, stroking the child's little head. "You are strong, and you are getting stronger with each passing day." Then, raising her head and looking me straight in the eye, she pronounced the letters more distinctly than usual, as though introducing herself for the first time:

"I am a *Ved-russ,* Vladimir."

I actually felt a kind of extraordinary sensation within me from the word Anastasia pronounced — it felt like a mild electrical current was running over my whole body like a pleasant heat wave, as though imparting some kind of news to every cell of my being. And something unusual, it seemed to me, had happened in the space around me too. The word itself meant nothing to me, but for some reason I rose to my feet upon hearing it. I stood there, as though trying to remember something.

Once again, this time quite joyfully, Volodya spoke up:

"You, Mamochka Anastasia, are a Vedruss beauty, and I too am a Vedruss..."

Then he looked at me with a happy grin and said:

"You are my Papa. Just like me, you are a Vedruss, only dormant. I'm talking too much again, eh, Mama? I'll go now. I've thought up something marvellous for you and Papa. Before the Sun sets behind the trees I shall create what I have thought up!" And catching an affirmative nod from Anastasia, off he went trippingly into the forest.

I looked at Anastasia standing there in front of me and thought to myself: *The Vedruss must be one of the Yugra minorities still living in the Far North and Siberia.*[1]

In 1994 in Khanty-Mansiysk Province there was an international documentary film festival devoted to the Yugra minorities. At the request of the provincial administration many of the festival participants were quartered aboard my ship on the Ob River. I had the opportunity to talk with them, watch the films in the competition and travel with the film-makers to some of the more remote Siberian settlements where shamans were still practising their craft. I couldn't remember much about the culture and customs of these minority peoples. But I did recall feeling a tinge of sadness over the fact that these

[1]*Yugra* — the original name of the *Khanty,* one of the two major aboriginal groups in the Province of Khanty-Mansiysk, located around the northern reaches of the Ob River, just before it flows into the Arctic Ocean. Together with the neighbouring *Mansi,* the Khanty are classified as part of the Siberian branch of the Finno-Ugric peoples, which include Finns, Estonians and Hungarians. Since the first recorded arrival of Russian explorers and colonists in the 11th century, the Khanty have co-existed with the Russian state, often with a greater degree of autonomy than other parts of the Russian empire or federation.

extremely small populations were dying out. And people were treating them as some kind of exotic curiosity which would soon be disappearing completely from the face of the Earth.

I did not recall hearing anything from the participants at this film festival (which could really be considered a major national event) about the Vedruss people, so I asked Anastasia:

"Have your people died out, Anastasia? Or rather, are there just a very few of them left? Where were they settled previously?"

"Our people have not died out, Vladimir, they are dormant. Our people happily thrived on the territories now known as Russia, Ukraine, Belarus, England, Germany, France, India, China and many other states both large and small.

"Up until quite recently, only five thousand years ago, in the real world our people were thriving on lands from the Mediterranean and Black Sea to the farthest northern latitudes.

"We are Asians, Europeans and Russians, as well as those who recently called themselves Americans — in fact, god-people, all from a single Vedruss civilisation.[2]

"There was an age of life on our planet known as the Vedic Age.

"During the Vedic Age mankind reached a level of sensitive knowledge allowing it to create energy images through collective thought. And then it underwent a transition into a new era of existence, known as the Image Age.

"With the help of energy images, created by collective thought, mankind was afforded the opportunity of co-creating in the Universe. It could have had the ability to create Earth-like life on other planets. And it *would* have, if it had not committed any mistakes in passing through the Image Age.

[2] *Ved* is a Slavic root signifying 'knowledge' or 'to know'. The words *Vedic* and *Vedas* are derived from this root.

"In the Image Age, however, which lasted for nine thousand Earth years, mistakes were repeatedly made in the co-creation either of a single image or several images simultaneously.

"A mistake occurred if there remained in the Earth's human society people with insufficient purity of thought, with an insufficient culture of feelings and thoughts.

"Such mistakes had the effect of obscuring the opportunity to create in the expanses of the Universe, and led mankind into occultism.

"The Occult Age of human life has lasted for one thousand years now. It began with an intensive degradation of human consciousness. Ultimately, a degradation of consciousness and an insufficient purity of thought, coupled with knowledge and opportunity at the highest level, would always lead mankind to a global disaster.

"This was repeated many times over billions of Earth years.

"Now we are in mankind's Occult Age. And, as always, a disaster of global proportions was supposed to take place. It was supposed to, but the deadline has passed. We have passed the end of the Occult Millennium. Now it is up to everyone to take stock of their purpose, their essence and where the mistake was made. We should help each other in mentally retracing the course of our history in the opposite direction and pinpoint the mistake. Then an era of joyous life on the Earth will be ushered in — an era such as no one has ever witnessed before in global history. The Universe is anticipating it with bated breath and great hope.

"In the meantime the forces of darkness are alive and prevalent, feverishly trying to control people's minds. But for the first time they failed to notice the Vedruss' unusual behaviour back five thousand years ago.

"When an image was born by a perverted consciousness upon the Earth — an image which desired to exercise control over everybody, that was when the first war began. It was under the influence of this image that people started killing each other. This has happened many times on the Earth just before a global disaster. But this time... For the first time the Vedruss civilisation did not enter the fray on a non-material plane.

"Instead, the Vedruss fell asleep on their territories both large and small, switching off a part of their consciousness and feelings.

"Man's life on the Earth seemed to carry on as before: children were born, houses were built, the decrees of the attackers were obeyed. It seemed as though the Vedruss had submitted to the dark forces, but therein lay a great secret: by falling asleep, the Vedruss, unconquered, remained alive on all planes of being. And this happy civilisation is dormant right to this day, and will continue to sleep until those who are awake search out the mistake in the image creation. That same mistake that led the Earth's civilisation to its present-day situation.

"Once the mistake has been identified with absolute precision, the dormant ones may hear the words of those who are awake and begin to rouse each other out of sleep.

"Just who thought up this particular move, I cannot say. It is probably someone very close to God.

"You, as a Vedruss yourself, should try to wake up, at least a little, and take a look at the course of history.

"Our people went to sleep on various continents. Three thousand years ago they were thriving only on what is now Russian territory. At that time the age of the dark forces had already come upon the whole Earth. And the Vedruss continued their happy existence only on the 'island' now known as Russia.

"They needed, very much needed to hold out another thousand years. They had to decide how to convey their knowledge to future generations, figure out what was happening on the Earth and determine how a repetition of the mistake could be avoided in the future. They managed to hold out another fifteen hundred years on this 'island'. They fended off the attacks, but not on a material plane. The darkness had already taken control of people's minds over the whole Earth. The priests placed themselves above God and decided to create their own world of the occult. They had already managed to intoxicate a third of the world.

"But all the forces of darkness could do no harm to our people on this 'island' that is today called Russia.

"It was only fifteen hundred years ago that this last 'island', too, fell asleep. The civilisation of the Earth, the people who knew God, fell asleep in order to awaken to the dawn of a new reality.

"The forces of darkness supposed that they had succeeded in destroying this people's culture and the aspirations of their soul forever. This is why they are trying so hard to conceal the history of the Russian people from those living on the Earth today.

"In reality there is much more to the story. In covering up the history of the Russian people, which can serve as a stepping-stone into the world of the beautiful, they are actually trying to cover up the joyously living civilisation of the Earth — cover up the culture, knowledge and feeling of knowing God which are inherent in that glad civilisation your forebears were a part of."

"Wait, Anastasia! Could you tell me a bit more specifically about this extinct — or, as you put it, dormant — civilisation using simpler terms, terms easier to understand? And can you prove the existence of this civilisation?

"I can try, using simpler words. But it will be a hundred times better if each one tries to visualise it for themselves."

"But is it possible for everyone to see what happened ten thousand years ago?"

"Yes, it is. Only in varying degrees and detail. But everyone can get an overall feeling of it, and even see one's forebears and one's self in this joyous world."

"How can everyone do that? How can I do it, for example?"

"It is all very simple. To start with, Vladimir, try to evaluate and compare events you are familiar with just with your own sense of logic. When questions come up, find your own answers to them."

"What d'you mean, by *logic*? How can one learn about the history of Russia, let's say, by logic? Anyway, you said that our Russian history and culture have been destroyed, or hidden from all the people of the Earth... But how can I — or anybody else, for that matter — verify what you say just using logic?"

"Let us try reasoning through this together. I can do a little to help you get in touch with history."

"Okay, then. What needs to be done to start with?"

"To start with, you should answer yourself a question."

"Which one?"

"A very simple one. Remember, Vladimir, the history textbook you brought for our son. It is called *A history of the ancient world.* There are chapters in it discussing the history of Ancient Rome, Greece and China. They describe what Egypt was like five thousand years ago. But nothing is said about what Russia was like during this time. Never mind five thousand years — Russia's history and culture even from a thousand years ago are kept in the strictest secret. The textbook is written in the Russian language, aimed at Russian children, but there is not a word in it about the Russia of only two thousand years ago. Why?"

"Why?" I echoed. "Indeed, a most peculiar situation. A Russian textbook on the history of the ancient world and nothing said about Russia itself. Not a word about the history of the Russian people, either during the time of Ancient Rome and Egypt or even later. Strange! Very strange... as though there were no Russian people living during those times."

In trying to recall what I knew of history, I remembered hearing about the existence of the ancient philosophers of

Rome, Greece and China. I never read their works, just heard about them. I also knew that their works were accepted by society as brilliant and outstanding. But I could not recall a single Russian philosopher or poet of that time. Indeed, why?

Aware that Anastasia wanted me to try to figure out the answer myself, I said:

"Neither I nor anyone else can answer this question, Anastasia. It's a question that's probably not possible to answer."

"It *is* possible. Only one must not be lazy in one's logical reasoning. You see, we have come to our first conclusion: the history of the Russian people is unknown not only to the world at large but to the Russians themselves. Do you agree with this, Vladimir?"

"Well, maybe not entirely unknown. We still have *descriptions* of what happened a thousand years ago."

"The description was written under censorship and with significant distortion. Besides, the commentaries are the same for every historical event. Russia's past millennium — the Christian era — is like a single day of history. We have Christianity in Russia still today, but can you tell me what preceded it?"

"They say that before Christianity, Russia was a heathen land. People worshipped various gods. But the description is very superficial. There are no writings or even any legends about that period. There are no descriptions either of the political system or of people's way of life."

"So, you have reached Conclusion Number Two: the Russian people had a different culture then. Now, use your logic and tell me under what circumstances do attempts arise to hide or distort history?"

"Well, there's a clear answer to that question. People try to falsify history when it's necessary to show the benefits of following a new order, a new authority, a new ideology. But to completely conceal any trace of it... Wow! That's incredible!"

"The incredible happened, Vladimir. It is an incontestable fact. Now, tell me something else — and do not slacken in your thinking, please. Did this fact come about all by itself, or is it the result of a deliberate effort on somebody's part?"

"Judging by the fact that people have always burnt books when they wanted to stamp out knowledge or ideology, I would say that someone deliberately stamped out all knowledge about pre-Christian Russian culture too."

"Who do you think would have done that — who?"

"Most likely the ones who were imposing a new culture and religion on Russia."

"One might say that. But possibly there was somebody behind it, somebody controlling the new religion and those who imposed it? Someone with their own agenda?"

"But who? Who can control religion? Tell me!"

"You are still looking for answers from the outside, you are too lazy to search for them within yourself. I can give you an answer, but an outside answer may seem to you incredible — it may provoke a degree of doubt. Everyone can hear the answer within themselves, once they have liberated their soul and logic and awakened even a wee bit from sleep."

"It's not that I'm lazy. It's just that searching for answers within myself will take a lot of time. Better you tell me yourself what you know about history. If I start having doubts, I'll question you further. I shan't just take your story for granted, but I shall verify it by logic, both now and later on, as you suggest."

"Let it be as you wish. But I shall merely give you a rough outline of the whole, and let everyone try to fill in the details as they perceive them. Today's reality, along with the past and the future, is something that needs to be determined only within one's self, with one's own soul."

Chapter Five

The history of mankind, as told by Anastasia

Vedism

People have been living on the Earth for billions of years. Everything on the Earth was created perfect right from the start. Trees, blades of grass, bees and the whole animal world.

There is a direct connection between everything living on the Earth and the entire Universe. The apex of creation is Man. And in the great pristine Harmony of all things Man was created harmonious.

Man's purpose is to learn about all his surroundings and create perfection in the Universe. To create the likeness of the world of the Earth in other galaxies. And with each new creation of his to add more splendour to earthly creations.

The way will open for Man to create on other planets when Man is able to overcome temptation — when Man is able to hold in unity the grand and diverse energies of the Universe inherent in himself. And when he does not allow one of them to take precedence over the rest.

The day when the whole Earth is a Paradise garden will mark the opening of the path of creation in the Universe. And once Man becomes aware of the whole harmony of the Earth, he will be able to contribute his own splendour.

Man takes it upon himself to take account of his actions once in every million years. Whenever he makes a mistake, whenever he allows one of the many diverse energies he contains to dominate at the expense of the rest, a global catastrophe takes place. Then everything starts again from the beginning. This has happened many times.

One of mankind's million-year periods may be divided into three ages: first, the *Vedic Age,* second, the *Age of the Image,* and third, the *Age of the Occult.*

The first age of human society on the Earth, the Vedic, lasts 990,000 years. During this age Man lives in Paradise like a gladsome child, maturing under parental care.

During the Vedic Age God is known to Man. All God's feelings are inherent in Man, and through them Man is able to obtain any advice he needs directly from God. And if Man should suddenly make a mistake, God is free to correct it simply by giving a hint, without disturbing the general harmony or infringing on Man's freedom in any way.

In the Vedic Age Man does not raise questions about how or by whom the world, the Universe, the galaxies — along with his marvellous planet called Earth — were created. Everyone is completely aware that everything around, either visible or invisible, has been created by their Father, namely, God.

The Father is everywhere! All that grows and lives — are His living thoughts, His programme. And one can use one's own thought to commune with the Father's thoughts. And one can contribute to His programme, provided one first understands it in detail.

During the Vedic Age Man did not bow down before God, nor was there the multitude of religions which sprang up afterward. There was a culture to life. People lived a Divine way of life.

There were no diseases of the flesh. Feeding and clothing himself in a Divine manner, Man simply did not think about food and clothing. Thought was otherwise occupied — with the excitement of discovery. And no rulers reigned over human society. There were no boundaries marking off states as today.

Human society on the Earth consisted of happy families. The various continents were inhabited by families. They were all united by their aspiration to create a Space of Splendour.

There were many new discoveries, and each family, upon making a splendid discovery, felt the need to share it with others.

Families were formed by the energy of Love. And everyone was fully aware that a new family would create one more oasis of splendour on their native planet.

There were many rituals, holidays and carnivals among the people of the Vedic Age, each imbued with great meaning, sensitivity and a conscious awareness of the real Divine existence on the Earth.

Each ritual served as a grand school and a grand examination for each Man that took part in it. An examination in the eyes of others, in the eyes of one's self, and, consequently, in the eyes of God.

I shall tell you about and show you one of these rituals. It was a wedding rite — or, rather, the recognition of the union of two people in love. Look and see. Try to compare the level of knowledge and culture with that of today.

A union of two — a wedding

The wedding rite — a bonding of two hearts — took place with the participation of the whole village, sometimes several neighbouring (or even distant) villages together.

The lovers-to-be could meet in various ways. It could happen that two young people from the same settlement might fall in love. More frequently this occurred at one of the major festivals where a number of villages got together, when two gazes met and a spark of feeling was ignited in their hearts.

It did not matter whether he approached her or the other way round. They could tell a lot about each other's feelings simply by looking into each other's eyes. But there were words too, which, when translated into today's language, might sound something like this:

"With you, my beautiful goddess, I could create a Space of Love to last forever," he would tell his intended.

And if the girl's heart responded in kind, she might answer:

"My god, I am ready to help you in your grand co-creation."

Next the young lovers would jointly select a location for their future home.

They would go together and visit the area around the settlement where *he* lived, and then visit a corresponding area near *her* village. And there was no need for the lovers to tell their parents of their plans. Everyone in both settlements knew what was going on and was fully aware of the grand happening that would soon take place.

After mutually agreeing upon a site where they would make their future life together, the lovers would often retreat there, just the two of them.

Sometimes they would spend the night there under the open sky or in a shelter they had constructed from tree branches. They would greet the dawn and bid farewell to the day there. After returning briefly to their parents' houses, they would hurry back to their chosen site. It called them, and drew them to itself, much as an infant inexplicably draws to itself a pair of loving parents.

The parents did not ask the young lovers any questions. They simply waited in eager and joyful anticipation for their children to ask questions of them, all the while watching as their son or daughter spent time in deep meditation.

And the children once more went off to their grand retreat. This might go on for months, or even a year or two. And all during this time there would be no physical intimacy between the lovers.

People in the Vedic settlements knew that these two lovers' hearts were creating a grand design, inspired by the energy of Love.

Right from birth both *he* and *she* had been absorbing from their parents the lifestyle, knowledge and mindfulness of the Vedic culture. They could share their deep knowledge either of the stars burning in the night sky or of the flowers unfolding their petals with the rising of the Sun, or of the purpose of bees, or the diverse energies existing in space.

From early childhood both *he* and *she* had been bearing witness to the marvellous domains, oases and Paradise gardens their parents had created in love, and now they were aspiring to co-create their own.

On their chosen plot of land, a hectare or more in size, the lovers laid out a plan for their *real* life ahead. The task before them was to mentally formulate a design for their home and work out an arrangement for a wide variety of plant life, where everything could work in mutual support and harmony.

Everything would be arranged to grow on its own, without requiring any physical effort on Man's part. There were a whole lot of factors to be taken into account here, including the disposition of the planets, as well as the day-by-day flow of air currents.

Come spring and summer, plants would exhale ethers and give off a delightful fragrance. The young lovers would try to arrange them so that whenever a breeze blew a bouquet of many different ethers would waft into their dwelling.

All this foreshadowed the birth of a grand and extraordinary complex. It consisted of Divine creations. Besides, the place the lovers selected was to be transformed into a scene of splendour which would delight the eyes. Not on a canvas, but on living ground — a living design was being created in thought, one that would last for ever.

Even today people can imagine how involved and concentrated thought can become when one is endeavouring to come up with a design for one's own home.

A dachnik,[1] too, will understand how, especially in the spring, one's thought can get absorbed in what one's plot of land will look like in the future. And a talented artist, in planning out a picture, also knows how he can get carried away by his thoughts.

All these aspirations were now concentrated in the two loving hearts. Their knowledge was enhanced by the energy of Love, fostering new inspiration. This is why they did not even think about what we call today the pleasures of the flesh.

Once the design was complete in their thoughts, the lovers first paid their respects to the bridegroom's home village, where they went around to every house and invited the residents to come for a visit. Each household awaited their arrival with great excitement and anticipation.

The people of the Vedic culture knew that when lovers came to see them, a new energy of Divine Love would visit their domain, albeit just for a moment. And the marvellous Space of each domain would smile at the energy of young love. There was no question of imagination or occult beliefs here. After all, even today anyone finds the company of a good person more pleasant than that of an angry one. Lovers cannot be angry, especially when they come visiting as a couple.

[1]*dachnik* — see footnote 1 in Chapter 2: "Conversation with my son ".

But in every family in the village there was also a feeling of anxiety. Whenever the young couple dropped in on a garden, a courtyard or a house, they would say just a few words to the residents. Just a sentence to each one. Something like: *Oh, what a splendid apple tree you have!* or *Your cat has a knowing look!* or *Your bear is a real worker, very considerate!*

To any resident hearing the lovers praise a tree growing in the garden or the household cat, this was a sign of respect shown by the younger generation to their elders' way of life. The appraisal was always sincere, for the one giving it was indicating that he too would like to have a tree or a bear of similar worth.

It was with great pride and joy in the face of the whole village that each resident aspired to present the young couple with the object of their praise as a gift. And all would wait with anticipation for the day the couple had selected, when they would present their gifts to the bride and groom.

In the meantime the couple would also go from house to house in the bride's village. Sometimes it took three days to visit every family in the two settlements. Sometimes more than a week. When the couple finished making their rounds and the selected day arrived, people both young and old would rise at dawn and begin hastening to the site of the young couple's new home for a visit.

People would take up a position around the perimeter of the couple's selected domain, marked out by dry branches. In the middle, next to the shelter, a little mound rose out of the earth, decorated with flowers.

Look now and you will behold a most extraordinary scene!

There he is! Look! Here is a young man coming out to greet the residents of two villages. He is magnificent, a virtual 'Apollo'! With hair of russet brown and eyes of bright blue, he ascends the mound. Now on top of the mound, Radomir[2] — that is his name — is excited. The eyes of all the people present are fixed on him alone. And in the ensuing silence he begins his speech.

In front of everyone assembled he sets forth the design of a new Space which he has co-created with his beloved. With the aid of hand gestures, Radomir tells where the apple tree will grow, as well as the cherry tree and the pear tree. He shows the location of future groves of pine, oak, cedar and alder, along with what berry bushes will grow in between, what grasses and herbs will send forth their pleasant fragrances. And how easy it will be for bees to build their home among the trees. And where that workhorse of a bear will hibernate during the winter.

He speaks quite quickly, with great inspiration, setting forth the carefully thought through design. He goes on speaking for about three hours, and the whole time the people listen with rapt attention. And each time the young man points to a spot where some living thing will grow, according to his grand design, someone from the group of people listening will go over and stand on the future site of the apple tree, pear tree or cherry tree. Sometimes this individual is a woman, sometimes a man or an elderly person, but it could also be a child with eyes full of awareness, wisdom and joyful contentment.

Those stepping forth from the assembly are already holding in their hands saplings of the tree or plant designated for the selected spots where beauty is to unfold.

As each one steps forth, the people bow to him, inasmuch as he has shown himself worthy of the young couple's appreciation — as they did the rounds of the village domains — for being able to bring forth beauty. Which means he has been

[2]*Radomir* — an ancient Slavic name derived from the roots *rad* (joyful) and *mir* (peace). The word *rad,* in turn, is a derivative of *ra* (Sun).

found worthy of appreciation on the part of the Creator — the Father of all, the all-loving God.

That is not a conclusion reached through superstition. It is quite logical.

People of the Vedic culture were wont to treat the young couple designing the splendid oasis as deities. Such treatment was not unfounded. After all, the Creator had performed His creations in an impulse of inspiration and Love. And these young lovers, likewise inspired by Love, have now created a splendid design.

Look — the young man has finished speaking. He comes down from the mound and goes over to where his bride is standing. She has been following the whole proceedings with great excitement and emotion. He grasps her hand and leads her to the mound, where they take up a position together.

And the young man utters these words in front of everyone assembled:

"I have not created this Space of Love in isolation. Here is my marvellous inspiration standing beside me before you all."

The girl — it would be better to refer to her as a *maiden*[3] — initially lowers her eyes in the face of the whole gathering.

Every woman has her own particular charm. But there come special moments in the life of every woman when she rises over everyone else. Such moments are not found in today's culture. But back then...

Look! Standing on the mound, Liubomila[4] (as she is called) has raised her eyes to greet the people around her. The cries of excitement of the whole crowd have merged into one. The girl's face has broken into a smile — a bold smile, not a saucy

[3]*maiden* — The Russian word *deva* (here translated 'maiden') is identical to the Sanskrit word denoting the nature spirits which help plants to grow.

[4]*Liubomila* — an ancient Slavic name derived from the roots *liub* (love) and *mil* (dear).

one. She is overflowing with the energy of Love. Her cheeks glow more intensely than usual. The maiden's clear eyes and body vibrant with health reach out to envelop the people and the whole space around them with a radiant warmth. For a moment the whole scene falls silent, still. The young goddess shines before the people in all her beauty.

And so there is no question of haste as the maiden's parents, accompanied by the whole family, both young and old, solemnly make their way to the mound where the young couple are standing. They pause at the mound and bow to the couple, then the maiden's mother asks her daughter:

"All the wisdom of our family line lies in you, my daughter. Tell me, do you see the future of the land you have chosen?"

"Yes, Mama, I see it," replies the daughter.

"Tell me, daughter dear," the mother continues, "do you like everything about the future you have been shown?"

A young maiden might answer this question in a variety of ways. Most often she would say:

"Yes, Mama. Here will be a splendid Paradise garden, a living home."

But look and see, this particular temperamental girl, her cheeks flush with a bright glow, comes forth with a non-traditional response:

"The design is not bad, I really do like it. But, you know, still I should like to add just a little something."

Quickly jumping down from the mound, she all at once runs through the crowd to the edge of her future garden, where she stops and says:

"Here is where an evergreen should grow, with a birch beside it. When a breeze blows from that direction, it will first meet the branches of the pine, then the birch, and after that the breeze will ask the trees of the garden to sing a tune. It will not be repeated exactly the same way each time, but it will always be a delight to the soul. And here," the maiden adds, running off a little to one side, "here flowers are to grow. First there will be a flush of red, then over here a little later violet will spring up, and burgundy over there."

The maiden, all aglow like a fairy, starts dancing around her future garden. And once more the people remaining in the circle set themselves in motion, hurrying about to carry the seeds in their hands to the spots on the ground the high-spirited girl has pointed out.

Upon finishing her dance, she once more runs up to the mound. Here, standing next to her chosen one, she says:

"Now the Space here will be splendid in its sheen. The earth will produce a most marvellous scene."

"Tell everyone, my daughter," her mother once more addresses her, "who will be crowned to reign over all this marvellous Space around? Of all the people living on the Earth, upon whom could you bestow the crown?"

The maiden takes a sweeping look at all the people standing around holding saplings and seeds in their hands. Each of them stands in a spot indicated by the young man according to his plan and the maiden's outline of the splendid scene to be. But no one is yet planting a seed in the ground. The sacred moment for that has not yet arrived. And at this point the maiden turns to the young man standing beside her on the mound, and says, almost in song:

"He is worthy to wear the crown whose thought is able to create a future that will be splendid all around."

With these words the girl touches the shoulder of the young man standing beside her. He gets down on one knee before her. And the girl places on his head a most beautiful crown, a garland woven from sweet-smelling grasses by the maiden's own hand. Then, running her fingers three times through her fiancé's hair with her right hand, she takes hold of his head with her left and draws it a little closer to herself. Upon her signal the young man stands up. Then the girl runs down from the mound, and bows her head ever so slightly in a sign of meekness.

Right at this moment the young man's father, accompanied by his whole family, is making his way over to the newly crowned groom. Approaching the mound, he stops and pauses in respect. Then the father begins speaking, his gaze fixed on his son:

"Who are you whose thought is capable of creating a Space of Love?"

Whereupon the young man replies:

"I am your son, and I am the son of the Creator."

"A crown has been placed upon your head, a sign of a great mission to come. You who are wearing the crown, what will you do as you reign over your domain?"

"I shall create a future that all around most splendid will remain."

"Where will you gain the strength and inspiration, my son, and crowned son of the Creator?"

"In Love!"

"The energy of Love is capable of wandering through the whole Universe. How will you manage to see the reflection of universal love on the Earth?"

"There is one girl, Father, and for me she is the reflection of universal love on the Earth."

With these words the young man comes down to where the girl is standing, takes her by the hand and leads her back up to the mound.

Holding hands, they watch as the two families merge into a single group, sharing hugs and jokes and laughter, from the youngest child to the eldest present. Everything becomes quiet once more when the young man holds up his hand and proclaims:

"My thanks to all who heard me in this place. My soul has spoken of the creation of a new Space. My thanks to all who have held the energy of Love in such high esteem. May what has been conceived by the soul's dream now sprout from the earth!"

These words have the effect of setting all the people standing around in joyful motion. And with pride and joy and great emotion the people plant the seeds and saplings in the ground. Each one plants just one sapling in the spot indicated by the young man as set forth in his plan. Those not assigned a specific spot set about to walk around the perimeter of the plot which has already been marked out, and to the song of the *khorovod*[5] throw the seeds they have brought with them into the ground.

Within the space of a few minutes a marvellous garden has been planted — the Space which has been created through a dream.

And now the people retreat once more beyond the plot's perimeter. Only two families remain surrounding the mound where *he* and *she* — the young lovers — are still standing.

Drops of rain from the skies are falling onto the ground. The very warm rain is unusual and lasts but a short time — these are tears of joy and tenderness falling from the Creator's eyes to water the marvellous Space co-created by His children.

What could be dearer for a parent than the marvellous creations of His children?

And once again the young man with the crown holds up his hand, and when all is quiet, says:

"Let all the creatures given to Man by the Creator live together with us in friendship!"

Whereupon the girl and the young man come down from the mound and head over to the shelter where they stayed while working out the design.

[5]*khorovod* (pronounced *hur-a-VOT*) — a circle dance accompanied by choral singing, traditionally popular among Russians, Ukrainians and Belarusians.

After these words, out from the circle of people standing around someone approaches the couple, accompanied by an old dog and a pup. The dog is one that greeted the couple in a friendly way on their tour of the domains and which they have taken a great liking to.

The visitor bows and presents the bride with the puppy. At his signal the old dog goes and lies down at the young man's feet. This dog has been trained to help Man teach all the other animals."

The young man orders the dog to sit by the entrance to the shelter, and presently the girl lets the puppy inside. Other people approach the shelter one by one, carrying in their arms a kitten or a lamb, or bringing a colt or a bear cub on a lead.

People quickly fashion tree branches into a wicker fence to attach animal pens to the shelter. And soon the dwelling which just a short time ago was used by people as sleeping quarters is now filled with young animals. And there is tremendous significance in this. For in mixing with each other this way, these animals will forever live together in friendship, caring for and helping each other. No mysticism in this. It is the law of the Creator of Nature. After all, you can find examples of this even today. If a puppy and a kitten grow up together, they will remain friends as adults.

One of the other characteristics of the Vedic period was that people were fully aware of the purpose of the various creatures. And all animals served Man.

Man did not bother feeding the animals; on the contrary, they fed *him*. During the Vedic age both Man and his household pets were vegetarians, and never ate meat — they would not even think of it. The tremendous variety of plants around were able to supply Man's taste abundantly — not only his, but that of the animals surrounding him.

In this instance the bride and groom are presented by the residents of the two villages with the best they have.

After accepting the gifts, the young couple once more ascend the mound:

"Our hearty thanks to everyone," the bridegroom expresses their gratitude to those gathered. "Thank you all for co-creating this Space. My descendants will care for it over the centuries to come."

"Our thanks to the mothers who bore the creator," says the bride.

And, turning to the young man, she adds:

"For the joy of the Creator of the Sun, the Moon, the sprinkle of stars in the sky and our most beautiful Earth, we shall co-create everything you are able to think of."

"Together with you, my splendid goddess, and with people!" the young man answers, and adds:

"You alone are capable of inspiring my dreams."

Once again the young couple come down from the mound. They are immediately surrounded by their respective families, all congratulating them.

And the people dance a *khorovod* around the plot, accompanied by a joyful song.

By this time it is getting on toward evening. The young people each go back to their own home. For two nights and a day they will not see each other.

Upon reaching home, after having spent so much effort creating, the young creator falls into a deep sleep. His beautiful bride does the same in her own bed.

Those who remain at the spot where the co-creation took place in love will go on singing songs in a *khorovod.* Older couples will go off by themselves with resurrected memories of how it all happened to them on a similar day of their own.

And over the course of the following night and day the best craftsmen from both villages will build the couple a little house to the accompaniment of songs and the *khorovod.* They will fit the rows of timbers tight together, the moss and grass between them making a sweet-smelling bouquet. And by the end of that day the women of the villages will place the best fruits of their harvest in the new home. The two mothers will cover the bed with a linen counterpane. And by the second night every last one of the visitors will be gone from the domain.

In the meantime, after a good night's sleep, the young man awoke on this day to see the Sun rise over the Earth, illuminating his parents' house with its glad rejoicing. His first thought was for the crown he had been given the day before. He took this and put it on his head, smiling at everyone, the picture of bliss.

Accompanied by his brothers and sisters he went over to a nearby stream to wash in fresh spring water. Passing through the garden on his way back to the house, Radomir caught sight of his mother.

With a restrained smile the mother began admiring her son.

Whereupon the young man, bursting with excitement, could no longer restrain himself at the sight of his own mother. He picked her up in his arms with delight. Spinning around like a child, he exclaimed:

"How marvellous is life all around, my dear Mama! Mama!"

"Oh!" his mother exclaimed, breaking into a laugh. Grandfather smiled behind his moustache. Grandmother then approached the happy pair, carrying a beautiful carved wooden ladle, and said:

"Young god of ours, stop right there. You must spare your gladsome energies. Drink this tea of calming herbs, so that your energy does not burn you. Its time will come the following day."

After drinking the tea, the young man began conversing with his grandfather about the Universe and the meaning of life. But the tea soon inclined him to sleep. And the young man whom his grandmother called a "young god" had soon nodded off to sleep on the hand-crafted counterpane.

What was happening? Why did the grandmother call her grandson a 'god'? Was she exaggerating, delighting in her admiration of the young man? Not at all! It was simply the case that her grandson had done deeds worthy of God's name.

God had created the Earth and everything living and growing upon it. And with all the knowledge he had assimilated from his forebears, the young man was able to distinguish the purpose and function of a multitude of creations, much to the delight of the Creator. This enabled him to create from them a marvellous living oasis, one capable of bringing joy not only to him and his beloved, but also to the generations of their children, and to people who would over the centuries look upon this splendid domain which was created with love.

Could any of all people's deeds on the Earth have delighted God more? What better and more significant thing could a Man do within the space of one human lifetime on the Earth?

In the Vedic culture the wedding rite was no occult ritual. As an aspiration to the likeness of the Divine being it is of tremendous practical significance.

In showing his knowledge and aspirations to the people gathered, the young man in love was, in effect, being tested in front of them. His deeds showed that he included the knowledge of all the generations of his family beginning with its pristine origins. And he added his own contribution too. His creation was appraised as worthy by all the people, and it was with great joy that they planted trees and herbs in the spots he indicated. And the marvellous co-creation will flourish each spring in ever more beautiful form.

Yet for all this, not a single neighbour would feel the slightest envy at the sight of it, since everyone has been involved in co-creating this marvellous Space of Love. Each one now has their own little shoot they planted in the new splendid domain. When domains like this begin to multiply, the whole Earth will be clothed in God's own flourishing garden. And in the Vedic culture everyone knew that Man has been given life eternal, and that a splendid life repeats itself when those living now aspire to beauty and perfection!

Domains! Domains of the Vedic culture! Domains that were to be known in subsequent occult books as 'Paradise', as people lost their vast store of knowledge and imagined that this Paradise could be perceived only over the distant horizon beyond the clouds. And all to enhance the significance of so-called 'modern science' and covering up the poverty of their own thought.

There's no point in debating this without practical proof. But debate-settling actions can be quite simple. Let all those 'worthy' scholarly luminaries now living on the Earth try, for example, to set up just a single oasis for a single family — a task which, in the Vedic culture, every young man in love had to cope with.

A domain which is home to a happy family should be able to satisfy all the food requirements of everybody living in it, hour by hour.

Disease should not be permitted to have even a foothold. The changing reality of the scene before Man should moment by moment gladden his gaze. It should delight the ear with an infinite variety of sounds, and the nostrils with flowering fragrances.

And provide ethereal food for the soul, nursing the newborn and preserving love for ever. And so no member of the family should be wasting their energies on mundane concerns — their thought should remain free. Thought is given to all people for creative purposes.

The world of academe takes pride in its illusions:

"See, our ships are flying into space for the benefit of mankind!"

"For mankind's benefit, you say?"

"See all those bombs going off? They are to protect you!"

"But are they really to protect us?"

"See how this learned doctor has saved your life!"

But up to that point life was in the process of being annihilated, moment by moment, by everyday concerns. They saved the life of a slave to prolong his suffering.

The world of academe is in no position to create even the similitude of a splendid domain because, again, there is a law of the Universe which says: A single Creator inspired by love is stronger than all the sciences combined, which are deprived of love.

Now the newly-wed young man has slept his second night, his deep sleep undisturbed by anything. Only the image of his beloved sparkled and flashed like the stars. In his sleep this image merged with the Space they had created, the might and infinite variety of the Universe.

Radomir awakes before dawn. And without a word to anyone, he puts on his garland and picks up a shirt that has been hand-embroidered by his mother. Then he goes to the spring-fed stream.

The moon illumines his path through the pre-dawn darkness, while garlands of stars twinkle in the heavens. After washing in the stream, he puts on his shirt, and quickly makes his way to his sacred creation. The heavens begin to brighten.

And there he stands alone on the spot where the two villages recently celebrated their joy — the place he created through his dream.

The power of the feelings and sensations within a Man at such a moment can scarcely be comprehended by anyone who has not experienced them at least once for himself.

It can be said that these sensations and feelings are Divine in nature. And they increase in quivering anticipation of the first ray of dawn, in which... *There she is! His marvellous Liubomila!* Illumined in the dawn's rays, she runs to greet him and their co-creation.

This vision incarnate runs to meet Radomir. While perfection, of course, knows no real limit, it seems as though time has suddenly stopped for the two of them. Enveloped in the mist of their feelings, they enter their new house. The table is spread with delicacies, and a tempting fragrance of dried flowers wafts from the embroidered counterpane on the bed.

"What are you thinking about right now?" she asks him in a heated whisper.

"About *him* — our future child," and Radomir gives a quiver as he looks at Liubomila. "My, how beautiful you are!" No longer able to contain himself, he very tenderly touches her shoulder and cheek.

Both are enveloped in the warm breath of Love and carried away to unknown heights.

Nobody in a million years will ever be able to describe in detail what happens between *him* and *her* when, merging into one in the impulse of mutual love, two people work out the likeness of themselves and God.

But the god-people of the Vedic culture knew precisely that after the inexplicable miracle takes place, merging two into one — each of them still retains their individuality. And at the same time, for one inexplicable moment the Universe quivers at the sight: the soul of a newborn child runs trippingly, barefoot, through the stars to the Earth, *embodying in himself the union of two — plus a third — as one*.

This act of sanctifying the union of two people in love during the Vedic age can by no means be considered a manifestation of the occult. It was an entirely rational act, corresponding to their way of life. The ever-increasing feeling of love for one another in every family coupling bore witness to the level of this culture.

In our modern day this feeling of mutual love in married couples always tends to dissipate after a while. The energy of Love is no longer within them. And this is something accepted as a given by human society. But this scenario is unnatural to Man. It tells us that the lifestyle people lead today is unnatural.

A loving couple in the Vedic culture realised not with their mind but with their heart and soul that the spark of the feeling of Love is a call to a Divine co-creation.

Take note of what the couple originally aspired to. Together, in an impulse of inspiration, they mentally worked out their design — the design of a Space for their love. It was in this Space they had created that their child was conceived. Three significant feelings of love merged into one for eternity. After all, a Man — for reasons he cannot explain, even to himself — retains a strong reverence all his life for his family domain — his Motherland, for his child and for the woman with whom all this was co-created. It is only three feelings of love, not a single feeling all by itself, that can live for eternity.

The birth of a son or daughter to a Vedic-age family was also the occasion for a grand celebration and a life-significant rite. And there were many other celebrations back in those days. And there was absolutely no marital infidelity. Millions of happy families made the Earth a delightsome place. It is the ranks of historians today, in their efforts to please the powers that be, who say that Pristine Man was once stupid, that this Man killed animals, ate their meat in a frenzy and dressed himself in their skins. A monstrous lie is necessary to people trying to cover up their monstrous deeds.

Raising children in the Vedic culture

Mankind is ever looking for a perfect system of raising children. It endeavours to seek out the wisest teachers, and then hands over its children to be raised by them. And you, Vladimir, in preparing to talk with your son, spent five years seeking out the best system of child-raising. A system capable of explaining everything to you and teaching you how to communicate with your own birth son. And you kept on asking advice from recognised teachers and various scholars. But not one piece of advice, not one system did you find satisfying or indicative of perfection. Doubts came to you with increasing frequency: *If there did exist a perfect system of education, many people would surely be using it. And somewhere on the Earth there would be living a people that is truly happy. But it seems that in every society all you find is the same or different kinds of problems. You have to search for a happy family — it is like looking for a needle in a haystack. So that means there is no miraculous system of child-raising, and there is no point in searching, since there is nothing to search for.*

Forgive me, please: I had no other choice but to keep track of your thought the whole time. I was trying to determine through you what leads people away from what is so obvious.

And then one day I felt you thinking: *Lack of trust and fear of making a mistake are what make people hand over their children to schools and academies so that afterward they can blame their teachers — anyone but themselves.*

On another occasion I saw how you turned pale and became scared stiff at the thought that children are raised by their parents' and society's lifestyle. Your thought was true and accurate. But you were afraid of it, you kept trying all along to forget about it. But you did not succeed in forgetting what is all too obvious.

Then you tried disagreeing with your own thought. You reasoned like this: *How is it possible to become a scholar, an artist or a poet? How can one learn about astronomy or history without studying at a special school?*

But you were thinking in terms of subject categories of knowledge, and they are not the most important in raising children.

Much more important is the culture of feelings, which are capable of compressing all knowledge into a tiny nucleus. You were in a position to understand this since you yourself are a vivid example of what I have been saying. After all, you were able to write a book without studying in a special school.

You and I spent only three days together in this glade, and now you are a writer, known in various lands. You can step out in front of a huge audience including prominent teachers, scholars, poets and healers. And you can go on speaking to them for as long as three hours or more. And people listen to you with rapt attention. You are often asked questions such as: *How can you hold an infinite store of information in your memory? How can you recite pages of your books from memory without a copy in front of you?* You generally responded to such questions with a mumble. But you concluded within yourself that I must have been working some kind of invisible charms on you. In fact, everything that happened to you is a good deal simpler than that.

During those first three days you were with me here in the taiga, on all three days it was the Vedic school that was exercising an influence on you. And it is certainly not pushy or intrusive, and it does not have any treatises or dogmas. It is capable of transmitting all information through feelings.

At times you would get angry, or get excited and laugh, or become fearful. And every time a new feeling arose in you, new information was taken in. That information was truly vast in scope. It is being revealed only later on, when you remember the feelings it aroused in you at the time.

Feelings, after all, represent a tremendous amount of concentrated information. And the clearer and stronger the feeling, the more knowledge of the Universe it contains.

For example, remember that very first night in the taiga, when you awoke and saw the she-bear beside you. Right off you were frightened. Please take note and think about those words "right off you were frightened".

But what *is* this feeling of fear? Let us try translating it into informational terms. What do we get then? You thought: *Here beside me is a huge beast of the forest. It weighs considerably more than my body weight. Its paws are far stronger than the muscles of my arms. A beast of the forest can be aggressive, it can attack me and tear my body apart. I am defenceless. I had better jump up and run.*

To make logical sense of this whole tremendous amount of information requires not just a moment, but a considerably longer time. But this same information, when compressed into a feeling — in this case, fear — allows one to react instantaneously to the situation. When one experiences a vivid feeling, a large amount of information passes through Man in a flash. It would require a whole scholarly treatise just to describe it, which could take years to work out without the aid of feelings.

A correct complex of feelings sequenced in the right order can multiply a Man's existing store of knowledge by a thousandfold.

For example, your fear of the bear passed as instantaneously as it arose. But what made it go away? After all, it was not natural for it to go away. You were still in the taiga as before, still defenceless, and the bear was not far away — besides, there might be a multitude of other beasts out there in the forest.

But that sense of fear in you was instantaneously replaced by a feeling of security. You felt this sense of protection even more strongly than when you were on your boat, or in the city, surrounded by armed guards.

This feeling of protection came over you just as instantaneously. It came over you just as soon as you saw that the bear took pleasure in carrying out my orders, reacting to my words and gestures. The feeling of protection enabled you to perceive information in a whole new way. A detailed description of everything that happened to you could fill a great many pages of a scientific treatise. And in your books you have devoted quite a few pages to the animals' relationship to Man. But the theme is infinite in scope. In terms of feelings, however, it can be expressed in the twinkling of an eye.

But something still more significant took place. Within the space of just a few seconds two opposite feelings turned out to be in perfect balance. I became to you someone in whose presence you could feel completely protected, even though at the same time one you could not fully explain and even found a little frightening.

The balance of feelings is very important. It is a confirmation of Man's equilibrium, yet at the same time, as though constantly pulsating, feelings engender more and more streams of information.

The culture and way of life of each family in the Vedic civilisation, as well as the way of life of the whole human society of the time, constituted a most remarkable school for the raising of the next generation, an intense régime of self-perfection for Man, advancing him to the act of creation in worlds of the unfathomable Universe.

In the Vedic age children were not raised the way they are in our schools today, but through participation in merry festivals and rites. These were either celebrations within a single family or ones where the whole community took part, or several neighbouring communities together.

More specifically: the multitude of celebrations during the Vedic age were crucial tests for both children and adults, and a means of information exchange.

The way of life in the family and the preparation for these celebrations afforded the opportunity to acquire a tremendous systematic store of knowledge.

Children were taught without the compulsion they feel when they are made to sit and listen to a teacher against their will. The learning process unfolded moment by moment for both parents and their children, cheerfully and not obtrusively. It was something desirable and fascinating.

But it did include some methods that would be considered unusual today. Ignorant of their tremendous significance for Man's education, modern scholars might call parents' actions during Vedic times superstitious or even occult-like.

For example, *you* thought that way and were very concerned when you saw our son, still so very young and helpless, as yet unable to stand on his own two feet, being picked up by the mighty eagle. The eagle held the little boy in its claws, and circled over the glade, rising and descending by turns.[6]

That happened with children in all Vedic families, though they did not always employ eagles for this purpose. They might be able to show the Earth from on high from the top of a mountain, if there happened to be a mountain close to where they lived. Occasionally a father might take his infant son or daughter and climb to the top of a tall tree. Sometimes they would build a special tower for this purpose. And yet the effect was more dramatic when an eagle circled over the ground with an infant in its claws. In just a moment or so the child would experience a whole gamut of feelings, and in that very moment he would take in a whole multitude of information. And when he was older, he could discover this information within him through these feelings whenever he wanted, whenever the need arose.

Remember, for example, I showed you what a perfect design the handsome Radomir created together with his bride Liubomila for their domain. I told you that the most recognised scientists in the world today are unable to create

[6]See Book 3, Chapter 15: "A bird for discovering one's soul".

anything like that. They would not be able to do it even if they all joined together as one.

But how could the young man bring about such a miracle back then? Where did he acquire the knowledge of all the plants, the significance of the winds, the functions of the planets and so much else besides? After all, he never sat at a traditional school-desk. He did not study science. Then how did the young man learn the purpose of each and every one of 530,000 species of flora? He might make use of only nine thousand of them, but he could accurately tell the interrelationship each species had with the others.

Naturally Radomir had been observing his father's and their neighbours' domains right from childhood. Yet he never wrote anything down, and did not consciously memorise anything. He never asked his parents what grew for what purpose, and they would never vex him by preaching at him. And yet this young man in love still managed to create his own domain, and even a better one than his parents had.

Please do not be surprised, Vladimir! Try to understand. You see, Radomir did not set forth a logical plan for his garden, although indeed it turned out that way in his domain. What happened was that Radomir outlined through his feelings a splendid picture for his loved one and his future offspring. And in this his flight with the eagle over his family domain contributed to his impulse of love, to his inspiration.

During the time the infant Radomir looked down from the height of the eagle's flight on the landscape of the domain, a picture was being imprinted on his subconscious just as on a reel of movie film. He was still not able to appreciate the beauty of the scene with his mind. *But his feelings!* His feelings were able to scan all the information from the variegated countryside below into a permanent imprint. And through his feelings, not through his mind or intellect, he was able to perceive what he saw as beautiful.

Not only that, but there amidst the beautiful landscape seen from the sky stood his very own Mama, smiling at him. What can be more marvellous for a little one than his mother's smile? And his mother was waving to him. Yes, that was *her!* The one whose breasts contained warm, life-giving milk. For a suckling child, nothing could be more marvellous than that. And from the height of the eagle's flight everything the young Radomir beheld seemed to him to be a single whole, inseparable from his Mama. In the twinkling of an eye the knowledge of this part of creation entered into him with a flash of exhilaration.

Young people displayed great competence in such modern sciences as zoology, agronomy and astronomy. People also appreciated their artistic taste.

Of course, there were also professional teachers in the Vedic age.

During the winter, elderly people who were especially learned in various disciplines would come to the community. Each settlement had a common meeting-hall, where they could set forth their wisdom. And if one of the children listening to them suddenly showed a special interest in astronomy, for example, the teacher would go and talk to the child's parents in their home. The teacher would always be warmly welcomed in the home. This scholar would talk about the stars with the child as many hours and days as the youngster wished. And there is no definitive answer to the question as to who learnt more from whom during these discussions. After all, it was with considerable respect that the great elderly scholar asked questions of the child. He could argue with him without being preachy. In the Vedic age there was no need to record the discussion, or the conclusions or discoveries arising therefrom. Free from daily routine and the multitude of concerns that occupy us today, the human memory could take in a great deal more information than the best computers that have been invented in our times.

Besides, any discoveries made, provided they were rational, were at once shared with everyone to use and put into practice.

The parents and other members of the household might also listen to these scholarly discussions, and sometimes even contribute to them, albeit tactfully. But still, it was the child who was inevitably the centre of attention. When a budding astronomer came to what the adults judged to be a wrong conclusion, they might say something like: "Excuse me, I can't understand you."

The child would try to explain. And it often happened that the child would prove himself right.

As spring approached each year, all the residents of the settlement would gather in the common meeting-hall and take note of their children's most recent achievements. Reports were given during these days. A six-year-old lad, for example, might astound everyone, telling about the meaning of life like a philosopher. Children might show everyone the marvellous things they had made. Others might delight the gathering with a song or an unusual dance. You could call these acts a kind of test, or simply a time of fun for all — the label was unimportant. What was important was that everybody derived joy from the act of creating. The stream of positive emotions and revelations during this event were joyfully put into practice. To the question as to who remained the most important figure in the raising of children, one could confidently answer that it was the culture and way of life lived by families in the Vedic age.

What lessons can be drawn from that culture for children of our present day? Which of our current systems of child-raising is the best, can we say? Judge for yourself, none of them is perfect. Mind you, when we distort the history of mankind, we cause children to lie to themselves. And we force their thinking into a completely false way. And that is why we suffer and cause our children to suffer too.

Above all, everybody ought to know the truth about themselves. Without truth, life bogged down in false dogmas is like a hypnotic sleep.

The sequence of three pictures in children's textbooks needs to be rearranged. The history of people living on the Earth needs to be presented to children correctly, for a change. First of all one must verify in one's own heart the accuracy of what has been reported. And then once children have learnt the essence of this history undistorted, a new path must be selected in consultation with them.

Children's books about the history and development of the Earth and its people tend to feature three pictures that are far from harmless. Consider what these pictures impress upon them from a very young age:

The first picture shows an impression of Primitive Man. Take a look at how he is portrayed: he stands there all covered with thick hair, with a beastly grin and a dumb expression on his face, holding a wooden club and surrounded by the bones of the creatures he has killed.

The second picture features a Man clothed in armour, carrying a sword, a dazzling decorated helmet on his head. He is off to conquer cities with troops under his command, while a crowd of slaves bows low before his hand.

In the third picture Man is shown with a noble face and an intelligent expression. He is healthy-looking, and dressed in a suit, and surrounded by a multitude of appliances, contrivances and mechanical gadgets to boot. Happy and delightful is the overall impression of modern Man.

All three pictures are false, as is the sequence in which they are arranged. This whole lie is stubbornly, rigidly and deliberately drilled into our children. Later I shall be able to tell you who is responsible and why they find this lie so indispensable. But first I want you try to verify the accuracy of these three pictures using your own sense of logic.

Judge for yourself: the trees, bushes and grass you can still see today in their primitive form. Even though they are billions of years old, you can still look at them and delight in their perfection.

What does all this tell us? The works of the Creator were made perfect right from the very beginning. And so? Did He make Man, the favourite of all His creations, to be some kind of monstrosity? Of course not! Right from the beginning, Man, the most perfect work of the Creator, was the most glorious creation on the Earth.

The first picture ought to show history as it actually was: it ought to show a family of happy people, with a look on their faces expressing both intelligence and child-like purity. And love on the faces of both parents. Human bodies in harmony with their surroundings, striking in their beauty and graceful power of spirit. A flourishing garden all around. Creatures always on the alert to render service with gratitude.

The second picture, too, should present to children an image of historical fact — two armies in monstrous armour rushing at each other, their commanders standing on a height of land, being entreated by priests. Some of their faces show fear and disorientation, while those of others, after yielding to the priests' entreaties, are inflamed with a beastly fanaticism. In just a moment a senseless slaughter will begin. People will start killing their own kind.

The third picture shows people in today's world. We should see a group of people of pale and sickly countenance in a room filled with an array of artificial things. Some have extremely obese figures, others are bent over, faces are full of heaviness and gloom. The kinds of faces you see on most passers-by along big-city sidewalks. Through the window one can see cars exploding on the street. And dirty ashes raining down from the sky.

All three of these true pictures of history should be shown to the child and the question asked: "Which of these lifestyles would you like to live?"

The pictures are only arbitrary illustrations. Of course the child should also be told the true account, sincerely and skilfully presented. The child should know the whole history of the human race without misleading distortions. Only after that can his actual education begin. The question should be asked: "How can we change the situation today?"

And the child will come up with an answer — not right off, not in the twinkling of an eye. But he will find it! Another thought will take over — a creative thought. Oh, the raising of children!... You see, Vladimir, just a single sincerely asked question, together with the parents' desire to hear their child's answer, is capable of uniting parents with their children — of making them happy — for ever. This joint quest for happiness is infinite. But even the beginning of the quest can be called a state of happiness.

Everybody today should learn their true history.

Rituals

At a later period the occult priests undertook tremendous efforts to distort and besmirch the significance of the ritual acts of Vedic times. They started a rumour, for example, that the Vedic people mindlessly worshipped the element of water. And that they held a yearly sacrifice of young girls who had not yet known love, throwing them into a lake or a river. Or that, tying them to a raft, they pushed them off from the shore and despatched them to their doom.

The element of water — a lake or a river — was indeed connected with many acts among the Vedic people. But it had a completely different significance — in support of life, not death. Let me tell you about just one of these. It is still practised today in a superficial form. But the resemblance is only superficial. In today's variant its great rational and poetic significance has been replaced by obscurity and occultism.

In various countries today there is a celebration involving water, whereby wreaths or small rafts with beautiful lanterns or candles are set afloat on a water surface and pushed away from the shore in a plea to the water to grant good fortune. But let us see where this particular celebration originated and how rational and poetic a significance it had in its pristine form.

In Vedic times it sometimes happened that one or two girls (how many is of no importance) did not find someone they could love within their own community. And even at large festivals involving several communities they did not succeed in choosing their intended. This would not have been on account of a limited selection. Indeed, they were presented with a whole array of splendid young men with intelligent countenances — almost like gods, who shone in their celebratory performances. But while the heart and soul of the girl in question were filled with great expectations, they were not visited by love. The girl was dreaming of someone, but of whom? She herself did not know. Even today, no one can explain the mystery or freedom of choice inherent in the energy of Love.

This is why on a designated day the girls would go down to the river, and in one of the little bays set a small raft afloat. Its edges were decorated with a garland of flowers. In the middle stood a small jug of wine or fruit infusion. Pieces of fruit were placed around the jug. The drink was to be prepared by the girl herself, and the fruit to be plucked by her from the trees she had planted by her own hand in her family garden. She might also place on the raft a woven linen headband, or some other object, but it had to be something made with her own hands. Lastly she would place on the raft a little *lampadka*.[7]

Around a fire burning on the shore the girls danced their *khorovod* and sang about a beloved of whom they were not yet fully aware. Then, taking one of the branches burning on the fire, they lit the wick of the *lampadka*. They pushed their rafts out of the bay into the mainstream of the river, where the current would catch it and tenderly convey it down to the river's farthest unknown reaches.

And each girl followed her raft with a hopeful gaze as it receded into the distance, until only the little light of the *lampadka* was still visible. But the girls' hearts were aflame with the fire of hope. A feeling of joy and tenderness grew within, directed to one whom they were yet to know.

Hastening back to their homes, the girls retreated to their rooms and excitedly began preparing for the anticipated meeting. He, the desired one, might come with the dawn or at sunset time — the hour did not matter. But how did it happen? What would draw him to her? Was the meeting the result of mysticism or rationality? Or perhaps of the knowledge to which the Vedic people had access through their feelings? Decide for yourself which way.

After all, the girls' rafts were carried along by the current on specific days. All the communities, even the distant ones, were aware of these particular days.

[7] *lampadka* — a small vessel filled with tree oil and a wick which could be lit.

Their journey might last a day, or two or three. On all these days and moonlit nights young men who had not yet known love were waiting hopefully in their loneliness all along the river's bays.

Upon seeing the little lights in the distance being carried along by the current, a young man would at once leap into the water and swim toward the little lights of love he had seen. The current did not inflame the young man's heated body, but tenderly cradled it with the transparent water of the stream. Closer and closer came the little lights and now the young man could make out the outline of the rafts — each one prettier than the next, it seemed. He chose one of them. It was not clear why this particular one fell under his special esteem.

He drew the raft from the middle of the stream to the shore, either pushing it with his hand or nudging it along by pressing his cheek to its side. It seemed as though the river current was engaging him in play. But his body was constantly being arrayed with strength, more and more, and he scarcely noticed the river's play. Besides, his thought was already on the shore.

Placing the little raft carefully on the land, the young man snuffed out the *lampadka,* took an excited drink from the jug and quickly headed home to prepare for his journey. He took with him whatever he had found on the little craft. Along the way he took a taste of the fruit, and was thrilled by its taste.

By and by he arrived at the village from where the raft had been launched, and was able to accurately determine which garden and tree whose fruit had sweetened his journey.

Aha! — some might wonder — *one cannot escape mysticism entirely: how on earth could young men of that time find their future loved ones with such accuracy?*

One could say that it was Love leading them by a path known solely to Love. But I can simplify the explanation — the *lampadka* also played a role. Notches had been cut in the small vessel carrying the brightly burning wick floating in the oil, so that everyone could tell how long the *lampadka* had been alight. The speed of the river's current was also widely known. It was a very simple calculation, and quickly executed. For a young man of the Vedic age, it was no task at all to find in the village the particular tree from which the fruit he had eaten had been plucked.

Pieces of fruit resemble each other only superficially. The fruit of trees and plants of the same species, even two trees growing side by side, can show marked differences in shape, colour, fragrance and taste.

There is only one thing that cannot be explained with complete accuracy. How was it that *he* and *she* always fell in love with each other upon meeting for the first time? And their love was extraordinarily passionate.

"It is all quite simple," a philosopher of the present day might say. "Their feelings for each other were already being set afire by their own dream even before they met."

But back then a wizened wise-man would have responded to such a question with a wink: "Our river has always had a mischievous streak in her!"

Of course, if he wanted to, the wise-man could always go into the details of each moment of the ritual I have told you about and explain the purpose of each one of those moments. He could write a great treatise on it. But no wise-man would bother wasting his thought on such a venture. The whole point is, Vladimir, that they... *They did not analyse life, they CREATED it!*

Feeding life in the flesh

People living in the Vedic age did not know a single disease of the flesh. Even at the age of a hundred and fifty or even two hundred years they maintained a lively spirit, a joy of living, and remained completely healthy. They had no doctors or healers such as exist in great numbers today. Diseases of the flesh were impossible because the way of life in one's own domain, the natural Space of Love which they themselves had established, completely regulated their intake of food. Man's body was supplied with everything it needed in the required quantity and at the time most favourable for its consumption, and at the most favourable planetary alignment for the intake of food.

Take note, Vladimir: in Nature it is no arbitrary phenomenon that during the whole spring, summer and autumn seasons the various plants mature and bring forth their fruit in a particular sequence.

First come the blades of grass — the dandelions, for example. They are also pleasing to the taste, especially when mixed with winter fare.

Then we see early currants maturing, wild strawberries and raspberries — both earlier in the full sun and later in the shade; sweet cherries; later sour cherries and a great many other fruits, herbs and berries, all of which, at the appropriate moment of their own choosing, attempt to attract human attention by their unusual shape, colour and fragrance.

There was no science of nutrition back then. What and how much one should eat and at what time — that was not something anyone even thought about. And still Man consumed everything needful for his body, with an accuracy down to the last gram.

Each berry, little herb and piece of fruit has its own day, hour and minute when it is the most beneficial to the human body — when it will complete the process of its own growth in conjunction with the celestial bodies. By this time it will have taken account of the specifics of what lies under the ground and of other plants growing around it, as well as of the Man that has bestowed his gaze upon it, and then evaluate and determine what his greatest needs are. And on that very day when it is ready to serve Man, Man will honour it by his acceptance, and allow perfection itself to become his food.

I have said that a woman with child should spend all nine months of her pregnancy in her own garden, in the Space she has created together with the one she loves. This is no occult mystery — it manifests the great rationality of the Divine being. Judge for yourself: in Nature there are many plants that can even painlessly terminate a woman's pregnancy — garlic, for example, oregano, the male fern, birthwort and many others. On the other hand, there are plants capable of helping the fœtus develop harmoniously in the mother's womb. Which ones should be taken and in what quantity is not something anybody will ever be able to tell. *He* is the only one who knows — the one inside the mother's womb. And he is taking care of not only himself but his mother too. That is why it often happens that after having a child a mother becomes healthier, younger-looking.

In order for this to occur, the pregnant mother must definitely be in her own garden, where every blade of grass is acquainted with her and every piece of fruit grows exclusively for her. She has also come to know each one's taste and fragrance. Her desires are quite natural and are in the best position to determine what kind of food she needs to take in and in what quantity.

Such accuracy is not possible in someone else's domain or garden, even if the vegetation in that garden is many times richer and more diverse. Besides, another factor making the ideal food intake impossible in another garden is that before consuming a particular berry or piece of fruit the woman will try it first.

Take an apple, for example. If she wishes to eat it, she plucks it from the tree and takes a bite. After swallowing the bite she at once feels that here is something her body does not need and has thereby caused harm to herself and to her child. Why does this happen? The fact is that even outwardly similar pieces of fruit can be made up of different substances. In her own garden, having tasted fruit from the various trees on a number of occasions, she could not make such a mistake. In another garden mistakes are inevitable.

What kind of law or knowledge provided such fine-tuned assistance in feeding Man at that time? It was the absence of laws and treatises! Man could depend only upon the Divine. Today they say that Man is in unity with — is at one with — Nature. But what is this unity right now — have you ever thought about it? In today's day and age Man consumes mainly artificial food — only what the system offers him as convenient to itself. And the schedule of consumption of food is also artificially determined by this artificial system.

Back then, in the Vedic age, everything was determined for Man by his God-given feelings. And the slightest sensation of hunger was satisfied by the Space of Love back then. After all, Man's feelings, in harmony with his Space of Love, could determine down to the minute — as accurately as the most perfect mechanical device ever invented or the smartest instructions ever penned — what food Man should take in and when.

Whenever Man walked through the Space of his own co-creation, his free thought could create or work out plans on the scale of the Universe. Temptingly beautiful fruit surrounded him. Intuitively he would pluck and eat a sample, or two, or three, without having his thought distracted by these sweet delicacies supplied him by God.

Back then, Man did not think about food. He fed himself in much the same manner as we today breathe. The Space he had created, in conjunction with his intuition, accurately worked out how and when the flesh should be fed.

In the wintertime the whole multitude of plants freed itself from its fruit and foliage in preparation for rest. Winter was for the creation of the spring to come.

But even in winter Man did not waste his time thinking of food, even though he did not prepare any comestibles in advance. All this was done for him by household creatures with great effort and love. Squirrels amassed a whole collection of nuts and mushrooms. Bees collected honey and flower pollen. Every autumn the bear would dig root-crop storage cellars.

Upon awakening in the spring, the bear would come to the Man's dwelling and either give a low roar or knock lightly with his paw upon the door. The bear would summon the Man, who would in turn show him which of the cellars should be dug up. Perhaps the bear had forgotten where he had stored away the food. Perhaps he was longing for communication with Man. Any member of the family might come out to him in response, but most of the time it was the child. After giving the hard-working beast a pat on the muzzle, he would go to the place designated by a marker and stamp his foot on the ground. The bear then began scraping the earth away in that spot and opened up the stores. Upon seeing his accomplishment he would jump all around for joy before delivering the stored food up to the surface with his paw. But he would not be the first to partake of the food — he would wait until Man began carting off at least some of the goods to the house.

Man himself could also prepare provisions, but this was not so much work as an art form. Many families would produce their own wine and infusions from different kinds of berries. Such wine was not strong and intoxicating like vodka. The result was a most healthful drink. Useful food provided to

Man by animals included milk, only not from just any animal. Man selected only those that were considered kind, tender and keen of mind — those who demonstrated an eagerness to offer Man what they produced.

Let us say one of the children or the elders of a household went up to a goat or a cow and touched its udder, and the animal suddenly began moving away. Man would not attempt to drink the milk of any animal that did not want to share it with him. This did not mean that the animal did not love the Man. It often happened that animals subconsciously determined that at that moment the composition of their lactic mixture would not be useful to the Man.

People of the Vedic civilisation would feed themselves from the various kinds of food growing only on their own plot or produced by their household animals. This approach was not determined by any kind of superstition or law. Rather, it was the result of a vast store of knowledge.

Though there is a difference between 'knowing' (*znat'*) and 'being fully aware of' (*vedat'*) something.[8] 'Being fully aware of' is not just to 'know'. It is to feel with one's whole being — body and soul — a multitude of phenomena, the purpose of each Divine creation, as well as His system.

And every Man of the Vedic culture was fully aware that what he consumed as food not only fed the body, but filled the soul with conscious awareness. At the same time it conveyed information directly to him from all the worlds of the Universe.

[8]The words *znat'* and *vedat'* in Russian are often used interchangeably in the sense of 'know', whereas in fact there is a significant distinction between them, as Anastasia points out here. While *znat'* specifically refers to 'knowing' through the mind or logic, *vedat'* (from an ancient Sanskrit root) covers other kinds of knowing as well — inspiration, intuition, emotional feelings etc.) — in other words, not just 'knowing' per se, but being *fully aware* of all dimensions of a subject through the various channels of knowledge available.

This is why these people were many times superior to their modern-day counterparts in terms of inner energy, keenness of mind and quickness of thought.

The animals and plants living in Man's family Space reacted to Man as to a god. The animals, herbs and trees were constantly thirsting for a tender look or a kind touch on Man's part.

And this power of the energy of feelings was what prevented unwanted weeds from growing in the garden or vegetable plot. Many people are now aware how a household plant can suddenly shrivel up when it meets with disfavour on the part of someone in the family. On the other hand, a feeling of love and communication directed toward the same plant can cause it to flourish.

This is why the Vedic people never went near their garden with a hoe. Even today, we have expressions such as 'give someone the evil eye'. It originated in those times. People could create a lot through their energy of feelings.

Suppose a Man is walking through his domain. Everything around catches his kindly gaze. He might look at a weed, and think: *Why are you here?* The weed would quickly wither from sorrow. On the other hand, if one were to smile at a cherry tree, it would cause its sap to run through its veins with twice the energy as before.

And if someone among the Vedic people happened to set out on a long journey, that Man would not bother to take along a supply of food. He would be able to find more than enough along the way to feed himself. Whenever he came to a settlement, he would see the splendid domains and ask for food and drink. It was considered an honour to serve tasty fruit, vegetables and drink to a traveller.

Life without violence and crime

Among the people of the Vedic civilisation, over the thousands of years of its existence, there was not a single act of violence or theft, or a mere fight. Even insulting words were absent from people's vocabulary. Yet at the same time there were no laws to punish such behaviour.

Laws can never protect one from evil deeds. But the knowledge and culture of the Vedic peoples completely ruled out conflicts in interpersonal relationships.

Judge for yourself, Vladimir: you see, every family living in their domain was aware that should any kind of unpleasantness happen to anyone, even a stranger, on the territory of their own domain or nearby, even on the very edge of the settlement, the whole Space would then suffer.

The universal energy of aggression would have an effect on every growing thing and on everyone living in that Space. It would upset the balance of energies. The energy of aggression might grow and leave its impression on adults and children alike, and infect their offspring with illness.

By contrast, if a passing traveller leaves a feeling of joy behind, the Space will radiate even greater beauty.

Not only that, but a Man visiting another settlement would be physically incapable of eating food plucked from a tree without the owner's permission or picked up from the ground in a garden upon which he had intruded.

People of the Vedic culture had a highly refined sensitivity. Their physiological makeup would immediately notice a significant distinction in the taste of pilfered food from that served by someone's generous hand. The whole range of foodstuffs sold in our modern supermarkets has nowhere near the fragrance and taste of the pristine produce of the Vedic age. Completely indifferent to Man, it has no feeling or soul. It does not belong to anyone and is beholden to no one. It is simply merchandise for sale.

If modern Man could actually taste and compare the food known in Vedic times, he could never eat the produce of today.

A newcomer could not, would not even think to take what was owned by somebody else without asking. Every single object, even a stone, contains information within itself known only to the family living in that particular domain.

In the Vedic civilisation, every domain was a fortress that loomed impenetrable to evil in whatever form. At the same time it served as a mother's womb for the family dwelling therein.

Nobody back then built high walls for fortification. The territory of each domain was protected by a living green hedge — a hedge which, along with everything living within its boundaries, protected the family from a whole host of harmful influences on the human body and soul.

I already mentioned to you that the bodies of deceased family members were buried only in the garden or among the trees of their own domain.

Those people were fully aware that while the human soul is eternal, the material body, too, cannot disappear without a trace. All objects, even those which appear to be soulless, carry within themselves a great deal of information from the Universe.

In the Divine nature nothing ever disappears into oblivion. It only changes its state and its fleshly form.

The bodies of the deceased were not covered with headstones, and even the places of their burial were not marked in any way. The Space created by their hands and soul served as a great monument to them.

And, changing their state, the now soulless bodies gave rise to trees, herbs and flowers. New children were born and walked among them. Oh, how everything around just loved the children! The spirit of their ancestors lingered over the Space, loving and protecting the children.

Children treated the Space of their Motherland with love. Their thought created no illusion about life being finite. On the contrary, the life of the Vedic peoples was infinite.

The soaring soul passes through all the dimensions of the Universe, and after visiting a number of different planes of being, it is once again embodied in conventional human form.

Upon waking in the garden of his Motherland, the child will once again give a bright smile. The whole Space responds to his smile. And the little rays of light, the breeze rustling the leaves on the trees, the flowers and the stars in the distant sky will sigh: "We are at one, embodied by you, child of Divine being."

Even today people cannot figure out why elderly people living on foreign strands ask to be buried in their Motherland.

Such people intuitively suspect that only their Motherland can bring them back to the Earth in a Paradise garden, while a foreign strand rejects their souls. To have their bodies buried in the Motherland has been the aspiration of people's souls for millennia. But can a cemetery be called a piece of the Motherland in any nation?

Cemeteries are a markedly recent phenomenon, designed to tear human souls apart in hellfire, demean and subjugate them, make them into lowly slaves.

Cemeteries are like... Well, they are like cesspits, where people go to get rid of their useless junk. The souls of the dead are tormented over cemeteries, while the living are terrified of cemetery plots.

Picture to yourself, by contrast, a kin's domain of Vedic times. Bodies of many generations are buried there. Every little herb aspires to tenderly care for those living therein, to be useful to Man's life in the flesh.

But every herb and every fruit in the garden can suddenly become poisonous when faced with aggression on the part of a newcomer. That is why nobody even thought of taking anything without asking.

The domains could not be seized by force. They could not be bought for any amount of money. Of course, who would dare trespass upon a place that is capable of destroying the trespasser?

And each individual here endeavoured to create their own marvellous oasis. The whole planet grew more beautiful with each passing year.

When modern Man surveys a city from on high today, what does he see, pray tell? The whole ground covered with an accumulation of artificially erected stones. Dwellings spread in all directions — upward and outward. Here, there and everywhere lie miles and miles of vast expanses blanketed by stone landscapes. There is no clean water anywhere, and the air is polluted. How many happy families can dwell under their own piles of stone?

If one compares modern families with those of the Vedic culture, the answer is: not a single one. And one could go further: amidst these piles of artificial stone people do not dwell — they sleep.

And yet in this hypnotic sleep a single living cell still strays like a tiny nucleus through the body. Sometimes at rest, sometimes in motion, this living cell touches teeming multitudes of others, attempting to awaken those that are asleep. Its name is *Dream*! And it will awaken them! Then human families will once again create marvellous oases upon the Earth.

As it was before, so will it be again. And in looking down on the Earth from on high, Man's gaze will once again be much charmed by a multitude of living scenes. And each of these marvellous scenes will mean that the Earth has been touched in that spot by the hand of an awakened Vedruss. And once again a happy family of people will be dwelling in their own plot of the Motherland — people who have learnt to know God and the meaning and purpose of life.

The Vedic people knew why the stars are in the sky. Their numbers included a great many poets and artists. There was never any rivalry among the communities. There was no cause for crime or violence. And there was a complete absence of hierarchical structures. The Vedruss culture flourished on the territories of our modern nations of Europe, India, Egypt and China, and there were no lines of demarcation dividing the various areas of land. There were no rulers, either important or petty. The sequence of grand celebrations provided a natural order of things.

People of the Vedic age possessed a knowledge of creation far in advance of modern Man. Their inner energy allowed them to enhance the growth of some plants and arrest that of others. Household animals endeavoured to carry out Man's commands not to obtain food, which they already had in abundance, but to receive from Man a reward in the rays of the energy of grace emanating from him.

Even today a word or gesture of praise from Man is pleasant to everyone — to people, animals and all growing things.

But in earlier times people's energy was immeasurably greater — all living things were drawn to it as to the Sun.

Chapter Six

Imagery and trial

Toward the end of the Vedic Age of human life a great discovery began to take place — a discovery unparalleled over the whole course of the history of human civilisations on the Earth.[1]

People became acutely aware of the power of collective thought.

And here we must clarify: what, exactly, *is* the thought of Man? The thought of Man is an energy unparalleled anywhere in space. It is capable of creating marvellous worlds on the one hand or, on the other, weapons capable of destroying the planet. And all the matter that we see today, without exception, has been created by thought.

Nature, the animal kingdom, Man himself, have all been created with great inspiration by the Divine thought.

And the proliferation of artificial objects, machines and mechanical devices which we see today are the creations of Man's thought. You may think that it is Man's hand that has produced them. Yes, today, hands must be employed. But to begin with, everything down to the last detail is created by thought.

It is believed today that Man's thought is more perfect now than in the past. But that is far from being the case.

For each member of the Vedic civilisation it was many millions of times superior to that of modern Man in terms of the

[1]This chapter is a continuation of Anastasia's narrative on the history of mankind, which, with one or two interruptions, carries through to the end of Chapter 8.

speed and fulness of information involved. This can be seen in the knowledge we have taken from the past about using plants for medicines and food. But Nature's devices are far more perfect and complex than anything artificial.

It was not just that Man summoned a whole lot of beasts to serve him. It was not just a case of defining the function of all growing things. Once he realised the power of collective thought, he found that he could use it to control even the weather, or cause springs to well up from the depths of the Earth. If he were not careful in handling his thought, he could make a bird fall from the sky while in flight. Or affect life on distant stars — either to plant gardens on them or to utterly destroy them. This is no fiction, but fact, and it was all given to mankind.

Everyone today knows how Man, having launched himself on the path of technocracy, has been attempting to build space ships capable of reaching the stars.

People have gone to the Moon, but only by wasting valuable resources and energies and with great harm to the Earth. But they have changed nothing on the Moon. This kind of approach is short-sighted — it is doomed to failure and is dangerous for everyone on the Earth as well as for other planets.

There is another approach which is much more effective. Through thought alone it is possible to grow a flower on the Moon, create an atmosphere capable of supporting human life, plant a garden there and find one's self with one's beloved in that garden in the flesh. But, before that can happen, thought must transform the whole Earth into a flourishing Paradise garden. And that has to be done through collective thinking.

Collective thought is indeed powerful — in the whole Universe there is no energy that can interfere with its operation. Matter and today's technology are the reflection of collective thought. It is this collective thought that has invented all the mechanical devices and armaments we have today.

But remember I was saying that in those Vedic times every living Man's thought had far greater power and energy than now. Objects such as rocks weighing many tonnes could be moved by as few as nine people gathered together. To make it easier to use collective thought for the benefit of the majority without wasting time getting a whole lot of people to congregate in one place, people invented images of various gods and began to control Nature with their help.

The Sun-god appeared in its own image, likewise the gods of Fire, Rain, Love and Fertility. Everything needed for life was created by people through images on which human thought was concentrated. It performed many useful acts. Rain, for example, was necessary for watering the ground, and so one person directed his thought just to the image of the Rain-god. When rain was really essential, then a whole lot of people concentrated their energy on the image of rain. When enough energy had been accumulated in the image, the clouds gathered and the rain fell, watering the harvests.

Unlimited opportunity has been given to Man by the Divine Nature. If mankind could only overcome the temptations associated with unlimited authority and hold all the energies of the Universe in perfect balance within themselves, then gardens — as the fruit of human thought — would appear in other galaxies. And Man would be capable of happifying other worlds with his thought.

What is called the Age of the Image was now coming into bloom. In it Man not only created, but felt himself to be a god. But then what else could the son of God turn out to be?

In what is called the Age of the Image, Man exists in the likeness of God and begins to create his own images. This period lasts nine thousand years. And God does not interfere in Man's deeds. All the diverse energies of the Universe are set in motion and actively try to seduce Man.

Particles of all the diverse energies of the Universe are to be found in Man. They exist in great numbers, and play opposite roles. But all the particles of the diverse energies of the Universe ought to be perfectly balanced in Man, brought together in a harmonious whole.

If one of these particles dominates, the rest are denigrated and their harmony is disrupted, and then... Then the Earth is transformed and becomes inharmonious.

Images can lead people to a many-splendoured creation, but if their inner unity is surrendered they can also lead to annihilation.

But what, exactly, is an *image*?

An image is an entity of energy invented by human thought. It can be created by a single Man or by several together.

A clear example of the collective creation of an image may be seen in stage-acting. One Man describes the image on paper, while another portrays the described image on the stage.

What happens to the actor who portrays the image invented? For a time the actor exchanges his own feelings, aspirations and desires for those inherent in the invented image. In the process the actor may change the way he walks, his facial expression, his usual clothing. In this way the invented image acquires a temporary embodiment.

The ability to create images is something only Man is endowed with.

The image created by Man can remain in space only so long as it is held in Man's thought — either by a single Man or by several at once.

The greater the number of people feeding the image with their feelings, the stronger it becomes.

The image created by the collective thought can possess colossal destructive or creative potential. It has a reciprocal connection with people and is capable of shaping character and behaviour on the part of groups of people both large and small.

In exploiting the great possibilities they have discovered within themselves, people became carried away with creating the life of the planet.

But it happened, back in the early stages of the Age of the Image in the life of Man, that there were six people — just six — who found themselves unable to hold within their bodies, hearts and minds the balance of those energies of the Universe which God gave to Man upon creating him. Perhaps they needed to make their appearance to test all mankind.

At first it was in just one of the six that the energy of grandeur and self-importance predominated — then in another, and then in a third, and finally in all six.

They did not meet together at first. Each one lived independently. But like attracts like. And they ended up concentrating their thought on how to become masters of all the people of the Earth. There were six of them, and in public they referred to themselves as priests.

Through the process of reincarnating themselves over the centuries, they are still living to this day.

Today all the peoples of the Earth are governed by just six people — these are the priests. Their dynasties are ten thousand years old. From generation to generation they have been transmitting their knowledge of the occult to their heirs, along with the science of imagery, which was also partially known to them. They have taken great pains to hide the Vedic knowledge from other people.

Among the six there is one who is considered chief, and he is called the High Priest. Today he considers himself to be the chief ruler of human society.

Through a few sentences I have uttered which you have recorded in your books, as well as through the reaction of many people to them, the High Priest has begun to suspect who I really am. Just in case, he attempted to destroy me by using a negligible amount of power. He did not succeed. He was surprised. And he has tried again, applying a greater amount of force, still not completely convinced of who I am.

Now I have uttered the word *Vedruss,* thereby exposing myself completely. The current High Priest living on the Earth today is afraid even of the word *Vedruss.* You can just imagine how shaken he is, since he knows what lies behind it. Now he will muster his soldiers — bio-robots to a man — along with the forces of all the dark occult sciences, to bring about my termination. And he himself will be working minute by minute on a plan of annihilation. Let him do that — it means he will not have time to be busy with his other plans.

You were telling me about the angry attacks in the recent press, Vladimir. Now you will see them intensify even more. And they will be even more cunning and sophisticated. You will see slander and provocation. You will see the whole arsenal of devices which the dark forces have been using over the millennia to bring about the devastation of our people's culture.

But what you will see at the beginning is only the tip of the iceberg. Not all people can witness the occult attacks at first hand. But you will understand them, you will feel them, you will see them. Do not be afraid of them, I beg of you. What is fearsome is powerless to affect a fearless Man. Whatever you see, you should forget immediately and forever. No matter how omnipotent a monster may seem, once it is forgotten it ceases to exist altogether.

This is an unusual fact, and I can tell you are doubting. Do not be hasty to give in to your doubts. Think it over calmly.

After all, even a small group of people who have gathered together for the purpose of building something inevitably has a leader — we may call him a ruler.

A small enterprise has an official in charge. A large enterprise has several people in charge, under a chief executive officer. There are many rulers over all sorts of territories which are known by different names: provinces, regions, states, communities, republics etc. The particular name is not important. Each nation has a ruler, who is aided by a whole host of assistants.

The *ruler of a nation* — is that the limit? That is what people often think. Does that mean nobody is governing the whole human society living on the Earth? And are there no claimants wishing to ascend the throne of the Earth?

There have indeed been claimants. There still are. You know from recent history many names of military commanders who have tried to dominate the world by force. But not one of them has ever succeeded in taking power over the world. Whenever they found themselves close to seizing universal authority, something would inevitably happen, resulting in the destruction of both the pretender to world dominance and his army.

And the nation aspiring to world domination, which before had been considered strong and flourishing, suddenly dropped to the level of a run-of-the-mill state.

That is the way it has always happened over the past ten thousand years. But why? All because there is already a secret ruler in the world, and has been for a long time. He toys with nations and their rulers, along with individual people.

He calls himself the High Priest of the whole Earth, while his five assistants refer to themselves as priests.

Consider one other fact, Vladimir. Think about how in various parts of the Earth over the millennia wars between people have never ceased. In every country crime, disease and various disasters are increasing day by day, but there has been a strict (indeed, the strictest) prohibition on discussing a particular question: *Is human civilisation really on the path of progress, or is human society being further degraded with each passing day?*

There can be but one simple answer to such a question. Only first take a look and see how the priests acquired their authority and how they have managed to maintain it to date.

Their first step leading to the accomplishment of their secret purpose was the creation of the Egyptian state. The Egyptian state is more familiar than others to historians of today. But once you eliminate personal commentary and mysticism and look only at the facts, you will be able to uncover many secrets.

Fact Number One — history calls the Pharaoh the supreme ruler of Egypt. And the many military achievements and defeats of the pharaohs of old have been well documented. Even today their magnificent tombs astound the imagination and prompt scholars to probe the mysteries they hold. Nevertheless, the grandeur of the pyramids distracts us from the most important secret of all.

Not only were the pharaohs considered as rulers over all the people, but they were worshipped as gods. It was to them that the people turned with pleas for an auspicious crop year, pleas for rain and an absence of pernicious winds. History can tell us about many of the factual accomplishments of the pharaohs, but after learning all these historical facts, you should ask yourself: could any of the pharaohs really have been a ruler over a large nation-state, let alone a god over the people? And once you weigh all the evidence, you will realise entirely on your own that the pharaoh was nothing more than a bio-robot in the hands of the priests.

Now here are the facts — they are also known to us from history.

During the age of the pharaohs there also existed priests in magnificent temples, and one of them was the High Priest. There were always several candidates for the pharaohship in training under their supervision. The priests would inculcate in the young boys whatever the priests desired — among them the notion that the pharaoh was chosen by God. Along with this they told them that the High Priest himself could hear God speaking to him in a secret temple. Later the priests would decide which of the candidates would become the next pharaoh.

And so the day of the coronation arrived. The new pharaoh, clothed in special robes and holding the symbols of office in his hands, took his place majestically on the throne. In the eyes of the people he was an omnipotent king, a god. Only the priests knew that it was their own bio-robot that sat on the throne. And having studied the new pharaoh's character from his childhood, they knew exactly how he would rule, they knew what gifts he would offer up to the benefit of the priesthood.

There was the occasional attempt on the part of certain pharaohs to come out from under the High Priest's authority. But none of them ever succeeded in becoming a free Man. After all, the power of the priests was just as invisible as the pharaoh's royal robes were visible to all. You see, the priests' authority did not require any verbal proclamation or manifest communication for its enforcement. After all, in exercising their power over any individual ruler the priests did not relent, even for a moment. And it was exercised over the masses in turn with the aid of invented suggestions as to what constitutes the order of the Universe. If only the pharaoh could have liberated himself from the images inculcated in him by the priests and reflect by himself in peace, perhaps he would have been able to become a real Man. But there was no way the pharaoh could free himself from the day-to-day cares and concerns — this had been part of the plan right from the start.

And what concerns there were! Couriers, scribes and local governors by turns brought in a daily flood of information from all over the vast nation. Situations calling for immediate solutions. And then a war would break out, absorbing the ruler's full attention. And the pharaoh would take his chariot and keep following his daily trajectories, respecting or rejecting the deeds of his subjects, often not getting enough sleep himself. The priest, on the other hand, would spend his time quietly reflecting, and in this lay his greatest advantage.

The priest directed his efforts to gaining single-handed control of the world as a whole. And even more than that — he meditated on how to resurrect his own world, distinct from the world God had created.

And did he care in the least about the stupid boy-pharaoh, not to mention the crowds which were subject to the pharaoh? For the priest they were all merely toys.

The priests studied the science of imagery in secret, while the masses of people remembered less and less about the law of Nature.

It was these priests, Vladimir, who channelled the energy of the interaction between people and the living Deity — the creations of Nature — into the temples they had invented. They fed on it — the energy of the people — giving nothing in return.

What had been surely clear to everyone in the age of the Vedic culture now became obscure and surreptitious. The people became stupefied, as though under a hypnotic spell, and unthinkingly followed the commands in a kind of semi-sleep. And they began to destroy the world of the Divine Nature, while building an artificial world for the priests' benefit.

The priests held their science under their strictest secretive control. They did not even dare write it all down on scrolls. They invented a language of their own for communication with each other — and this is a fact you can also learn from history. They needed a different language lest someone should inadvertently overhear their conversation with each other and become party to their secrets. And so even today these simple truths which have now become shrouded in a cloak of secrecy are passed down to new generations of the priesthood.

Six thousand years ago the High Priest, one of the six, decided to take control of the whole world.

He reasoned as follows: *There is no way I can seize power by military force, with the pharaoh's armies — even if I taught the commanders how to make use of weapons more advanced than others possess. Besides, what could an army of raving mindless dullards do? Go and plunder gold, but there is so much of that as it is. There are slaves aplenty, but there is an unfavourable energy emanating from them, and it would not be proper to accept food from the hands of a slave. The food would be savourless and harmful to health. I must bring human souls into subjection, and direct all their love and tremulous affection back to myself. But in this case it is not an army that is needed, but scientific thought. The science of imagery — that is my invisible army. The deeper I become acquainted with it, the more faithfully this army ought to serve me. The less that is known by the crowd, immersed as it is in occultism and unreality, the more it will be in subjection to me.*

The High Priest devised his plan. Even today it finds its reflection in the historical events of the past six thousand years.

You and everyone else are aware of recent events. The only difference is in their interpretation. But you should try and give your own, and then the truth will be made known to you. Look and see.

There in the council of those six priests the plan was laid out, and was later revealed to many — it is mentioned in the Bible, in the Old Testament. By order of the High Priest the priest Moses led the Jewish people out of Egypt. The people were offered a most marvellous life in the Promised Land, prepared by God especially for them.

The Jewish people were declared to be God's chosen ones. The tempting news set minds afire, and a part of the people followed Moses, who for forty years led his people about from region to region in the wilderness. The priest's assistants constantly preached sermons about their being a chosen people and inspired the people to make war and plunder cities, all in His (God's) name.

If anyone should happen to awake from his psychosis and demand a return to his former life, he was declared a sinner to be reformed, and given a deadline by which he had to be reformed. If he failed to do this he would be killed. The priests acted not in their own names, but by pretending they were carrying out the deeds of God.

What I am telling you is no fantasy or dream. This may be clearly seen by everyone for themselves by looking for answers in the Old Testament of the Bible — a great historical book. A reliable portrayal of historical events can be learnt by anyone who wakes at least a little from the millennia-old hypnotic sleep and reads how and by what means the Jewish people were programmed and turned into troops of the priesthood. Later Jesus tried to deprogram his people and to use his manifest gift for acquiring new wisdom to prevent the priests from carrying out their designs. In his journeys among wise-men, he endeavoured to glean inklings into the science of imagery. And after he had learnt a great many truths, he decided to save the Jewish people, his own people. He succeeded in creating his own religion — one which could serve as a counterbalance to the terror.

His religion was not for all the nations upon the Earth. It was intended only for the Jewish people. He himself mentioned this more than once. His words were written down by his disciples, and you can still read them to date.

See, for example, St Matthew's gospel, Chapter 15, verses 22–28:

> A Canaanite woman from that vicinity came to him, crying out, "Lord, Son of David, have mercy on me! My daughter is suffering terribly from demon-possession.
>
> Jesus did not answer a word. So his disciples came to him and urged him, "Send her away, for she keeps crying out after us."
>
> He answered, "I was sent *only* to the lost sheep of Israel."[2]

What does it mean: "I was sent only to the lost sheep of Israel"? Why are Jesus' teachings only for the Jews? Why did he consider the Jewish people to be lost?

I tell you, Vladimir: Jesus knew that as a result of the forty-year programming in the Sinai wilderness, the majority of the Jewish people were lost in a hypnotic dream. This part of the people as, indeed, Moses himself, thus became a tool in the hands of the High Priest. They were his foot-soldiers, whom he compelled to seize power over all the Earth's people to satisfy his own vainglory.

And they will be running their battles in various parts of the Earth for thousands of years. Their weapons will not be primitive swords or bullets, but cunning and the creation of a way of life subjecting all the world's peoples to occultism — in other words, to the selfishness of the priests.

And they will do whatever it takes.

But any battle presupposes the presence of two opposing sides, you may well be thinking. *And if so, then where are the victims? In any battle there have to be victims on both sides.*

[2]Matth. 15: 22–24 (*New International Version;* emphasis added by the author).

You could probably find evidence of these battles yourself through searching by the dates mentioned in the various historical sources. But to make it easier for you to locate these fearful dates I shall cite just a few of them right now. If you wish, you can look up their historical confirmation for yourself.

Everybody knows today, including you, Vladimir, how children and elderly people are perishing from terrorism in Israel. It was not all that long ago that what you call the Great Patriotic War[3] took place. And it is well documented how during that war the Jews — old people and children, mothers and young pregnant women, young men who had not yet known love — were systematically burnt in ovens, poisoned with gas and buried alive in common graves.

Not just one person, not an hundred, not mere thousands, but millions of people were brutally slain during this brief period. Historians lay the blame squarely on Hitler. But who was to blame back in 1113, in Kievan Rus',[4] when popular hatred of the Jews suddenly boiled over? Jewish houses in Kiev and other parts of Rus' were plundered and burnt, while Jews — even children — were killed. The people of Rus', caught up by a brutal rage, were ready even to topple the ruling princes from their thrones. And when the princes gathered together within council, they decided to pass a law expelling all Jews from the whole territory of Rus' and henceforth letting none in. An order was given to rob and kill any who surreptitiously entered therein.

[3]*Great Patriotic War* (Russian: *Velikaya Otechestvennaya voina*) — the common Russian term used to refer the events of the Second World War that directly involved Russia or the Soviet Union.

[4]*Kievan Rus'* (pron. *ROOSS*) — the name given to the East Slavic state dominated by the city of Kiev between 880 and the mid-12th century.

In 1290 there was a sudden move to effect the physical extermination of all Jews in England. The rulers were obliged to eject the whole Jewish population from the country.

In 1492 Jewish pogroms began in Spain. A threat of physical annihilation hung over all Jews living in Spain, and once again they were obliged to leave the land.

Right from the moment when the Jews left the Sinai wilderness they became the target of hatred by peoples of various countries. The hatred kept increasing, and here and there manifested itself in cruel pogroms and murders.

I have cited just a few dates of these fearful pogroms — ones that you can easily verify for yourself in histories people have written down. There have been many more conflicts besides for the Jewish people. Any one of them by itself is naturally not as significant as the instances everybody knows about. But when the range of small-scale conflicts is examined as a whole, it takes on an unprecedented scale and proportion, perhaps the most extreme of all the most terrifying phenomena in human history.

If something like that has happened throughout the millennia, one could conclude that the Jewish people are to be blamed in people's eyes. But what are they to be blamed for? Historians both ancient and modern have said that the Jewish people have conspired against authority. That they have aspired to deceive everyone, from the least unto the greatest. In the case of the poor, to try to trick them out of at least a little, in the case of the rich, to bring them to utter ruin. And this is evidenced by the fact that among the Jews there are many wealthy people capable of even influencing governments.

But there is one question you should ask yourself: How righteous are the ones who have been deceived by the Jews? The ones that had amassed such wealth, did they acquire it all by honest means? As for those condemned to be in authority, can we believe them to be so smart if they could be so easily deceived?

Besides, most rulers are dependent on someone else, as the Jews have demonstrated quite clearly. One could go on exploring this topic for a long time, but the answer is simple: in the Occult world *everybody* lives by deceit. Then should we only condemn the one who has succeeded in achieving more than the rest?[5]

And as far as the Jewish people are concerned, we could easily substitute any one of the other peoples we know today. Any one — if they were subjected to the same totally unprecedented programming as the Jews were during their forty years of wandering in the wilderness, heeding only occultism and not seeing what had been created by God.

Jesus tried to remove this programming and save his people. He came up with a new religion for them — one different from what they had before. For example, in contrast to the previous saying: "an eye for an eye, a tooth for a tooth", he said: "whosoever shall smite thee on thy right cheek, turn to him the other also".[6] In contrast to the verse which said: "God hath chosen thee to be a special people unto Himself" he called his people "the servants of God."[7]

[5]Vladimir Megré has always emphasised in his writings and public speeches that any individual should be judged by his actions and not by his religion, ethnicity, nationality or race. The raising of the 'Jewish question' in this chapter is aimed solely at exposing the roots of (and thus helping to alleviate) the inter-ethnic conflict and the anti-Semitic feelings so prevalent in today's Russia and elsewhere in the world. See also Book 7, Chapter 16: "To Jews, Christians and others".

[6]See Exod. 21: 24; Matth. 5: 38, 39 (quotation from the *Authorised King James Version*).

[7]Quoted from Deut. 7: 6; I Peter 2: 16 (*Authorised King James Version*); see also Rom. 6: 22.

Jesus could also have told the truth to his people. He could have told them about Vedic times, about how Man was able to live happily in his domain, in contact with the creations of the Father-Creator. But the Jewish people were already programmed. They believed only in occult deeds, their consciousness was oppressed by the world of the unreal. And so Jesus decided to act in an occult manner himself. He founded an occult religion.

The High Priest at the time was able to guess Jesus' intention. The High Priest racked his brains for many a year before he found what he considered the smartest solution: *There is no point in fighting Jesus' teachings. Through the minds of the soldiers I have selected from among the Jews I must spread them through all the peoples of the Earth, while maintaining the old religion for Israel.* And so it happened, exactly as the High Priest had conceived.

And two essentially different philosophies began to coexist.

According to one, the Jews are a chosen people, as Moses taught, and all other peoples ought to be subject to them. According to the other, expressed in Jesus' words, all are equal before God, and people should not try to take precedence over others; instead one should love one's neighbour and even one's enemy.

The priest realised that if the Christian religion, which calls everyone to love and humility, should succeed in spreading throughout the world, and at the same time Judaism, which elevates one over the rest, is preserved, the world would be subdued. While the world might bow before the Jews, they are but foot-soldiers. The world would actually be bowing before the priest.

And the priest's preachers went out into the world as earnest teachers of the new doctrine.

The doctrine of Jesus? Not quite. The priest had by now added a great deal of his own teachings to it. What happened thereafter you already know. Rome fell. It was not external foes, however, that destroyed the great empire. Rome was destroyed from the inside after adopting Christianity. The emperors were under the impression that Christianity would enhance their power and authority. They were quite flattered by one of the postulates, namely, that all power was derived from God, and that the ruler was ordained to the Emperor's throne by God's grace.[8]

In the fourth century A.D. Christianity celebrated its victory in Rome, both officially and in actual fact. In great delight the High Priest gave a silent, non-contact command to the Byzantine emperor. And Christian Rome burnt the Library of Alexandria* to the ground. Altogether 700,033 volumes were lost. Bonfires of books and ancient scrolls burned in many cities. The burnt books were largely from the heathen period, but they also included the few that recorded the knowledge of Vedic people. These were not burnt — they were salvaged, concealed and studied in turn by a narrow circle of the devoted, and only afterward were destroyed.

It seemed to the High Priest that now that people were getting further and further away from a knowledge of their pristine origins, he would encounter no more obstacles on his path. Feeling bolder, he issued yet another tacit command, resulting in an anathema being issued at the Second Council of Constantinople[9] against the doctrine of reincarnation. For

[8]Compare Rom. 12: 1: "...there is no power but of God: the powers that be are ordained of God. " (*Authorised King James Version*).

***The Library of Alexandria* [footnote appearing in the Russian edition] — the most famous library of antiquity, containing every single work in existence at the time. In Cæsar's time its collection numbered something on the order of 700,000 items. In 391 A.D., during the time of bloody wars between the heathens and the Christians, the Temple of Sarapis, which housed the library, was destroyed. — *Slovar' antichnosti* (Dictionary of antiquity), Progress Publishers [Moscow], 1989.

what reason? — you may ask. To keep people from thinking about the essence of earthly life.

To keep them thinking that a happy life exists only beyond the Earth's borders. And many peoples of the Earth began believing precisely that.

The priest was truly delighted. He knew what would happen next. He construed that since nobody had experienced other-worldly life, Man would have no idea of how to reach Paradise the Good or how to avoid ending up in a fearsome Hell. So now he would offer to Man a little occult hint which would favour his own plan.

And so the priests have kept on giving out hints to the world which bring benefit to themselves. But they were not able to immediately obtain full power over the world, even when it seemed to them that the strongest bastion of heathen culture, Rome, was destroyed. Even then, there still remained on the Earth one small island which was impervious to the priests' usual charms. Even back before Rome, even before the appearance of Jesus' teachings, the High Priest had aspired to destroy the culture of the last Vedic state — Rus'.

---

[9] *Second Council of Constantinople* (also known as the *Fifth Ecumenical Council*) — an assembly held at Constantinople (5 May–2 June, A.D. 553), summoned by the Byzantine Emperor Justinian and attended mainly by Eastern bishops. Its purpose was to head off 'contamination' of official Christian doctrines by 'heretical' Christian-based teachings such as reincarnation and Nestorianism (a belief in Jesus as two persons, human and divine).

Chapter Seven

The secret war with Vedic Rus'

The war with Vedic Rus' began long before Jesus' appearance on the Earth, long before the fall of Rome. This thousand-year war was not waged with iron swords. Occultism executed its military raids on a non-material plane.

Preachers of the occult religion came to Russia — dozens of their names are mentioned in various ecclesiastical books. But they actually numbered in the tens of thousands. They were not to blame for their ignorance. They were fanatics, which means their mind was unable to fathom even the millionth part of creation. As foot-soldiers to the priest, reverently carrying out his orders without so much as a murmur, they attempted to explain to people how to live. They tended to say exactly the same things they had said when preaching to once-majestic imperial Rome.

They tried introducing ritual. And proposed the construction of temples, instead of paying attention to Nature or earthly existence. Then the kingdom of heaven would come for everyone. I shall not burden you by reciting their sermons. If you wish, you can still read their words today. I shall tell you why for thousands of years they did not succeed in doing anything with Vedic Rus'.

Every other person living in Rus' at that time was a poet and a wit. And there were bards in Rus' — they were called *bayans*[1] back then. And this is how it all took place in those times. For decades the priest's foot-soldiers waged a propaganda campaign to the effect that God had to be bowed down to. And here and there people began to listen and reflect on the message. Upon seeing this, the bayan would simply laugh and make up a parable, which he would then sing. And the parable would quickly spread throughout Rus'. And over the next ten years or so Rus' would have a good laugh at the priests' sermons.

The priest was furious and launched new attacks. But once again in Rus' a parable would be born, and Rus' would laugh once more. Of all the many parables of those times I shall tell you just three.

In which temple should God dwell (Anastasia's first parable)

In one of the many populated settlements on the Earth people went happily about their daily life. In this particular community lived ninety-nine families. Each family lived in a splendid house decorated with fanciful woodcarvings. The garden around the house brought forth fruit every year in abundance. Vegetables and berries grew all by themselves. Every year people met the spring with joyful greeting and delighted in the summer. A series of cheerful friendship celebrations brought forth songs and *khorovods.*[2] In the

---

[1] *bayan* (pron. *bah-YAHN*) — see footnote 4 in Book 4, Chapter 33: "School, or the lessons of the gods". On the role of bards, see Book 2, Chapter 10: "The ringing sword of the bard".

[2] *khorovod* — See footnote 5 in Chapter 5: "The history of mankind, as told by Anastasia"..

wintertime people rested from their daily exhilarations. And they looked up to the heavens and tried to decide whether they might be able to weave the Moon and the stars into even better patterns.

Once every three years in July those people gathered in a glade at the edge of their community. Once in every three years God would respond to their questions in an ordinary voice. Even though He remained invisible to ordinary eyes, each one could feel Him. And He, together with all the residents of the community, decided how best to build their life in the days to come. The people's conversation with God might be philosophical, but sometimes quite simple and even funny.

So, for example, one middle-aged man stood up and addressed God this way:

"C'mon, now, God, for our celebration this summer, when we all gathered together with the dawn, You decided to drench us all with a monsoon? The rain poured down like a waterfall from heaven, and the Sun began to shine only around noon. What, did You sleep in till noon?"

"I was not asleep," God replied. "At this morning's dawn I thought about how to make your celebration truly glorified. I saw how some of you on their way to the celebration were too lazy to wash themselves with clean water. How so? Such reprobates would spoil the show with their appearance. And so I decided to first wash everyone, and then have the clouds sweep in and allow the rays of the Sun to caress the water-washed bodies with tenderness."

"Well, okay, if that is how..." the man agreed, brushing off food crumbs from his moustache and wiping the blackberry stains around his son's mouth.

"Tell me, God," asked an elderly and pensive philosopher, "there are many stars shining in the sky overhead. What does their fanciful alignment mean? If I should select a star that is pleasing to my soul, and then when I get bored with my earthly life, could I remove there with my family?"

"The alignment of the heavenly bodies twinkling in the dark tells about the life of the whole Universe. An alertness in your soul, but without tension, allows you to read the Book of the Heavens. This Book will not open for idleness or curiosity, but only for pure and meaningful thoughts. And yes, you can settle on a star. And each of you can choose for yourself a planet in the heavens. There is only one condition that you must observe. You must become capable of producing on your selected star creations more perfected than those produced on the Earth."

A very young girl jumped up from the ground and tossed her light-brown braid of hair over her shoulder. Raising her little face with its turned-up nose heavenward, she placed her hands saucily on her hips and suddenly declared to God:

"I have a complaint to make to you, God. For two years now I've waited patiently to tell you about it. Now I shall tell you. Some kind of disorder or abnormality is taking place on the Earth. All the people are living as people — falling in love, marrying and being happy. But am I to blame for something? Every year, just as soon as spring arrives, my cheeks break out into freckles. There is nothing that'll wash them off, and I can't paint them over. Did you think this up as some kind of a joke, God? I demand that as of next spring not a single freckle ever appears on my face again!"

"Oh, My daughter! Those are not freckles, but spring speckles that appear on your beautiful little face each spring. But I shall call them as you wish. If you find your freckles to be such an annoyance, I shall remove them come next spring," God answered the spunky girl.

But then a handsome young lad got up at the other end of the glade, and meekly addressed God, though not in a loud voice:

"We have a lot of work ahead of us in the springtime. You, God, try to take part in everything we do. Why would you waste your time on removing her freckles? Besides, they are so beautiful that I cannot picture a more beautiful image than a young maiden with freckles in the spring!"

"So what am I to do?" God thoughtfully responded. "The maiden asked, and I promised her..."

"What's this about 'what to do'?" the girl once more broke into the conversation. "You heard the people say it's not freckles, but other more important things, that we should be concerned about... But while we're on the subject of speckles, I'd like to ask for two more — right here, on my right cheek, so that it's all symmetrical."

God smiled — this was evident from the fact that all the people were smiling. Everybody knew that it would not be long before a new splendid family would be lovingly born into their community.

So the people lived with God in that remarkable community. And then one day a hundred wise-men came to see them. The hospitable residents always greeted guests with all kinds of good things to eat. The wise-men tasted their splendid fruit and were amazed at its extraordinary flavour. Then one of them said:

"Oh, people, what a splendid, orderly life you lead! You have abundance and coziness in every home. But your communication with God lacks sophistication. There is no glorification or adulation of Deity."

"But why?" the residents tried to protest in alarm. "We talk with God the way we talk with each other. We talk and reason with Him every three years. But every day He rises with the Sun. As a bee He busies Himself around the gardens beginning in every spring. Every winter He covers the ground with snow. His tasks are clear to us, and we are glad for all the seasons."

"You are doing things the wrong way," said the wise-men. "We have come to teach you how to talk with God. All over the Earth an array of temples and palaces has been built in His honour, where people can talk with God every day. And we shall teach you to do the same."

For three years the residents of the settlement heeded the words of the wise-men. Each of the hundred insisted on his own theory about how to best construct a temple to God, and what should be done in the temple each day. Each of the wise-men had his own theory. The residents of the community had no idea which of the hundred wise theories they should choose. Besides, how could they choose without offending the wise-men? And so they decided to heed them all and build all the temples proposed. One for each family. But there were only ninety-nine families in the village, and there were a hundred wise-men. When they heard the decision of all the residents, the wise-men became very concerned. It meant one of them would not get his temple built, and would not receive the anticipated offerings. And they began arguing among themselves as to whose theory of worshipping God was the most effective. And they began dragging the residents into the dispute. The dispute heated up, and for the first time in many years the villagers forgot about their time of communication with God. They did not gather as before in the glade on the appointed day.

Another three years went by. Ninety-nine magnificent temples were scattered about the settlement, and it was only the villagers' huts that had lost their lustre. Some of the vegetables lay uncollected on the ground. And the fruit of the garden began to become infested with worms.

"This is all because," the wise-men preached in the various temples, "you do not have full faith. Bring more and more gifts to the temple, try harder and bow down to God more often."

But there was one wise-man — the one who had been left without a temple — who whispered first to one, then to another:

"You have been going about everything the wrong way, people. All the temples you have built are of the wrong construction. And you do not worship the right way in your temples, you are not saying the right words as you pray. I am the only one who can teach you how you can communicate with God every day."

Just as soon as he managed to bring someone over to his side, a new temple would be erected, and one of the existing ones would fall into disrepair. And again one of the wise-men, the one newly deprived of the people's offerings, tried to surreptitiously slander the others in front of the villagers.

A number of years passed. Then one day the people remembered about the gatherings they used to have in the glade where they heard God's voice. Once again they gathered in the glade and began asking questions in the hope that God would hear them and give an answer as before.

"Answer us, how did it happen that our gardens are bringing forth worm-infested fruit? And why do our vegetables no longer yield an abundant harvest every year? And why do people quarrel, fight and argue amongst themselves, but cannot possibly choose the best faith? Tell us in which of the temples we built for you do you dwell?"

For a long time God did not answer their questions. And when a voice finally sounded in space, it was not a happy voice, it sounded weary. God answered those gathered:

"My sons and daughters, the reason for the desolation in your houses and the gardens around them is that I am simply not able to do everything by Myself. Everything has been designed by My dream right from the start in such a way that I can create splendour only in conjunction with you. But you have in part turned away from your homes with their gardens. Creation is something I cannot ever manage on My own — there must be co-creation by the two of us together. Moreover I want to say to you all: you yourselves include love and freedom of choice, and I am ready to follow your aspirations with My dream. But you must tell me, My dear daughters and sons, in which of the temples I am to dwell. Before me you are all of equal worth, so where abouts should I reside so that no one feels left out? When you have decided on your own in which of the temples I should make my home, I shall be glad to follow your collective will."

After responding to all with these words God fell silent. The people of the once beautiful village are continuing their conflict even to this day. Their houses are filled with desolation and dust. Around them the temples rise higher and higher, even as the conflict grows bitterer and bitterer.

"Well, Anastasia, that is quite an unrealistic, fairy-tale parable you told. There must have been some pretty dumb people in that settlement. Didn't they realise that God wants to work with each one of them to care for their garden? Besides, you say that those dullards in the settlement are still arguing, even today. And where is that settlement, in what country? Can you tell me?"

"I can."

"Then tell me."

"Vladimir, you along with people from different lands are living in this very settlement right now."

"Eh? Oh, I see, precisely: we are the ones! We are still engaged in a dispute about whose faith is better. While our gardens are full of worm-infested fruit!"

The best place in Paradise (second parable)

Four brothers came to a gravesite to honour the memory of their father who had died many years before. The brothers wanted to know whether his soul was dwelling in Paradise or in hell. They were all eager for their father's spirit to appear before them and tell how it was doing in the next world.

Their father's image appeared before them in a wondrous radiance. The brothers were awed and their hearts were afire when they saw this miraculous vision. When they finally regained their composure, they enquired:

"Tell us, Father, does your soul dwell in Paradise?"

"Yes, my sons," their father replied, "my Soul delights in a wondrous Paradise."

"Tell us, Father," the brothers started asking, "what fate awaits our souls after our own flesh dies?"

And the father responded to each of his sons in turn with a question of his own:

"Tell me, my sons, how do you appraise your deeds to date upon the Earth?"

And each brother answered his father in turn. The elder son began:

"I have become a great military leader, Father. I have defended my native land against its foes, and never allowed an enemy foot to tread upon it. I have never offended the poor and infirm. I have endeavoured to take good care of the soldiers under my command. I have always honoured God, and therefore I hope to enter into Paradise."

The second son replied to his father:

"I have become a prominent preacher. I have preached goodness to the people. I have taught them to worship God. I have reached great heights and achieved high standing among my peers, and therefore I hope to enter into Paradise."

The third son replied to his father:

"I have become a prominent scientist. I have designed a great many devices to benefit people's lives. I have raised a large number of handsome buildings for mankind. Each time I start a new construction project, I give praise to God and celebrate and honour His name, and therefore I hope to enter into Paradise."

The youngest brother answered his father:

"I, Father, cultivate a garden and work daily at raising vegetables. From my splendid garden I send fruits and vegetables to my brothers and try not to do anything dishonourable or displeasing to God, and therefore I hope to enter into Paradise."

The father replied to his sons:

"Your souls, my sons, will indeed dwell in Paradise after your flesh dies."

The vision of their father faded. Years went by, the brothers died and their souls met in the Garden of Paradise, only the soul of their younger brother was not among them. The three brothers then began to call out to their father, and when he once again appeared before them in his wondrous radiance they asked him:

"Tell us, Father, why is the soul of our little brother not among us in this Garden of Paradise? It has been a hundred earthly years since we last spoke with you at your gravesite."

"Do not be concerned, my sons," replied the father. "Your little brother's soul, too, is dwelling in the Garden of Paradise. Only he is not here with you right now because your little brother is at this moment communicating with God."

Another hundred years went by, and once again the brothers met in the Garden of Paradise. But again their younger brother was not with them. And again the brothers called for their father. When he appeared, they asked:

"See, another hundred years has gone by, but our little brother has not come to meet us, nor has anyone seen him in the Garden of Paradise. Tell us, Father, where is our little brother now?"

And the father answered his three sons:

"Your little brother is communicating with God, and that is why he is not among you."

And the three brothers began asking their father to show them where and how their younger brother was communicating with God.

"Take a look," the father replied. And the brothers saw the Earth, and there was the marvellous garden which their little brother had cultivated during his life. In this wondrous earthly garden their brother, looking so much younger, was explaining something to his child. His beautiful wife was busying herself nearby.

The brothers asked their father in astonishment:

"There is our little brother in his earthly garden as before, not in the Garden of Paradise as we are. What is he to blame for before God? Why has his flesh not died? Several centuries have passed in Earth years, and here we see him as a young man? Does that mean God has somehow changed the order of the Universe?"

And the father answered his three sons:

"God has not changed the order of the Universe, which He established right from the start in great harmony and inspired love. Your brother's flesh has died, and on more than one occasion. But the place of one's soul in the Garden of Paradise is best created by one's own hands and soul. Just as for any loving mother and father the child of their own creation is always the most glorious. According to the Divine order of things, the soul of your little brother should assuredly be granted entrance to the Garden of Paradise, but seeing this garden is on the Earth, it is immediately incorporated into a new body in the earthly garden so dear to it."

"Tell us, Father," the brothers went on, "you were saying that our little brother is communicating with God, but we do not see God with him in his garden."

And the father responded to his three sons:

"Your little brother, my sons, is looking after God's creations — the trees and the grass — they are the Creator's own materialised thoughts. In treating them with love and conscious awareness, your brother is thereby communicating with God."

"Tell us, Father, shall *we* ever return to the Earth in fleshly form?" the sons asked their father. And they heard him answer:

"Your souls, my sons, now dwell in the Garden of Paradise. They can take on earthly form only if someone creates a garden for your souls on the Earth similar to the one in Paradise."

The brothers exclaimed:

"Gardens are not created with love for *other* people's souls. We ourselves, once we are given a fleshly form, shall cultivate a Garden of Paradise on the Earth."

But the father replied to his sons:

"You were given that opportunity already, my sons."

After this response the father began to quietly withdraw. But once again the three brothers cried out and asked their father:

"Dear father, show us *your* place in the Garden of Paradise. Why do you withdraw yourself from us?"

The father stopped and replied to his three sons:

"Look there! Do you see that leafy apple tree flowering beside your little brother in his garden? Under that apple tree is a little cradle, and in that cradle is the beautiful body of a tiny infant that has just wiggled its little hand as it begins to awake. My soul is alive in that little body. After all, that was the marvellous garden I began creating myself..."

The wealthiest groom (third parable)

I shall make a few changes in this parable to put it in a modern-day context.

In one village lived two neighbours. The families were friends with each other, and enjoyed working their land. Every spring gardens bloomed on the two plots, and their little groves of trees grew taller.

Into each family a son was born. After their sons had matured, one day, while gathered around a festive table, the fathers took a firm decision and handed everything over to their sons' control.

"Let those sons of ours now decide what to sow and when," one of them said to the other. "And you and I, my friend, shall not oppose them, or even give them hints or questioning looks."

"Agreed," replied the other. "Let our sons even make changes around the house if they wish. Let them choose the clothing they like, and let them decide what livestock and other things to buy."

"Fine," replied the first. "Let our sons become self-sufficient. And let them choose worthy brides for themselves. We shall go together, my friend, to seek brides for our sons."

And this is the decision that emerged from the two friends and neighbours' conversation. Their idea was supported by their wives, and the families began living under their grown-up sons' administration. But thereafter the two families' lives significantly diverged.

In one family the son became an active member of the community and paid his respects to everyone, which led to his being defined as the 'first citizen' of the village. The other son seemed to be slow and serious of mind to all around; he came to be called the village's 'second citizen'.

The first neighbour's son felled and sawed up the trees of the grove his father had planted and hauled them to market. He bought himself a family car in place of his horse, along with a small tractor. The first son here was considered very enterprising. The new entrepreneur calculated that the coming year would see a sharp increase in the price of garlic, and he was not mistaken. He pulled up all his plantings and sowed his fields with garlic. His father and mother did their best to help him in everything — they had made a promise and it was not forsaken.

The family sold the garlic at a profit. They set about building a huge mansion using the most modern materials invented and hired construction workers. And the enterprising son did not relent — he spent from morning 'til night trying to figure out what the most profitable crop would be to plant in the spring. And by winter's end he had calculated that this spring's most profitable crop would be onions. And again he sold his harvest at a profit, and bought himself a fancy new car.

One day the two neighbours' sons met along the road. One was driving a car, the other a wagon harnessed to a frisky mare. The successful entrepreneur stopped his car and the two neighbours had a conversation.

"See, neighbour, I'm driving a fancy car, while you're getting around in a horse-drawn cart just like before. I'm building a big house, while you're still living in that old house of your father's. Our fathers and mothers have always been friends, and I too am ready to help you in a neighbourly way — if you like, I can tell you what is the most profitable crop to plant your whole field with today."

"Thank you for your willingness to help," responded the second neighbour from his wagon, "only I happen to cherish a great deal my freedom of thought, indeed I do."

"I certainly don't want to encroach on your freedom of thought. It's just that I sincerely want to help you through."

"I thank you for your sincerity, good neighbour. But freedom of thought is eroded by non-living things — that car, for example, you are sitting in."

"How can a car erode...? It can easily overtake that old farm-cart of yours, and by the time you get to the city I'll be able to have my business all taken care of. And all thanks to my motor car."

"Yes, your car, of course, can certainly overtake my wagon, but it requires you to sit behind the wheel and hold on to it constantly as you drive, while you as the driver have to keep jerking some kind of stick with your hand and looking continually at the dashboard and the road. Maybe my horse is slower than a car, but it doesn't require any attention, and doesn't distract my thought either. If I should take a snooze, the horse will find its own way home. You say you have problems with fuel, whereas my horse fills itself up in the pasture over there. Anyway, tell me, where are you in such a hurry to get to in your car?"

"I want to buy some spare parts to keep on hand. I know exactly what could go wrong with my car at any moment."

"So, you know enough about technology that you can accurately predict all your breakdowns?"

"Yes, I'm pretty good at that! I took special mechanics courses — for three years in all I swotted through. If you recall, I asked you to join me in those courses too."

"So for three years of your life you had only this technology to give your thought to. Something that can get old and break down."

"Your horse, too, will get old and die."

"Yes, of course, she will get old. But before that happens she will be able to give birth to a foal. The foal will grow, and I shall be able to ride him. What is living will eternally serve Man, never fear, while what is dead only shortens his years."

"The whole village makes fun of your ideas," remarked the entrepreneur. "They all think of me as successful and wealthy, while they see you just sit and live off your father's fortune. Besides, you haven't introduced any new species of trees or bushes on your father's land, not even a bit."

"But I've come to love *these.* I've been trying to understand each one's purpose and how they interact with each other. And I've been able to invigorate the ones starting to wither, just by looking at and touching them. Now, come each spring, everything is blossoming in harmony, all by itself, requiring no outside attention. It's just waiting eagerly for summer, and then for the fall when it will offer up its fruit for the year."

"Really, friend, I must say you *are* queer," sighed the entrepreneur. "You walk around entranced with your domain, your garden and your flowers. At the same time, you say, you are giving freedom to your thoughts."

"Yes, I am."

"What do you need a free thought for, anyway? What's the point in freedom of thought?"

"So that I can make sense of all the grand creations. So that I can be happier myself, and help you."

"Me? What's got hold of you? I can marry the best girl in the village, any one of them will go for me. They all want to be rich, live in a spacious house and ride in my car."

"Being rich doesn't mean being happy."

"And being poor?"

"Being poor isn't so good either."

"So if you're not poor and not rich, then what?"

"You ought to have just enough of everything. Being self-sufficient — that's not bad either. And be consciously aware of what's going on around. After all, it's not by chance that happiness can be found."

The entrepreneur grinned and quickly went on his way.

A year later the two neighbouring fathers got together to talk. They decided it was time to be courting brides for their sons. When they asked them which of the village girls they would like to wed, the entrepreneuring son replied to his father:

"The daughter of the village elder really appeals to me, Father. I would rejoice to have her as my wife."

"I can see, my son, that you have made an excellent choice. The village elder's daughter is renowned as the most beautiful girl in the county. All the visitors to our village from both near and far are entranced at the sight of her. Mind you, she can be quite capricious. The girl has a mind of her own that even her parents can't figure out. Some people might think her strange — more and more women keep coming to her from various settlements for advice and to be healed of their ills, and they even bring their children to see this young girl."

"What of it, Father? I'm made of sterner stuff. In all our village there is no more spacious house or better car than mine. Besides, twice now I have seen her give me long and thoughtful looks."

On being asked which of the village girls *he* most fancied, the second son told his father:

"I love the village elder's daughter, Father."

"And how does she act toward you, my son? Have you noticed a look of love in her eyes?"

"No, Father. Whenever I happen to meet her, she lowers her eyes."

Both neighbours simultaneously decided to woo the maiden for their sons. Arriving at their house, they seated themselves sedately. The village elder summoned his daughter and told her:

"Look, my daughter, two matchmakers have come to see us. On behalf of two young lads, each wishing to have you to wife. The three of us have decided that you should choose from the two. Can you tell us your decision now or would you like to think about it until tomorrow morning?"

"I have spent many mornings thinking about it in my dreams, Father," the young girl quietly said. "I can give you my answer right now."

"So tell us. We are all eagerly awaiting your decision."

The beautiful girl answered the matchmakers like this:

"Thank you, fathers — thank you all for enquiring. I thank your sons for desiring to join their life with mine. You have indeed raised splendid sons, and it might have been very difficult to choose to which of two destinies I should myself resign. But I do want to have children, and I want my children to be happy, to stand tall in prosperity, freedom and love, and so I have fallen in love with the one who is wealthiest of all."

The father of the entrepreneur rose to his feet in pride, while the other father sat glumly in his chair. But the girl went over to the second father, knelt down before him, and said, without raising her eyelids:

"I wish to live with your son."

At this point the village elder rose to his feet. He wanted to see his daughter living in what was deemed by all the richest house in the village, and so he said to her rather harshly:

"You spoke correctly, my daughter — your smart reasoning brought gladness to your father's heart. But you for your part did not go and kneel before the richest man in the village. Someone else here is the wealthiest. This is he."

And the elder, gesturing to the entrepreneur's father, added:

"Their son has built a spacious home, honey. They have a car, a tractor... and money."

The girl went over to her father and responded to his harsh and bewildering words:

"Of course you are right, Papa dear. But I was talking about children. What use will our children have for those things you mentioned? The tractor can break down while they are still growing up. The car may rust and the house fall into decay."

"That may be — maybe what you say is true, granted. But your children will have *a great deal* of money, and they can buy for themselves a new tractor and a new car and new clothes."

"And just how much is 'a great deal', might I ask?"

The entrepreneur's father proudly stroked his beard and moustache, and answered solemnly and seriously:

"My son has heaps of money — enough so that if he needed to buy three of everything our household already has, he could do so all at once. And those horses our neighbour keeps, we would be able to buy not just two, but a whole stable full."

The girl meekly lowered her eyelids and responded:

"I wish you and your son great happiness. But there is no amount of money on the Earth that would buy a father's garden where every branch reaches out in sheer love to the one cultivating it. And no money in the world can buy the loyalty of a steed that has played with a child as a colt. Your domain may indeed make money, but my beloved's domain will make a space for sufficiency and love."

A change of priestly tactics

During the thousand-year war the priest changed his tactics a number of times, but all to no avail. Rus' still laughed, as before, at his occult intrusions. The people referred to those preachers as miserable wretches. At that time wretchedness was not equated with physical affliction but with occultism. People in Rus' took pity on the wretched preachers, they fed them and offered them shelter, but did not take any of their sermons seriously.

After four hundred centuries the priest realised he would never achieve victory over the Vedic land. He accurately determined wherein the extraordinary power of Vedism lay.

Vedism was based solidly on a Divine culture. Everyone's way of life was Divine. And every family created in its domain a Space of Love, they felt the wholeness of Nature and, consequently, of everything God had created.

What happened in Vedism was that people spoke with God through Nature. Instead of bowing down before Him, they attempted to understand Him. They loved God as a son and daughter love their kindly parents.

And so the priest came up with a plan which would be able to break this dialogue with the Divine. To this end it was necessary to separate people from their domains, from the Divine gardens, from their co-creation together with God. It was necessary to divide the whole territory where the Vedic people lived into different states and to destroy their culture.

New preachers went to Rus'. They put a new approach into practice. This time they sought out people in whom selfishness — pride — dominated even just a little over the other energies of feelings. Whenever they found such a Man, they tried enhancing the sense of pride within him. This is how they operated:

Imagine a group of stately-looking elders arriving at the home of a happy family. But there is no attempt, as before, to preach or teach them how to live. On the contrary, they all at once bow down before the head of the household, present him with outlandish gifts and say:

"In our far-off land we climbed to the top of a high mountain — the highest mountain on the Earth. Standing at the summit, above the clouds, we heard a voice from heaven telling us about you. And it was told to us that you are the wisest of all people on the Earth. You alone were chosen, and we are honoured to bow down to you, present you with our gifts and wait upon your words of wisdom."

And if they saw the Man taking their bait, they would continue their sly talk:

"It is your duty to make all other people happy — the voice told us so on the mountain-top. You should not waste your valuable time on other concerns. You should be in charge of people and make decisions for them — decisions that have been entrusted to you alone. And here is your heavenly head-dress."

At this point a head-dress decorated with precious stones was presented to the Man as though it were the grandest treasure.

And so the head-dress was placed upon the head of the Man who now believed in his own majesty and his chosen status. And at that very moment all the visitors fell to their knees before him in great reverence. And they began to praise heaven for the honour of being worthy to bow before this majesty. Next, the foreign visitors built him a separate house to live in that looked very much like a temple.

This is how the first princes rose to power in Vedic Rus'.

The new prince's neighbours looked upon this Man sitting on his throne in the temple as some sort of curiosity. They watched as the foreign visitors bowed before him, indulged his every whim and plied him with all sorts of questions.

At first they took this scenario for some kind of game from overseas, and some decided, either out of curiosity or out of compassion, to play along with the foreigners and with their neighbour. But people gradually got drawn into the game. And little by little they sank into a state of serfdom, and without their realising it, their thoughts turned more and more away from co-creation.

It was not easy for the priest's emissaries to get the princedoms established. In the beginning, for more than a hundred years, their attempts proved unsuccessful. But still it finally came about, and Vedic Rus' was carved out into princedoms.

And then events took their natural course: the princes began fighting over who was greater, and dragged their neighbours into internecine feuds.

Later historians would claim that grand princes arose who managed to join the isolated princedoms of Rus' together into one mighty state. But think for yourself, Vladimir — could that really have been so? And what kind of unification exactly do the historians have in mind? It is all very simple, in fact. Yes, one prince was able to kill or conquer others. But people can be united only by culture and a way of life.

The setting up of borders always indicates separation. Once a state was established, not on the basis of a cultured way of life but on the artificial greatness of one or more people by virtue of their armies, a whole lot of problems immediately made themselves heard: how to maintain those borders and expand them as the opportunity occurred — and so arose the need for a sizeable army.

A large state cannot be governed by one Man alone — so clerks and scribes soon appeared, and they have been multiplying each day right up to the present time. The princes, clerks, scribes, merchants — and all their servants — together form a category of people who have been separated from God's creations. Today their functional designation is the creation of an artificial world. They have utterly lost the ability to perceive true reality, and so constitute fertile soil for occultism.

Only a thousand years ago Rus' was considered pagan. Paganism still carried within itself a lingering sense of the Divine Vedic culture. With the advent of the princes and their princedoms — first little princedoms, and later large ones — the rulers found they needed a force more powerful than an army. A force capable of creating a type of Man inclined to unquestioning submission to authority.

Here too the priest's messengers came to the ruling princes' assistance and offered them a suitable religion.

The essence of this new development was very much to the princes' liking. Though there was hardly anything new in it. It contained everything that Egypt had had five thousand years earlier.

Like the pharaoh, the prince was considered to be appointed to his position by God. The occult ministers of the new religion were his advisors — again, just as in Egypt. Everyone else was a mere slave. It was not a simple task to inculcate the new order into the minds of free people whose memories could still savour the celebrations of Vedic culture. And so once again the priest came to the princes' aid. His foot-soldiers began spreading false rumours to the effect that there were pagan settlements where people were being more and more frequently sacrificed to God.

It was noised abroad that pagans sacrificed to their gods not just various animals but also beautiful girls, or young men, or even little children. This false rumour is still rampant among us today. More and more it became a source of anger to the pagan people. And now here was this new religion being offered which placed a strict prohibition on burnt sacrifices. It talked about equality and brotherhood — exempting, of course, the princes. Thus this new religion was little by little introduced into pagan Rus'. Eventually one of the ruling princes decreed that Christianity be recognised as the only true religion in the land, Rus' came to be called Christian and all other religions were banned.

Now let anyone whose forebears — mothers and fathers — were called pagan just a thousand years ago ask themselves this question: did pagans really sacrifice either animals or people to their gods? And the true picture of events will become clear to anyone who is able to do at least nine minutes of logical reasoning.

And you, Vladimir, once you have applied your own logic to the discovery of the truth, can see the facts for yourself. I shall be glad to give you a little help.

First ask yourself a logical question: If pagans, as their accusers claim, actually offered up someone as a sacrifice to God, then why did the mere rumour about such offerings so greatly trouble their mind and feelings? It would have been more logical in that case to welcome such claims and enthusiastically try to repeat them, instead of greeting them with outrage and accepting the new religion's entreaties. But the people were outraged — why? Naturally, because the pagans could not entertain even the thought of sacrificing animals, let alone people.

That is why no one can come up with even a single source in support of burnt sacrifices among the people of pagan Rus'. It was only the chroniclers of Christianity that claimed that. But then they never lived in pagan Rus', and did not even know the language of pagan Rus'. And what about the sources and manuscripts of pagan Rus' itself? Some of them were hidden, some were burnt in bonfires, just as in Rome. What exactly was seditious in those scrolls? What did they disclose? Without being able to read them, everyone today can make their own guess. They would have exposed the falsity of the accusations against paganism. And they could have transmitted the knowledge of Vedism. There was more to it than the fact that none of the people of pagan Rus' ever indulged in burnt sacrifices. They did not eat meat at all. They could not even imagine such a thing. They were friends with the animals. Their daily diet was varied enough, but it was strictly vegetarian. Who can come up with a single recipe from ancient Russian cuisine that even mentioned meat? No one!

Even our epic folk tales tell about how the turnip was respected in ancient Rus', about how the people drank mead-beer. Let anyone today, even meat-eaters, try drinking this warm mead made from flower pollen and herbs — after drinking that, you will not want to eat anything else, certainly not meat. Those who force themselves to do so may find the meat will only make them vomit.

Besides, judge for yourself, Vladimir, why should anyone eat meat when all around them a whole lot of easily digestible, high-energy food was available?

During the winter bees feed on nothing but honey and pollen, and so can go the whole winter without excreting at all. The whole intake is assimilated by the bee's body. And *sbiten'* — a drink made with boiled honey — was always served to guests directly they entered the home. And who would start eating meat after tasting a sweet drink?

It was the nomads that introduced meat to the world. There was hardly any edible fruit to fend for in the prairie-lands and deserts they moved about in, and this is why they ended up killing cattle. And the nomads ate the meat of those animal herds that served as their beasts of burden — animals that carried their belongings, fed them with milk and gave their wool for clothing.

Thus the culture of our forebears was destroyed, and Rus' was plunged into religion. If the people had learnt genuine religion, purely Christian, it is possible that life would have turned out differently. But the priest managed to inject his own twists into the Christian teachings. And the one religion became subject to various interpretations. And the Christian world became divided into a multitude of denominations, often in conflict with each other.

The High Priest spent a great deal of effort on Rus'. In other places on the Earth people saw what he was doing and did not permit his preachers within their borders. Japan, China and India did not become Christian. But the High Priest won them over by another way. The Age of Occultism began one thousand years ago. People all over the Earth lived in the Age of Occultism. And are still living in it today.

Chapter Eight

Occultism

It lasts only a thousand years.

During the Age of Occultism mankind is plunged into a world of unreality.

Mankind begins to direct its tremendous store of diverse energies toward made-up images and abstract worlds existing beyond the boundaries of real life. The real world with its diversity receives less and less of the life-creating warmth of Man. It maintains its existence only at the expense of past accumulation and its original charge from the Divine.

Mankind ceases to fulfil its main purpose. It becomes dangerous for the Universe, and planetary-scale disasters take place.

Today all mankind still lives in the world of the occult. But that age ended in the year 2000. Of course, in reality the name *2000* is a misnomer.

You know yourself that only recently the traditional year-count was radically changed. The latest temporal borderline represented the millionth anniversary of civilisation on the Earth.

And as always a global disaster was slated to happen. More specifically, mankind was supposed to launch a new attempt toward populating the Universe through its own perfection. But no disaster occurred during any year of the Occult Age.

It took only three of the Vedic people who were not asleep to partially remove the soporific occult spells from people today. Remember how the hearts of those reading your books began to flutter and recall their love for the Earth? They are still asleep, but the power of God's Vedic culture is coming back to them. And God is gaining new hope. While still not fully awake, they through their love averted a disaster. Now it will not happen on our planet.

Soon all people will come out of the hypnotic occult sleep. They will start coming back to reality.

Are you surprised that mankind today is either asleep under a hypnotic spell or dwelling in an unreal world? You might wonder: *How can that be? Here I am, and in the cities both large and small there are millions of people living. Cars go up and down the streets.*

You should not be all that surprised by my words, Vladimir. Think about it and judge for yourself — at what times, on what day or at what hour do people actually live in a real world? Think, for example, how many different religions there are on the globe. They all have a different interpretation of Man's being and the order of the Universe, and each has its own set of rituals, distinct from the others.

Let us say that there is indeed one religion which is truer than all the rest. But that would mean that the worlds the rest of them are creating are unreal. But after all, people believe in them too. And if they believe, they live in submission to the laws of the unreal world.

All over the Earth greater and greater numbers of people are wanting to have more money. But what is money? It is simply a convention. People think that everything can be bought with money. That is an illusion. No amount of money can buy the true energy of Love, or a mother's feelings, or one's Motherland, or the taste of fruit intended only for the one who grew it with mindful attention.

As a convention, money can be used only to buy conventional, conditional love — along with a multitude of soulless things around — but in the process you are dooming your soul to a state of loneliness.

In the Occult Millennium mankind is completely disoriented as to the Space created by God. And people's souls simply flounder about as though in darkness.

Look closely, Vladimir. Just over the past hundred years in the country where you live, look how society has kept changing its direction.

There was a tsar, the social élite functioned according to prescribed behavioural rites, and people of prominence were decorated with various emblems, medals and orders with coloured ribbons. They wore gold-embroidered uniforms. And monasteries and temples were built throughout the country where you live now. And then all of a sudden that was considered contemptible. Uniforms, medals and the ribbons attached to them came to be considered no more than clown outfits. Temples were part of the dark ages. Those who served in the temples were called swindlers.

And people enthusiastically sacked the temples and angrily slew the occult servers therein. Later it was announced to all that only the Soviet authorities were to blame. Yes, the authorities did officially encourage the people to do this. But then the people did not protest — they simply responded to the call of their ruling idols.

After all, you know from documents existing today how in the Kuban'[1] forty-two Christian priests were brutally slaughtered. Not just killed, but brutally tortured. Their bodies were tossed in cesspools. This was not just the work of the rulers, the people themselves willingly participated in such acts. The rulers' only role was to allow them to happen. As a result, priests were slain by the thousands in different parts of the country. The ones that could not run ended up

[1]*Kuban'* — the area around the Kuban' River in the northwestern Caucasus, which flows from Mount Elbrus to the Sea of Azov.

renouncing their faith. Very few in those times managed to save both their life and their faith.

The majority of the people in the country became sincere atheists. They changed their clothes; the emblems and ribbons on their uniforms became different, with different colours. Many analysts and historians have written books about the Soviet years, but… In the future Lenin and Stalin will be remembered for just one thing : *For the first time mankind has been shown clearly that occultism is obsolete. Even in their sleep people do not accept occult religions. Occultism is supported only by artifice and force.* But, you see, it was not their faith in God that was destroyed. It was only the occultism that had infested their faith that was brought down.

Over the past millennium, in Russia alone a startling change of philosophy has managed to occur among the people as a whole. Religion became significantly denigrated and people's faith in it was transferred to communism, though that too is a faith.

Quite recently, you saw yourself how once again the people in the country where you live sharply changed their direction. The path everybody in the country had been enthusiastically following was declared to be the wrong one. And priorities changed once more.

Did the people choose a new way? No way! The path is not at all clear to the people. In the unreal world of the occult the people do not choose their own path. Someone always points it out. But who? The High Priest, who still today rules the world.

How does he rule the people of the modern world? And why can nobody ever overthrow him? Where is he located? Take a look — I can show him to you.

The priest who still rules the world today

Now you see an elderly man. Do not be surprised at his modest appearance. In terms of clothing and behaviour he is indistinguishable from most other people, and as you can see, he is surrounded by ordinary things. And his house is not that big — his staff comprises just two servants. He has a family: a wife and two sons. But even his family do not know who he actually is.

And yet he does have one outward distinguishing feature: if you observe him closely, you can see that he spends the whole day in isolation. And on his face you can see the depth of his meditation. Whenever he eats, or talks with his wife (although their conversations are rather rare), his eyes look as though they are concealed behind a foggy film. And even when he watches television, his eyelids are slightly lowered, he never shows surprise and never laughs. In fact he hardly watches any television at all. He merely pretends to watch, and during this time he is deep in intensive thought. He is working out grandiose plans. And exercising control of events in whole countries. He is the High Priest from a dynasty of priests, having inherited from them a knowledge of the occult, which he will also be able to transmit to one of his sons. It will take him just a year to convey everything orally to his successor, whom he is training in secret without his even knowing it — the priest has long been developing specific abilities within his son.

All the world's money belongs to the High Priest. All the world's money works for him — including what you have in your pocket right now. Do not be surprised. I shall show you how this happens, and by what means and for what reason the High Priest prefers not to live in a castle surrounded by an army of guards, why he prefers commonplace routines to special luxury.

The High Priest has no bodyguards because he knows perfectly well that the more visible authority is to all, the greater the need for armed protection. Besides, there is no guarantee that any number of bodyguards, even hundreds of thousands, will succeed in protecting any earthly ruler. Indeed, there have been instances where the guards themselves betray or even kill the ruler. Besides, having bodyguards may entail a lot of problems. There are times when the ruler is compelled to submit to the guards' terms. Compelled to tell the guards about his intentions — forthcoming trips, for example.

With a bodyguard a ruler is always under observation, and so meditation becomes more difficult for him.

It is much simpler and more reliable to conceal one's identity. This also wards off intrigues on the part of one's adversaries, fanatics and challengers to one's authority.

Now you may well be thinking: *But how is it possible to control huge numbers of people without assistants, managers and deputies, without drafting laws and disciplining those who fail to carry them out?*

It is all very straightforward. The vast majority of the people have been immersed in occultism for a very long time.

The High Priest knows all the tricks of occultism. He does have assistants, managers, drafters of laws, prisons and executioners. He has armies and commanders, though not a single one of those who carry out his missions has any suspicion himself of who is secretly commanding him and by what means the orders are issued.

It is a simple system of control without visible and personal contact.

In cities both large and small of any country there are people who all at once start to hear voices from a source they cannot pin down. And this voice from an unknown source may order a Man to carry out some kind of action, and the Man obeys the order.

Sometimes there is a clearly audible voice, sometimes this Man does not know himself what is happening to him — it is just that he feels some kind of attraction within and he carries out the action ordered.

This kind of phenomenon is known to modern science. Psychiatrists along with other scientists have been attempting to study it for a long time, but to no avail.

Modern science classifies this kind of phenomenon as a type of mental disorder. People who go to doctors and report hearing voices coming out of nowhere and giving them orders are invariably carted off to a hospital. What kind of hospital? A psychiatric institution. In many countries these are very much like prisons. There are a great many of them today in America, Europe and Russia. Patients are treated with all sorts of pills and injections to quiet the mind — this dulls their sensations, making them sleep a lot and become extremely sluggish. And some of these people stop hearing voices as such. Others feign cure in an attempt to procure their release.

But not everyone who hears voices will go see a doctor. Just imagine now that someone submitting to a voice command is in charge of an atomic missile, or in command of an army, or assigned to guard a container of deadly bacteria. And this voice then gives him a bizarre order...

Science has not been able to define the exact nature of this unusual phenomenon. It definitely exists today, and they are afraid to publicise it, but that does not help. In the meantime, they should have been focusing their attention on something more basic: if there is a signal receiver, there must somewhere be a signal transmitter as well.

The High Priest and his assistants know how to transmit voice-commands. They also know what kind of Man each of the many religions is capable of shaping. The priests are the originators of these religions, of occultism itself. They need it in order to control people. The fanatic who believes in the unreal world is like a bio-robot, predisposed to hear the voice-commands and to carry out any order unquestioningly.

The High Priest and his assistants know how to set people at odds with each other and start wars among people of different faiths.

Wars may have different specific causes, but in any war the basic weaponry has consisted of discrepancies in people's beliefs.

All technology and all artificial information channels are similarly controlled by the priests through people. And for this they do not have to control every television broadcast themselves or look over every reporter's shoulder as he writes. They need only create a general condition whereby all media are out to make money.

Television advertising, for example, has become more and more sophisticated, intrusive and aggressive. Any psychologist will tell you that it is nothing less than aggressive mental suggestion aimed at individual viewers — often not to their benefit, but to their harm. People are shamelessly told that commercial advertising cannot be helped — that is what pays for the programmes people watch. But then every TV viewer pays for all these adverts by purchasing products at the suggestion of the advertisers. Advertising costs are included in the retail price of the product. What can be more sorry than a situation like that?

And money acts as a huge and powerful lever for the priest's influence.

I told you that even the money you have in your pocket right now serves the High Priest. Here is how it all happens.

A simple pattern may be observed in the convoluted banking system we have: money withdrawn by someone from a bank increases the bank's capital. For example, let us say Russia as a country borrows on credit from an international bank. It is then obliged to pay back with considerable interest much more than it originally borrowed. How is the difference made up? From the taxes you pay — or, let us say, even when a pensioner buys a quarter-kilo of bread, a tax is also included as a percentage of the price. And that percentage, or at least a part of it, goes to the international bank. Thus capital flourishes, but whose? The High Priest's. Without even touching the capital himself, he is able to direct the flow of money into wars, occult activities or the production of deadly medicines.

His goal is simple. Pride dominates in him, and it constantly aspires to create its own world, distinct from the world God made, and hold it in subjection. And the priests partially succeed in achieving the objectives they desire. People's concerns about their everyday lives are a great help to them in this. And they themselves stir up concerns among the people to distract them.

Note how when people are distracted by everyday concerns they do not notice that less and less information is being provided them. There are stricter and stricter prohibitions on bringing up the one basic question: is the path to which all mankind is now aspiring the right one?

If they could only free themselves from distraction, many might be able to come to a conclusion for themselves: seeing how every year diseases are on the rise, wars are not ceasing and each day brings greater and greater disasters, the path we are on is doubtful, to say the least. But oh the distractions! They do not allow for any kind of contemplation. The priest, on the other hand, is engaged minute by minute in meditation, creating designs and having them carried out by the hands of millions of people...

I spent a long time listening to Anastasia's emotional narrative. I refrained from interrupting her or asking her for clarification along the way. This time I stayed longer than usual in the taiga. As I was leaving, I realised I was suffering from information overload and that it would be difficult for me to set everything down in a book. Besides, the things she said were so extraordinary, raising questions about religion and authority. In our religious denominations today there are a great many fanatics, all kinds of them. They are ready to go after anyone who encroaches on their beliefs! What do I need these problems for?

Chapter Nine

A need to think

After I got home and was preparing this book to submit to the publisher, I still couldn't decide, even up to the last moment, whether or not I should include all of Anastasia's sayings in the manuscript.

When Anastasia spoke of a splendid future for Russia which could be realised through the establishment of family domains, everything she said made sense. Her idea quickly caught on among my readers. People began to act.

Then in the book *Who are we?* when in an emotional answer to a question she referred to Christ Jesus as her older brother, and I wrote about it,[1] a number of readers, mainly faithful Christians, began to object.

In the book before that, I had written how, in answer to my question as to whether she might name any clerics who could understand her, she replied that Pope John Paul II would help her.[2] This prompted fresh doubts on the part of a few Catholic readers.

Such sayings of hers left me with a constant series of doubts of my own: should I write in my books about Anastasia's unusual actions, words and behaviour? Are they beneficial or harmful? Will they not cause some readers to entertain doubts about the obvious practical ideas of transforming society through the improvement of the living conditions and way of life on the part of individual families?

[1]See Book 5, Chapter 23: "Your desires".

[2]See Book 4, Chapter 24: "Take back your Motherland, people!".

Besides, I wasn't completely free of doubt in regard to the content of her sayings — now I ask you, what am I to make of phrases like "Christ Jesus' sister" or "Pope John Paul II will help"? If you look through the Bible, there is no mention anywhere that Jesus had any brothers or sisters.

And then all at once there occurred an event that could be called super-sensational, and in connection with this Anastasia's unusual sayings again and again gave me pause for reflecting on the tremendous scope of Man's true possibilities. This is what happened.

All at once I heard that the Vatican had publicised sources mentioning two of Christ Jesus' sisters. Only I don't remember whether they were sisters or cousins... I heard this brief news report while I was alone in my apartment, taking care of some routine tasks.

The radio and the television were both on at the time, and so I can't say for certain where I heard it. I think it may have been the TV news.

After hearing this, each time I sat down at my desk I couldn't help picking up my notes with Anastasia's unusual sayings, which I had previously decided not to include in the new book. Now I was having second thoughts about whether I had made the right choice. Among these sayings there was this one in particular:

The American President, George Bush, in a highly unconventional move, without being aware of it himself, will save his country from a terrible disaster and protect the world from a war unprecedented in its potential destructive influence over the whole Earth.

Following the disastrous acts of terrorism in America on 11 September 2001 and the subsequent military operation (war, in fact) in Afghanistan with direct American involvement, this saying of Anastasia's seemed to completely contradict what actually happened. However, upon analysing the information available in the press and on the TV, I became more and more convinced that the events of 11 September in America could help people uncover a major mystery — could help head off even larger-scale, global acts of terrorism in various countries of the world. And they will be averted only providing this secret is exposed. Again and again I read over all Anastasia's extraordinary sayings. And here is what I discovered.

On 11 September 2001 in the United States of America there occurred a series of large-scale acts of terrorism. Several jets with passengers aboard took off with unknown pilots from New York airports and immediately altered their scheduled flight path. One after the other the planes tore into the twin towers of the World Trade Centre along with other strategic targets.

Over and over again gruesome images of the crashes lit up TV screens all over the world. Soon afterward Osama bin Laden and his organisation were declared to have masterminded the attack. A little while later the American President and government secured the support of a number of European countries and Russia and began bombing Afghanistan, where, according to available intelligence, the chief culprit and members of his organisation were hiding out.

So then, what is the mystery here? After all, images of the results of these terrorist acts and the ongoing anti-terrorist military operation were shown many times over and are still being used in TV news clips several times a day.

The mystery lies in the complete absence — or cover-up — of the *causes* of the acts of terrorism — in the complete absence of logic, not on the part of those who carried them out but of those who thought them up.

The mystery lies in the fact that the press didn't even try to make even a half-way significant analysis of the causes of what happened, as though somehow all the mass media had been issued an injunction not to investigate them. What we see and hear in the media on a daily basis touches upon only the fact of what occurred. The constant repetition tends to make the extraordinary commonplace, something as routine as the daily reports of highway accidents.

According to media briefings this is what happened: Some extremely wealthy terrorist – generally assumed to be bin Laden, planned and carried out through his agents a series of notorious acts of terrorism which resulted in a huge number of casualties and exerted an unprecedented effect on people the world over.

Just what, in sum, did the mastermind behind these terrorist acts achieve? A significant part of the world community, on the head-of-state level, united against him. The most up-to-date technology and well-trained military units were employed to capture and destroy him.

According to the official version, terrorist Number One is hiding out in caves in the Afghan mountains. These mountains have been bombed from the air, along with Taliban forces, considered as collaborators with the mastermind.

The developed countries, led by the USA, have joined forces to put an end to all the camps of terrorist organisations, no matter what country such camps are located in.

Could the mastermind have failed to foresee the subsequent development of events? Sheer nonsense! Of course he knew that it would happen precisely that way. For a man able to evade capture by the special forces for such a long time, to plan and carry out terrorist acts requiring serious analysis and calculation, it should not have been a difficult task to calculate the course of events which followed.

Thus it turns out that this mastermind, from one point of view, is an astute strategist and tactician capable of meticulous analysis, while from another standpoint he is an utter fool. It turns out that through his terrorist activities he has brought doom upon himself, his organisation and all terrorist organisations, even those not connected with him.

The situation is utterly illogical and, consequently, the actions of the world community in the struggle against terrorism may not be effective — and, if the full truth be told, dangerous, since logic dictates that the mastermind behind a terrorist act remain above suspicion.

Be that as it may, one thing is clear: the picture of events that emerges from the facts reported in the mass media is a highly illogical one.

In the beginning, of course, I, like many other people, didn't pay much attention to this, but... The news from America immediately resurrected in my thought several of Anastasia's sayings — sayings which I had decided to refrain from publishing because of their strange and extraordinary nature. But now, after what happened in America, these same sayings explain a lot. Though it didn't become clear right off, by any means. Here's one example:

> Right from the time of the Egyptian pharaohs, the rulers of states both large and small have been the least free people on the Earth. They spend the greater part of their time in an artificial information field, compelled to submit to accepted rituals of behaviour. They constantly receive a tremendous amount of routine and monotonous information, but time constraints do not allow them to analyse even that. If a ruler should make the transition from an artificial information field to a natural one even for just three days, this is something dangerous for all levels of the priesthood. Dangerous, too, for the ruler's secular rivals. The danger lies in the possibility that the ruler might start analysing a whole range of processes on his own, thereby freeing himself from the yoke of occult influences and freeing his people from them.
>
> A natural information field is Nature at large — its appearance, fragrances and sounds. It is only the Nature of

one's own domain — a place where flora and fauna treat Man with love — that can protect Man from occult influences on him.

Now, as I sat at my desk (made of the cedar wood which Anastasia had given to me), I recalled these words, though this time they no longer seemed strange to me, as they had before.

Indeed, look at what is happening, even with our own President of Russia. He is constantly meeting either with foreign heads of state or with officials from our own country. None of them just stop by to take tea — they come with all sorts of problems, and are impatient for an immediate solution. And the press? No sooner does some sort of unusual event happen in the country than immediately the press wonders what the President's reaction will be. Or more bluntly: *Why didn't the President himself go to Ground Zero?* And he wins approval ratings when he actually visits the place where a flood or something else happened. But is that a good thing?

And when does he have time to calmly think about and analyse the information coming in? *Give us the President!* the people demand the moment something occurs. That's the way it happens. That's the way it's scripted. But what if it were scripted another way? The President should not be dashing off in all directions like a firefighter. He shouldn't be briefing officials, wasting time on meetings.

It is essential that he be given the opportunity to sit in his own garden, and from that perspective follow what is going on in the country, then analyse the incoming information, and from time to time take some kind of decisions. Perhaps then the people, too, would start to live better.

"What kind of nonsense is that?" many might react, as I did at first. Nonsense? But is it normal not to give someone the chance to think? Indeed, there is someone who finds it very profitable for the presidents of various countries to think as little as possible. What would happen in our country if our President were given uninterrupted time to quietly think about things? What if he were afforded the opportunity to step out of the artificial information field, at least for a time?

And all at once... I was struck by a thought which made me feel as though an electric current was running through my whole body. All at once I could feel my desk warming up. An incredible stroke of intuition hit me... For some reason in my excitement I grabbed the telephone receiver and, without dialling any number (since she doesn't have a telephone) I cried into the mouthpiece: *Anastasia!*

There was no customary dial tone. And a moment later I heard a familiar voice, easily distinguishable from all other voices in the world — the calm, pure voice of Anastasia, saying:

"Hello, Vladimir! You should try not to get so excited. You see yourself what unnatural actions excessive excitement can lead to. I shall not talk with you on the telephone. Please, calm down. Get up from your desk and go out into the fresh air, into the grove of trees near your house."

The dial tone returned. I put the receiver down.

Wow! I thought, *I really did get stirred up. I wonder whether that was really Anastasia talking to me or was I just hallucinating from excitement? I really must go outdoors into the fresh air and calm down.*

A short time later I got dressed and went out to the grove of trees next to the house. Deep in the grove I caught sight of... her! There was Anastasia, standing under a pine tree, just by the side of the pathway, and smiling. Not paying any attention to her extraordinary arrival, I began talking immediately.

Who saved America?

"Anastasia, I've got it... I did some analysing, comparing your sayings with the events which took place in America, and it all became clear... Listen to me, and correct me if I'm wrong. The series of terrorist acts which occurred on 11 September in America – it wasn't complete. The organisers were preparing something a lot bigger, weren't they?... Of course they were. Only I can't fill in the details. In general, I think, I've got it. But the details... Can you help me here?"

"I can."

"Then tell me."

"The mastermind behind this was counting on six terrorist groups to act in succession. Each of the six groups was to act independently at its appointed time, without knowing anything about each other. And their leaders did not know who was behind it all or what the ultimate goal was. Each group was made up of religious fanatics, ready to die for the cause.

"Only one group was comprised of people who had agreed to carry out the dirty deeds for money.

"The first group was to simultaneously seize control of all civil aircraft in the skies over the country, as well as those taking off from airports and those approaching American airspace. All the seized aircraft were to be used to destroy targets of national importance.

"Six days prior to this another group was to infect the water-supply system in twenty major hotels. The plan was drawn up in such a way that it would be virtually impossible to trace the source of the infection and the location of the perpetrating agents. Each agent was supposed to take a room in one of the hotels, place a special device on the cold-water tap and open the tap. Instead of water flowing from the tap, the air pressure would force a deadly powder back into the whole system. After this the tap would be shut off and the following morning the perpetrator would be making his way to a hotel in another city.

"The bacteria released into the water-supply system would become glutinous upon contact with the water, sticking to the sides of the pipes, swell up, multiply and flow downward. In twelve days they would have proliferated a great deal. In an ordinary, natural-water setting they would be incapable of proliferating — they would be destroyed by other bacteria. But such a balance is absent in an artificial supply system, where Man has deprived the water of many of its natural properties.

"During peak consumption periods — when people would be washing themselves in the morning, for example — the water flow would cause a part of the bacteria to come loose, and contaminated water would come out of the tap. People washing themselves would feel nothing at first. But after eight to twelve days small abscesses would appear on their skin at an increasing rate. They would grow in size and suppurate. The disease would be highly infectious and very difficult to cure, though the attack organisers possess an antidote...

"A lot of people would be infected in many countries. Soon it would be discovered that these people had all stayed at hotels, but this would become evident only after the planes crashed.

"It pains me to talk about the wretched deeds to be carried out by the other perpetrators. The net result of all the acts of terrorism taken together were designed to produce a climate of panic and dread.

"Many people would begin leaving the country, taking their families with them. They would attempt to relocate their capital to banks in lands where they considered it less dangerous to live. But not every nation would agree to accept refugees from the USA. Most countries' populations would be gripped by fear and terror — especially if what had been considered the most powerful state in the world could not cope..."

"Stop, Anastasia! Let me try to guess. After that the masterminds would announce themselves — I mean, put forward their demands through some kind of intermediaries."

"Yes."

"But they didn't succeed in carrying out all the attacks they had envisaged. They didn't succeed in wholly frightening Americans. They didn't manage to do everything they had planned because they were forced to start acting quite a bit before they were fully prepared. That's how the illogicality arose. The terrorist acts took place, but they didn't follow through with any demands. The whole process got cut off! And I think I can guess why. Because the real masterminds are to be found among the priests who are alive today. And they were frightened by Bush's actions and were obliged to jump the gun. Right?"

"Yes. They..."

"Wait, Anastasia! I've got to understand all this for myself — I've got to learn *how* to understand. This is very important. If *I* can get it, that means others like me will also be able to discern the reality we live in. That means everybody will understand what must be done to better our lives."

"Yes, Vladimir. If you have been able to understand, other people will too. Some right off, with others it will take time, but people will start building their lives in a splendid reality. Go on, only a little more calmly — there is no need to get so emotional about it."

"But I've almost got myself calmed down now. Or maybe not. This is hard to talk about without getting emotional. But hey! — The President of America, Bush, has really stirred things up for those smart asses. I realised how horrified they must have been when he... When President Bush all at once upped and left for his ranch in Texas.

"Just six months after taking office, the President takes a holiday and goes away for close to a month! And where does he go? Not to some fashionable resort. Not to some exotic castle. He goes to his ranch, where he has a small house. Even the usual lines of presidential communication are missing. All he's got there is one very ordinary telephone. And no proliferation of TV channels, seeing he hasn't got a satellite dish. The media commentators mentioned these facts, but nobody realised what was behind them. I read on the Internet everything I could about Bush's trip to his ranch. Just the fact was stated. They were surprised that he took a holiday so early in his mandate. And for such a long time. He spent twenty-six days at his ranch. He didn't allow any press people to visit, and didn't invite a bunch of officials.

"Nobody, but nobody, understood! Here was George Bush, the President of the United States of America, taking a colossal step which not a single president had ever taken before in the whole history of the country. Maybe not a single ruler has ever thought of doing something like that over the past five or ten thousand years!"

"You are right, they have not."

"The beautiful thing is that for the first time the ruler of a huge country, the most important country in the world, much to the horror of all the priests, suddenly tore himself away from his artificial information field. He simply picked himself up and left it behind. And with that he came out from under the control of the occultists.

"Now I understand: rulers are always kept under control. Their daily pronouncements are vigilantly followed, right down to their intonations and facial expressions. Their actions are subject to correction through all kinds of information tossed their way. But when Bush escaped from that field they were horrified. They tried reaching him through occult means — you know, the way you put it, through remote voice commands. But that didn't work — they didn't reach him! Just as you said — d'you remember? You said that Nature — the flora and fauna — constituted the natural world, and it does not permit harmful occult influences to reach Man. It protects Man, provided Man has made contact with the natural world — the one he has created himself."

"Yes, that is it, exactly."

"George Bush, of course, evidently did not create what was growing on his ranch. But he was the one who selected the location. He treated it with love — love for the Nature there, which is obvious from many facts. And Nature reacted to his love. It responded to him in kind. It protected him in the same way as the vegetation growing in one's family domain. Is something like that possible, Anastasia, when someone hasn't planted things himself, yet they still react?"

"It is possible. Sometimes they will react when Man treats his surroundings with sincerity and love. A similar thing happened in the case of George Bush."

"So there! I was right. Here was the President on his very own ranch. Everybody thought he wasn't receiving any information. But in actual fact the flow of artificial information from the artificial world significantly lessened. And the flow of natural information from the world around him significantly increased. The President took it in through the rustling of the leaves, the splashing of the water, the singing of the birds and the whistling of the wind, and he meditated. He analysed! He thought! This fact is something they will try to 'wipe out', to forget, or to refrain from talking about. They'll try to change the subject. But they won't succeed! Bush will still go down in millennial history.

"I've got it, Anastasia. Of course one can say a lot of intelligent things and write a lot of songs and poems, like King Solomon did in the Bible. Or one can act more radically and convincingly, like Bush, and thereby say to the world: *Look here, people. I'm rich, I have supreme power over the strongest country in the world. But none of this is the most important thing for Man's being. Man's soul, along with its Divine essence, prefers something else: not an artificially created world, but the natural world, created by God. My ranch is dearer to my soul than gold and technocratic achievements. And that is why I am going to my ranch. You too should be thinking, people, about your aspirations in life!*

"The American President has come up with the best, the strongest and most convincing advertisement for the family domains you spoke of. The future family domains of Russia — of the whole world! If people don't understand it after this, then mankind really *is* asleep. Or just about everyone's under somebody's hypnosis. And that's why they're sick and in agony, that's why they use drugs and go to war and kill each other. If mankind doesn't come out of this hypnosis after your words, after Bush's actions, then it's going to take a disaster.

"Bush is the President. He's the most informed person in our technocratic world, since he has access to information from special services and various think tanks. And he is aware of the information offered by the natural world. He can do comparisons and analyses. He did this and showed with his actions...

"Wait — another incredible coincidence. No, a whole series of coincidences — if, indeed, they are coincidences. You were saying... You say things, and they come to pass... You told me that at the start of the new millennium the Russian President would pass a law concerning the land, to grant every Russian family a hectare of land free of charge.

"Well, on the 21st of February 2001 all the TV news programmes carried a report on a session of the State Council of governors under the chairmanship of the Russian President, Vladimir Vladimirovich Putin. The session looked at the land question — specifically, private ownership of land, including farmland. The various governors assembled had different opinions on the question. The majority of regional leaders — members of the State Council — were in favour of making land available to Russians as private property.

"Judging by his remarks and his address, as well as by the fact that he was the one who had put the land question before the State Council, it appeared that the President was also in favour of allocating land to people as private property with the right of inheritance.

"And so the upshot of the session was a directive to the government to prepare draft legislation on the land issue by May of 2002 and present it to the State Duma for consideration.

"Of course they're talking about *selling,* not giving the land away for family domains, and farmland isn't even on the table, but all the same, it's a palpable step in the right direction.

"Anastasia, is all this a chain of coincidences or did you exert some kind of influence on people? Eh? You can give remote voice commands too, can't you? Of course you can. And you do. Have you been talking with them?"

"Vladimir, I have not been talking with anyone except you, and that has only been today, on the telephone. I have not talked with anybody at a distance, as you suppose. And I never influence anyone against their will."

"But one time when I was in Moscow I could hear your voice, Anastasia. You weren't around, yet I still heard your voice."[3]

"Grandfather, Vladimir, was near you at that time. Many people can catch thoughts existing in space. It is a natural ability of Man. Earlier all people could do this, and there is nothing bad in it. Because there is no forcing. One Man can touch another at a distance with his thought-ray, send him warm cheer and thereby speed up the thinking process. Every Man possesses this thought-ray, only in varying degrees."

[3]A reference to Book 2, Chapter 25: "The Space of Love".

"But your ray is very strong — have you tried touching people with it?"

"Yes, I have. But I shall not mention their names."

"Why not?"

"The touch of the ray is not important here. What is important is their ability to perceive reality."

"All right, then, don't name names. Only... Hey, I've got an idea! You know what I just thought of? It's terrific! After all, you're able not just to warm people with your ray at a distance, but to burn them too. You can even turn a stone into dust — you demonstrated that once.[4] So what you should do is burn up the perpetrators of terrorist acts. Burn up the priests — along with all the demonic forces. You were telling me. I remember writing it down: 'With my Ray I shall take but a moment to burn up the murk of age-old dogma. Stand not between the people and God...'[5] And so forth. You remember those words of yours?"

"Yes, I do."

"Then what are you waiting for? Why don't you burn them up? After all, you said that..."

"I was talking about dogmas. I would never dare burn up *people* with my ray."

"Even the masterminds behind acts of terrorism?"

"Even with them I would not dare."

"Why not?"

"Think about what you are saying, Vladimir."

"What's there to think about? Everyone knows the terrorism masterminds and their accessories need to be destroyed, right away. Armies of various countries have already been mobilised to this end. Special forces. People are dying."

[4]See Book 3, Chapter 7: "Assault!".

[5]See Book 3, Chapter 24: "Who are you, Anastasia?".

"Their efforts are to no avail. They will never find and never destroy the real masterminds. They will never be able to stop terrorism that way."

"All the more reason. If you can pinpoint and burn up the masterminds and their accessories in a flash, then do it. Burn them up!"

"Vladimir, perhaps you might give some thought to — you might determine — just who are the masterminds' accessories, and how many of them there are?"

"Well, sure, I could think about that. Only I doubt I'll be able to come up with an answer. If you know who, tell me their names."

"Very well. One of the accessories to terrorism is none other than *you,* Vladimir — along with your neighbours, friends and acquaintances."

"What? What are you saying, Anastasia? As for myself, and my friends too, I'm absolutely certain that we are not accessories."

"The lifestyle of most people, Vladimir, is fertile soil for terror, disease and all sorts of catastrophes. Is not someone who works in a factory producing machine guns and cartridges an accessory to killings?"

"If they manufacture weapons, well, maybe, indirectly. But you were talking about me. And I don't work in an arms factory."

"But you smoke, Vladimir."

"Well, yes. But what's that got to do with it?"

"Smoking is harmful, hence it follows that you are terrorising your own body."

"My own...? But we were talking about terrorising other people..."

"Why bring up other people right off? Everyone should carefully examine his own lifestyle. Especially those who live in cities. Do people who ride in motor cars not know what deadly gas their motor car is polluting the air with? Do people who live in large buildings divided up into a whole lot of flats not know that it is harmful and dangerous to live in these apartments? The way life is organised in big cities is aimed at destroying Man and disorienting Man in respect to natural space. The majority of people who live that way — they are the ones who are accessories to terrorism."

"Well, let's say you're right. But now many are beginning to understand, and they're going to change their lifestyle. So help people, burn up the masterminds of terrorism with that ray of yours."

"Vladimir, in order to carry out your request, I would have to charge my ray with a great deal of malicious energy capable of destroying Man."

"So, what of it? Go ahead and do it. After all, this Man is a mastermind of terrorism."

"I understand that. But before I can aim malicious energy at another, I would need to concentrate and produce in myself a large amount of this energy. Afterward it can inject itself into me again or be scattered in particles among other people. Yes, I can destroy the High Priest, but his program will continue to operate. And evil will find another priest, and he will be even stronger than the one I destroyed.

"You must understand, Vladimir, that terrorism, murders and crime are many thousands of years old. In Egypt the pharaoh was poisoned by the priests for trying to oppose their actions. When scientists opened his grave in the past century, they discovered that Tutankhamen was only eighteen years old.

"You have read in the Bible about the war of the priests. You yourself might remember that it talks about it in the Old Testament. Before all the Jews were to come out of Egypt, the priests quarrelled among themselves.

"The priest Moses asked for exclusive authority over the Jews, but the other priests would not accede to his request, and then the locusts came and attacked the Egyptian crops. Then a plague came over all their children. Many people and cattle fell victim to the disease. And finally the pharaoh let the Jews go. The residents of Egypt were so frightened they gave them cattle and weapons, as well as gold and silver.

"In the Old Testament it says that God was behind these attacks in Egypt. But could such attacks really have come from God? Of course, they could not have. God creates life to be happy for everyone. The priests caused the terrorism in Egypt when they were attempting to divide the authority among themselves. And then they blamed God for their evil deeds.

"Remember, too, Vladimir, how Jesus was crucified on the cross. Who was crucified along with him, on the crosses next to him? Criminals! That is what the New Testament says. And that was more than two thousand years ago. But they had crime back at that time too. They executed criminals. But what was the result? Crime still exists today. It goes up with each passing day. Why? Spending thousands of years in constant commotion, people have not realised that you cannot fight evil with evil. In that kind of a fight evil will only get bigger. That is why, Vladimir, I cannot respond to evil with malice."

"Well, either you can't or you don't want to — I don't suppose it makes much difference overall. When you speak, Anastasia, your arguments are very weighty indeed. It is quite true that mankind has not been able to cope with lawlessness for thousands of years. Maybe they've been using the wrong methods all this time. Only when you look at the current situation in the world, no alternative to suppressing terrorism by armed force comes to mind.

"And another thing: more and more often today we hear the term *religious extremism*. You've heard about that?"

"Yes."

"And they even say: *Islamic religious extremism*. They say it's the strongest religious extremism of all."

"Yes, so they say."

"So what's to be done? After all, I have heard Islam is the fastest-growing religion today. Many of my acquaintances are Muslims, and these aren't bad people, but on the other hand, there are also extremists among the Islamists. They engage in large-scale terrorist activities. How can we counteract them except with military force?"

"The first thing is, not to lie."

"Not lie to who?"

"To yourself."

"How so?"

"You know, Vladimir, you have heard about Muslim religious extremism. Many people have been called terrorists. You are not the only one who knows that — people have been deliberately spreading the news all over the world. It is not difficult to make a lot of people believe a notion like that, when acts of terrorism are actually taking place and Muslims participate in them. But when we talk about Muslim terrorism, we forget about another weighty argument."

"Which one is that?"

"Those that are called extremists and terrorists believe that it is *they* who are attempting to put an end to terror and save their people from calamities. And their arguments have substance to them. They believe that they are saving the whole world from the plague brought on by the Western, non-Muslim world."

"You said that their arguments have substance to them. But I have never heard anything about their arguments. If you know about them, please tell me."

"Fine, I shall tell you. But try to reason things through for yourself, and then tell me which of the two warring sides is right. The Muslim spiritual leaders say something along this line to their flock: *Look, people, look at what the unfaithful bring. The Western world has sunk into the mire of promiscuity and adultery. It wants to inject its fearful diseases into our children too. Allah's troops must stop the invasion of the unfaithful.*"

"Wait, Anastasia, those are mere words. Where are their arguments?"

"They cite facts showing that promiscuity, prostitution and homosexuality are widespread in Western, non-Muslim countries. Crime is prevalent. And every day more and more people are using drugs. And they are unable to stop terrifying diseases — AIDS, for example, and drunkenness."

"And you mean to say they don't have any of that in the Muslim countries?"

"Vladimir, in the Muslim world, in the Muslim countries, there are far fewer drunkards and smokers. There are far fewer cases of AIDS. Their birthrate is not falling as it is elsewhere and there is much less marital infidelity."

"So, it turns out, both sides are convinced they are fighting for a right cause?"

"Yes."

"So, what's ahead?"

"The priests believe they have already done everything necessary to initiate and spread large-scale war. The Western countries, the Christians, have joined together to attack the Muslim world. Following this, the Muslim world will come together, ready to fight. But the sides will not be equal: the Muslims have no modern weapons. Then, upon seeing their faithful brethren perish, they will get ready thousands of terrorists to make the Western world quit. War will start, but it will be stopped — *they* will not let it go ahead."

"Who will stop it?"

"Your readers. A new world-view is being formed in them, different from the one that has prevailed throughout the past millennia. They are creating in their dreams. Once dreams begin to turn into reality, all wars and diseases will cease."

"D'you mean to say that this will come about when construction of family domains begins? But how do family domains relate to the cessation of conflicts and religious opposition throughout the world?"

"The glad tidings of these domains will keep spreading throughout the world. People all over the globe will be roused out of their hypnotic incarceration, they will awaken from their millennial sleep. They will change their way of life and build a Divine world on the Earth with inspiration."

"Of course, Anastasia, if what you say begins to take place, and takes place everywhere on the Earth, then the world will indeed change. I know that you dream about this. You believe in your dream and will never betray it. And many people have understood your idea in regard to the family domains. These people are really starting to take action.

"But, Anastasia, you don't know everything. Come! Come to my flat, to my office. I have something I want to show you right now, and you will see, you'll understand for yourself what these people are up against."

"We shall go, Vladimir, and you will show me what has troubled you so."

Who is for, who is against?

Upon entering the flat, Anastasia took off her cardigan and kerchief, letting her golden hair fall to her shoulders. She gave her head a light shake, and the flat was at once filled with the enchanting fragrances of the taiga.

I took a chair and put it next to my own arm chair by the desk, turned on my computer and logged on to the Internet.

Not all people in Russia today will know what that is. And so I shall give a brief explanation. The Internet is an electronic information network, or 'web', which has been developing at an intensive pace in many countries of the world. With the aid of a computer one can tap in (or 'log on') to this network through a telephone line connected to a server. A server is a special powerful computer containing all sorts of information pages. On most servers one has the opportunity of posting one's own messages.

The Anastasia Foundation for Culture and Assistance to Creativity, based in Vladimir,[6] together with the Moscow firm known as *Russki ekspress* (Russian Express) has also set up its own server and its own site at the address: *Anastasia.ru*.

Thus any readers with a computer can type in the address on their keyboard and not only visit our site, but they can send us an electronic message expressing their opinions about the books, find out what other readers have said about them, and argue or discuss any particular question.

Those that do not have their own computer can gain access to our website through one of the Internet cafés which now operate in all the regional and provincial centres of Russia, as well as, I am sure, in most major cities.

From time to time I too log on to the Internet and look up what my readers have been saying. I have not been able to do this very often, as I simply have not had time to respond to all the correspondence I receive by regular mail. And last year the *Anastasia.ru* site received more than fourteen thousand

[6] *The Anastasia Foundation for Culture and Assistance to Creativity, Vladimir* — see Book 5, Chapter 15: "Making it come true".

postings. People discussed concrete questions connected with Anastasia's ideas on family domains. They suggested draft changes to the Russian Constitution; some were thinking to hold a referendum on this issue.

The substance of Anastasia's idea about granting every willing family no less than a hectare of land on which to organise a family domain was set forth in appeals to President Putin more accurately and with more cogent back-up arguments than I had expressed in my own appeal, published in the book *Who Are We?*[7] In any case, you can judge for yourselves. For those readers without Internet access I am reproducing here an excerpt from one of the appeals.

Open letter to the President of the Russian Federation Vladimir Vladimirovich Putin

Dear Vladimir Vladimirovich,

Over the years of Soviet power, which even today many of us still remember as the best years of our lives, a most frightful thing, you know, happened: we — the citizens of this Great Country, Russia, historically a mighty Power, which emerged victorious from the terrible Second World War and in an incredibly short period of time was able to build up its war-ruined economy — we transformed ourselves, without our even being aware of it, into weak-willed... parasites and welfare bums.

Look back — in Soviet times we all went to work without ever worrying about a job opening, and received a stable salary on which we could lead a normal life. We handed over our children to be schooled and were assured of their future. We knew that upon reaching retirement age we as pensioners would receive a stable pension and quietly live out our years... And this stability,

[7]See Book 5, Chapter 16: "Open letter to the President".

this mighty totalitarian system, played a dirty trick on us: having got accustomed to social passivity, social apathy and indifference, and now no longer enjoying access to a stable source of income, we have begun to get very upset. You see, we did not start to take action or improve our lives — we just started vilifying and railing like the blazes at the powers that be — each President and each Government in turn — blaming them and them alone for our Present Situation. After all, we figure it is up to them to pay us a stable salary and take care of our present and our future, while we simply live our lives for our own pleasure, and do nothing to support this Stability and Prosperity. I think you will agree that when there is movement only in one direction — that is parasitism. If all we want to do is receive and give nothing in return, well, that's parasitism for you.

And now something *amazing* has happened: thousands and tens of thousands have risen up under the impulse *to make something happen, to create!*

To create — a splendid flourishing corner of their Motherland — *Russia.*

To create — a splendid Present and Future for themselves and their children.

To create — their own Material and Spiritual Prosperity.

To create — Russia to be the wealthiest and most flourishing country in the world!

And for that these people need nothing more than a small plot of land a mere hectare in size. Along with the assurance that this land will not be subsequently taken away from them — their Motherland, where they will Create for ever a Space of Love for themselves and their children. A *Space of Love* — which will be comprised of all the flourishing corners of our vast Russia and proclaim to the Whole World the Great Miracle — the Renaissance of Russia the Great!

It seems to me that even now in Russia a situation has come about that any Ruler — you can call him a President, if you like — might dream about: a situation where people themselves desire to work and create their own material and spiritual well-being, asking nothing from the state except a plot of land and a sign of stability expressed in Law.

Isn't this the dream of any state — to open up an *inexhaustible source* of wealth and well-being within itself, to find *stability* within itself and independence from external troubles?

Dear Vladimir Vladimirovich! Like thousands of other Russian citizens, I should like to affirm once more my intention to *create* my little corner of my Motherland, Russia, to make it into a flourishing garden for many generations of my descendants.

Like thousands of other Russian citizens, I hereby reaffirm my intention of labouring for the good of my family and for the good of my Motherland.

Like thousands of other Russian citizens, I have stopped unthinkingly and relentlessly criticising either you or our Government, realising the complexity and responsibility of your work.

Like thousands of other Russian citizens, I believe in your wisdom and far-sightedness, and am confident that you will take a responsible approach to appraising the current situation.

The time has finally come for you and us to work together as a fraternal team, a team of like-minded thinkers, for us to *understand* and *accept* you as a close friend, and then you will feel our love and support and look after us, too, with love, as the People entrusted to your charge.

And together we shall create a splendid Present and Future for our children, for our Russia!

20 July 2001 Vadim Ponomaryov, citizen of Russia

They defamed our forebears too

One day on my computer I opened up an Internet search engine, which lists all the various websites containing any key word you type in. I typed in the word *Anastasia*. And the monitor immediately lit up with an impressive list: 246 Russian-language sites, together with links to their web addresses.

Still not believing that they all related to the Siberian Anastasia, I began following the links and familiarising myself with the content of these pages. It turned out that the vast majority of them did in fact discuss at varying length the Siberian Anastasia. Her ideas were treated favourably on many of the sites. At first I was delighted by this, but as I delved deeper into the volume of information available on the Internet, I began coming up against an even more incredible phenomenon. Several of the sites offered a selection of articles from the press, along with anonymous messages, claiming that the movement associated with Anastasia was a sect, and all the readers of the books were categorised as sectarians. One of the sites featured a list (either full or partial) of the existing sects in Russia, and the list included 'Anastasia' and her supporters. There was no mention of the basis for such a conclusion or of who was spreading such rumours — they were simply set forth as though they were a given fact that apparently everybody had known about for a long time.

The articles and brief comments from various national and regional publications posted on different websites were very similar to each other, and they always came to the same conclusion: that the *Ringing Cedars of Russia* movement was either a sect or a business. The Anastasia movement was lumped in with such sectarian organisations as *Aum Shinrikyo*,[8] and classified as a 'totalitarian sect'. They even used words like 'bigots' and 'destructivism'. No concrete facts were cited, just the conclusion, and that was it.

Not knowing the exact definition of the word *totalitarianism,* I looked it up in my Great Encyclopedic Dictionary[9] and read the following:

> Totalitarianism is one of the forms of domination, characterised by its complete control over all spheres of a society's life along with the virtual liquidation of constitutional rights and freedoms, also by repression of political opposition and dissenters (for example, the various forms of totalitarianism in Fascist Germany and Italy or the Communist régime in the USSR).

Now that's pretty steep! What they're saying in effect is that I or Anastasia have been in control of some flashy totalitarian sect ready to overthrow authority, abolish constitutional freedoms and institute a fascist régime. But I categorically deny that I have had any governing role in any kind of organisation, all the more so in the case of Anastasia. Throughout the past six years I have been working exclusively on my books, and once or twice a year I give talks at readers' conferences which are open to anyone who wishes to attend. My talks have been recorded on tape, and anybody can have access to them.

But why, for what purpose and by whom is this bald-faced lie being spread abroad? In one of the newspaper articles,

---

[8] *Aum Shinrikyo* (also spelt *Senrikyo*) — a Japanese Buddhist religious group founded by Shoko Asahara; some of its members were held responsible for the 1995 gas attack on a Tokyo underground (subway) line. In 2000 the organisation's name was changed to *Aleph* (the first letter of the Hebrew and Arabic alphabets). In 2006, after years in prison, Shoko Asahara was sentenced to death.

[9] Great Encyclopedic Dictionary (*Bol'shoi Entsiklopedicheski Slovar'*), edited by A.M. Prokhorov, 2nd ed. Moscow & St Petersburg, 2002.

this one in the Vladimir-region supplement to *Komsomol'skaya pravda,* it says that in the Anastasia books readers are encouraged to give up their city apartments and go off into the woods.

How can that be? I thought. After all, Anastasia says the exact opposite. Here are her direct words: "There is no need to go live in the forest. You need to clean up the place you have been polluting first."[10] And she calls upon people to build their family domains near big cities, and gradually change their lifestyle to one more civilised and more favourable to one's soul and physical health.

Not having the opportunity to personally review the tremendous amount of information, let alone analyse it, I turned to several well-known experts in political science to examine the situation independently of each other and draw their conclusions. Each of them asked considerable compensation for their work, given that they had to read through all five books plus the huge amount of information connected with the books which had been posted on the Internet. I had no choice but to accept their terms.

Three months later I received the first expert's conclusions and, not long afterward, the remaining reports. Even though they expressed their findings in different words, since they did not know each other and were working independently, they came to pretty much the same conclusions. I shall cite a few typical excerpts from one of the reports:

> There is a whole targeted, clearly formulated campaign directed against the *Ringing Cedars of Russia* series of books, with the aim of preventing the spread of these books among the population at large...

[10] Quoted (from two separate sentences) from Book 3, Chapter 21: "Should we all go live in the forest?".

The pivotal ideas of the books are the strengthening of the state, the achievement of the greatest possible unanimity in the various social strata of the population through the well-being of each individual family. This condition of well-being is achieved by virtue of each willing family being allotted no less than one hectare of land for lifetime use. In the context of the books this idea is the most persuasive and takes precedence over all others. Consequently, the series' opponents, whatever the arguments they put forward, are in fact denouncing this particular idea.

The next question raised by the *Ringing Cedars of Russia* series — the Divine nature of Man, his spiritual origin — may provoke animosity on the part of many religious denominations. The book's main heroine declares that Man's existence in Paradise should be built here on the Earth and by Man himself. Man is eternal, only changing his fleshly form from one century to the next. Our whole natural environment is created by God and comprises His living thoughts. It is only by making contact with Nature that Man can comprehend what God has programmed and the substance of His purpose for Man on the Earth...

This whole concept, the reasoning behind it and its extreme persuasiveness cannot fail to provoke opposition, especially among religious fanatics who believe that the end of the world is inevitable and that some people will be transported into a Paradise beyond the clouds while others are sent to hell. Such a concept is favourable to many people who have been unable to make their own life happy during their existence here on the Earth.

The opposition to the ideas of the series' main heroine (Anastasia) is being effected by the circulation, through the mass media, of rumours that its readers, who have taken the initiative to put a number of the projects suggested by the books into practice, belong to some sort of totalitarian sect.

This approach is quite deliberate, inasmuch as it serves to distance the authorities from contacts with enterprising readers and from examining their specific proposals, as well as from discussing the problems raised in the books in the mass media. It also serves to interfere with the circulation of the books and the ideas put forward in them. It should be pointed out that the opposition has achieved their aim. According to reports on hand, claims about the readers belonging to a sect are being circulated in many government agencies.

The specific objectives of the opposition are not clearly presented — they remain quite enigmatic.

As a rule, when candidates competing for office use dirty tricks in their campaigns, it is easy to guess who is instigating them. Similarly in the economic sphere, when individual firms are competing for business, it is not difficult to determine who is behind a smear campaign and why. The goal is always clear — to knock off or weaken the competition.

Anastasia talks about a new consciousness for Man, a new way of life, establishing the state on a more perfect foundation.

Who would oppose an aspiration like that? Only forces interested in the destruction of individual families, states and society as a whole. The existence of such forces can be traced through their conspicuous opposition — in this case, in launching actions directed at Anastasia herself and her ideas, as well as against the readers of the *Ringing Cedars of Russia* series. To all appearances they are acting through agencies either directly or indirectly under their jurisdiction, as well as through individuals.

I showed Anastasia isolated excerpts from the discussions of the subject on the Internet, and read her the expert's conclusions, in the hope that the situation portrayed would somehow move her or rouse her into taking corrective action.

But Anastasia continued sitting quietly beside me on her chair, her hands resting on her knees, her face showing absolutely no concern. On the contrary, it even betrayed a little smile.

"What are you smiling for, Anastasia?" I enquired. "Doesn't it bother you at all that they are slandering your readers? The fact that they are blocking their initiatives to obtain land for the family domains?"

"I am delighted, Vladimir, by the inspired impulse on the part of so many people, by their understanding of the essence and significance of what they are undertaking. See how thoughtfully they are setting forth their thoughts and drawing up plans for the future. And the appeal to the President is better than the one you formulated in your earlier book. As well as their making plans to hold a conference with that wonderful title: *Choose your future!*[11] It is very good when people start reflecting on their future."

"They certainly are making plans, Anastasia. But don't you see how their plans are being thwarted? What a tricky move someone thought up — to call them all sectarians, striking fear into the population and discouraging administrative bodies from contact with them? Don't you see that?"

"I see it. But there is nothing new or sophisticated in such opposition. The same approach was used to destroy the culture, lifestyle and knowledge of our forebears. And now the dark forces are using the old methods again. And they will even come up with provocations, and then spread frightening rumours. This has happened before, Vladimir."[12]

[11]The conference later took place in February 2002 in Moscow's Palace of Youth (*Dvorets molodiozhi*) and was attended by hundreds of readers from all over Russia and abroad. The conference's Proceedings, including presentations on economics, law, ecology, public policy and other subjects were subsequently published as a separate volume.

"Exactly — this happened before. And they won. You said yourself — they destroyed the culture of our forebears. They distorted history. That means that now, too, using a tested method, they'll win again. If they haven't won already. Hey, just a simple question like granting every willing family a hectare of land — it's been impossible to solve for a year now.

It would have been okay if they'd asked for that hectare for something obscene. But it's impossible to get land for the purpose of organising one's family domain, for normal living conditions and a supply of food. Those refugees that have been living in tent cities for more than three years now[13] — if they — at least the ones who wanted it — had each been given a hectare of land, by now they could have turned it into a decent human place to live. I've thought quite a bit, Anastasia, about what colossal changes could take place in our country, if only the authorities would not oppose but help people aspiring to create their own domains. But such a simple little question regarding the allocation of land is not being solved."

[12]In October 2006 a central Russian daily newspaper with a circulation of 1.6 million featured an article (subsequently reprinted in other editions throughout the country) claiming that destructive behaviour on the part of readers of the Series had reached the point of feeding their children to wild beasts and copulating on tombstones of the dolmens — all at Vladimir Megré's instigation. Similarly, a thousand years earlier Christian 'historians' alleged that pagans were offering human sacrifices and engaging in public orgies.

[13]A reference to the hundreds of thousands of people displaced by the war in Chechnya — see footnote 4 in Book 5, Chapter 17: "Questions and answers".

Glad tidings

"This question is far from simple, Vladimir. It actually involves major changes on our planet and in the Universe. When millions of happy Earth families begin to consciously transform the planet into a flourishing garden, the harmony reigning on the Earth will have an effect on other planets and the whole space of the Universe. Right now the planet Earth is sending a poisonous stench into the Cosmos. And more and more garbage is piling up in orbit. And a malicious energy is radiating from the direction of the Earth. A different energy will be emitted when there is a change in the conscious awareness of Earth dwellers. And then the grace emanating from the Earth will bestow flourishing gardens upon other planets."

"Wow, how grand! And has there never been such an opportunity before in human history? After all, in Russia back before the revolution landlords had their family estates. And now in many countries there is private ownership of land. We have farmers too who rent out land for extended periods. But nothing comes of it. Why not?"

"There has been no conscious awareness — the kind that is growing today in human minds and souls as little shoots of the Divine. What you called a straightforward question, Vladimir, during the occult millennia was the greatest secret held by the priests. Many religions through the ages have talked about God, but not one of them has ever stated the obvious: in consciously communing with Nature, Man communes with the Divine thought. To understand Space is to understand God.

"And even the thought or the dream of a family domain, where everything is in harmony with you, embodies much more closeness to God than a whole lot of convoluted rituals.

All the mysteries of the Universe will be unfolded to Man. And all at once Man will discover within himself capabilities that he cannot even imagine today. And Man will become truly Godlike — the Man that begins to create the Divine world around him.

"Think, why do not 'wise-men' ever mention this anywhere? All because once Man understands his earthly essence and his capabilities, he will become free from occult spells. The power of the priests will disappear. Nobody and nothing will ever have power over a Man who has created a Space of Love around him. And no harsh and threatening judge will the Creator be for such a Man, but rather a father and a friend.

"This is why through the centuries they have come up with so many tricks to turn Man away from his purpose. Land! Such a straightforward question, you say, Vladimir. But think about how centuries have passed and Man still does not have family land of his own. You were mentioning farmers and landlords. But with their family domain they hired other people to work the land. They have endeavoured to get as much profit as possible out of their land. People who did not work the land themselves could not treat it with love. And often seeds were sown in the ground in anger, and malice grew.

"For thousands of years simple truths have been hid from the people. Other people's hands and thoughts should not be compelled to touch one's family land. In different ages rulers have offered people land allotments, but in such a way that the meaning of their earthly deeds has not been clear to people.

"If a Man is given just a small piece of land — a quarter of a hectare, for example — his family will not be able to build an oasis there which will serve him effortlessly. A large tract of land is too much for a Man to govern independently and he will end up hiring helpers, thereby involving other people's thoughts. So people have been drawn away by trickery and chicanery from what is important."

"Does this mean, Anastasia, that not a single religion over thousands of years has ever called upon people to create Divine oases on the Earth's land? On the contrary, they have spent all their time calling people's thought away from the land, somewhere else. So it turns out that they..."

"Vladimir, do not say unflattering words about religion. Your spiritual father, the monk Feodorit,[14] led you to where you are today. And it is largely thanks to him that you and I met in the first place. The time has come today when congregations of all the various denominations need to think about how to save our spiritual leaders from disaster."

"What kind of disaster?"

"The same kind that happened in the past century — when people sacked the temples and put ministers of various faiths to death."

"You mean under the Soviet régime... But now, you see, we have democracy, freedom of religion and the authorities treat all religions — or at least the major ones — with respect. How could the events of bygone years all at once repeat themselves?"

"You should take a closer look at what is happening today, Vladimir. You know that many countries have joined together in the struggle against terrorism."

"Yes."

"They have pointed their finger at *other* countries as the ones promoting terrorism. And they have publicised the names of the instigators. They have accused, among others, some spiritual and religious leaders, and special forces have been assigned to hunt them down. But that is only the beginning. Reports have been given to the leaders of countries both large and small exposing the nature of many religions, and they include a whole lot of examples of how these

[14]*Feodorit* — see Book 2, Chapter 24: "Father Feodorit".

religions themselves were responsible for fomenting acts of terror and wars on the Earth. In these reports, which have already been prepared, analysts have set forth everything accurately and convincingly. Information about many terrible crimes will now gradually come to light. They will remind people of an endless succession of wars like the Crusades, intrigues, perversions and greed among the ministers of the occult. When anger builds up in a whole lot of people, pogroms may be launched in many places, and these may include the destruction of temples.

"At the moment, clerics from a number of religions are trying to put a stop to religious extremism, making declarations to the effect that the extremists have nothing in common with them — indeed, these clerics openly condemn extremism. For the moment, these declarations are being accepted. Or, rather, the political leaders feign ignorance... and say they are satisfied with the declarations.

"In the meantime, these secret reports are already claiming that religions are programming people, using any kind of pretext. The pretext may be well-intentioned — calling the faithful to good works, for example. But any faith in something a Man cannot see, especially one which he accepts unquestioningly as truth from a preacher, is always fraught with the danger that the thoughts of the programmed believer may be redirected at the will of the preacher, and so today's believers may easily be transformed into tomorrow's suicide bombers. And a whole lot of different facts from both past and present are cited in the reports as evidence in support of this conclusion. Before long the rulers will become inclined to the opinion that they should select one religion and put it completely under their control, at the same time declaring all others harmful and deserving of elimination.

"Subsequently, if they do not succeed in drawing all the people into one religion, then the next step is to destroy *all* religions, at least within their own borders. Such a decision will lead to a never-ending war. This war has already started, it is already going on. It must be stopped. And this can only be done in one way — by giving birth to a conscious awareness on the part of our spiritual leaders. Only glad tidings can restore peace to all the Earth. Those that accept the glad tidings and proclaim them in temples both great and small — they will fill the temples with multitudes of people. Those that do not perceive the sayings will find themselves in temples that are empty and decaying."

"What glad tidings are your referring to, Anastasia? Can you explain it a little more simply?"

"People who call themselves spiritual leaders, who talk of God and teach children in the schools today, should recognise as a God-pleasing deed the co-creation of a Space of Love in the personal domain of every family dwelling on the Earth. Not only to recognise this but to create designs as well for future projects together with their parishioners. To endeavour, along with the people, to bring back the knowledge of pristine origins. To dream and discuss such a theme, and then to bring the design to perfection in all its detail. The process of creating the dream will take many years. Then, when all this comes to prevail upon the Earth, people will live in harmony, in a real, Divine Space of Love."

"I've got it, Anastasia. You want everyone to begin studying Nature in all the temples of whatever religious persuasion, and in the schools and in institutions of higher learning. To master the science of creating a family domain according to a special design. Let's say this can actually bring various religious denominations together into a common alliance — not just in words but in deeds. Let's suppose it could really awaken people from their hypnotic sleep, put an end to terrorism, drug use and a whole lot of other negative tendencies in society.

"Let's suppose. But... How will you be able to convince all the patriarchs and all the clerics, and in so many different denominations? How will you be able to convince all the secular educational institutions? A lot of things you say come true, Anastasia, but what you're talking about at the moment is completely unfeasible, sheer pie in the sky!"

"It *is* feasible. They have no other choice now."

"But that's just what *you* think. Just you. These are mere words that you're saying."

"But the One who allows me to utter these 'mere' words, as you put it, possesses power unsurpassed. You may remember back seven-plus years ago, back when you were still an entrepreneur, that I stood before you and drew letters in the sand by the lake in the taiga."

"Yes, I remember, but what of it?"

"And then all at once you began to write books, and now a whole lot of people are already reading them. Who do you think was mainly responsible for this? The sand by the taiga lake? Or the stick I drew with? Or the words I articulated? Or perhaps your hand created the books all by itself? And later poetry welled up like a sacred spring in human hearts. Who was the chief Creator behind these works of art?"

"I don't know. Possibly all the factors played a part."

"Believe me, Vladimir — please try to understand. It is His energy that stands behind everything that was created. It is His energy that inspired human hearts. And it will continue to inspire them."

"Perhaps, but somehow it is hard to believe that church ministers will start to act the way you say."

"You should believe in this. And visualise a gladsome prospect within yourself, and then it will come to achievement. All the more so, since that is no longer hard for you to do. You remember how an Orthodox village priest came to you to cheer up your crestfallen spirits.[15] Another priest paid for your books with his own money and then distributed them to the prisons. And your Father Feodorit talked with you about a lot of things... Do you remember?"

"I do."

"And you should realise, too, that not all church ministers share the same world-view. There are those who will proclaim the glad tidings."

"Yes, I think you're right. But there will be others who will begin to oppose them. Especially the High Priest you spoke about — his occult agents will think up some kind of new intrigue."

"Of course they will, but all the dark forces' endeavours will now be in vain. The process has begun and it has already attained the point of no return. People will learn first hand of their earthly Paradise. These are mere words, you will say. But here, I shall now utter two simple words — and a part of the darkness will be illumined with light. Let the rest of the darkness tremble and begin to conceal their names, as they fail to win the possibility of turning into reality. And these words are utterly simple: *The Book of Kin*."[16]

---

[15]See Book 4, Chapter 24: "Take back your Motherland, people!".

[16]*The Book of Kin* — a translation of the two-word Russian phrase *Rodovaya kniga*.

Chapter Ten

The Book of Kin

"Yes, the words are certainly simple, all right," I observed. "And just why are all the forces of darkness supposed to tremble at hearing them?"

"They are afraid of what is behind the words," replied Anastasia. "Do you know who will write this book? And how many pages it will have?"

"How many? And who will write them?"

"Just a few days will go by, and millions of fathers and mothers in many a land will be writing the Book of Kin, filling in its pages with their own hand. There will be a vast multitude of them — these Books of Kin. And all of them will contain the truths which begin in the heart, for their children. There will be no room in these books for artifice or guise. Before them all the lies of history will fall.

"You can surmise what would happen, Vladimir, if you could take into your hands today a book which your ancestor of old had begun to write especially for you. Then another would continue the writing, eventually your grandfather, and your father and your mother.

"The books read by Man today include many that are devised with a specific aim in mind — namely, the distortion of history and of the meaning of life. Many false dogmas are especially designed to disorient Man in space. This is not easily discernible all at once. But clarity comes directly a son reads a book of his forebears, which his father and mother have continued personally for him."

"But wait, Anastasia, not everyone knows how to write a book."

"Everyone can if they feel the demand to do so — if they are looking to protect their children, and in the future themselves, from false dogmas. In Vedic times every father and mother would write a book of kin for their future children and grandchildren. This book was not comprised of words, but of deeds. Children could read created space like a book, and understand the deeds and thoughts of their parents, and were happy to inherit a happy space. Only one thing was missing from that book — children were not alerted to the world of the occult. It was not part of the complete awareness of the omniscient Veduns.[1] Now that all mankind has been able to detect in their own experience the devastating influences exerted on themselves by the occult dogmas, they will certainly be able to protect their children from them.

"Even if there are not yet any domains to bloom in the spring, thoughts about them are already alive in many human hearts. They need to start writing a book precisely about their thoughts, for their children."

"And why, Anastasia, does every parent need to write? Look, I've written books about domains and an architect from the suburb of Medvedkovo[2] is working on a design for a whole settlement. Besides, there is a flurry of Internet discussions on the subject — isn't that enough?"

"It is not enough, Vladimir. Take a closer look at what has been going on. You have been writing books, but other people are writing books too, to counteract yours. There are so

[1] *Vedun* (pron. *ve-DOON*) — in Slavic and Hindu traditions: a revered wise man. Like the word *Vedic,* it is derived from the Old Slavic (originally Indo-European) root *ved-* meaning *knowledge* or *full awareness.*

[2] *Medvedkovo* — a northern Moscow suburb, founded in the 16th century as the estate of Vasili Fiodrovich Pozharsky, who bore the nickname of *Medved'* (Bear). Note that this word includes the roots *med-* (honey) and *ved-* (know) — the bear was originally named in Russian for his knowledge of where honey could be found.

many books that a Man could not hope to read even half of them over his lifetime. And look, there is a daily flow of information to Man that does not come from books. And even though it seems very diversified, all that information really comes down to the same result: it justifies and glorifies the unreal world of the occult. What can help the newcomer to the world determine where the truth and where the falsehood lies?

"The holy temple of the family will help in this — the Book of Kin. In it a mother and father will write for their son and daughter about what is the most important thing that needs to be created for happiness in life. The children will continue to record the Book of Kin. There will be no wiser and truer books for families anywhere on the Earth. All the knowledge of their pristine origins will be poured into it."

"But how, Anastasia, how can knowledge of one's pristine origins turn up in a book which people are only beginning to write today? Where are they to find such knowledge? You said that the culture of our forebears, their books, were all destroyed."

"Those that will begin to write already have this knowledge concealed within themselves. It is preserved within each one of us. When people think deeply and begin to write not just for anyone, but for their children, all the knowledge of their pristine origins will be revealed within them and come to light."

"So that means that before they start to write, they first need to *think*, so that wise thoughts may be set forth right from the very first pages of the book?"

"The first pages may be outwardly very simple."

"Can you give me some examples?"

"When was the Man who began to write this Book of Kin born? What was his name? For what purpose and with what thoughts did he take pen in hand and approach the pages of this most important book? And what did he plan to create in the future?"

"Such a book," I observed, "would be easy to begin for anyone who, let's say, has been a famous artist, or a governor, or a scholar, or a die-hard entrepreneur. But what about someone who has simply lived a life? Say someone's been working and can barely make ends meet, he scarcely earns enough for food and clothing. What could he possibly write for his children, what advice could he give them?"

"The rulers of today, and those who bask before the public in rays of glory, and those who have accumulated a whole lot of money, will find it difficult from now on to have an answer for their children. People quickly forget their deeds of yesteryear. But what a Man has contributed to his future will be appreciated by future generations. Are you or anyone else in the habit of recalling past governors, famous artists or entrepreneurs?"

"Not very often — or, rather, I don't really think about them at all. I don't even know their names. But children will take great pride in remembering what their parents did."

"And their children will try to forget — they will be ashamed just at the mention of their parents' names."

"Why should the children be ashamed?"

"Because fate offered their parents such great opportunities, but they could not grasp the fact that fate is affording us opportunities only — invariably — for the purpose of creating the future. In his one lifetime, Man should be endeavouring to create the next life for himself — a life in which he can embody himself anew and live for ever.

"Every Man can even today plan out a domain and a Space of Love, they can create their design and try to obtain the land. They can use that land to plant a few saplings or plant seeds of family trees. Perhaps they will not be able to grow to maturity, say, a whole grove, or a green hedge, or a splendid garden, in their lifetime. Perhaps a poor old man will not even be able to lay a foundation for his house. But he will be able to write in the Book of Kin for his grandchildren, for his children: *I was poor, it was only in my old age that I began to think on the meaning of life, on what I have handed to my children. And I have created a plan for a space for our family, I have described it for you, my children, in a book. I have been able to plant nine fruit trees in the garden, as well as just one tree on the spot where a grove will grow.*

"The years will flow on, the grandson will read that book and remember his grandfather. He will go up to the mighty, majestic cedar or oak growing amidst a lot of other trees on the land of his kin's domain. His thought, overflowing with love and gratitude will soar into space, will merge with his grandfather's thought, and then a new plane of being will be born for both of them. A whole life in eternity is afforded to Man. The settling of the Earth and the planets of the Universe is nothing more than a transformation for each Man within himself.

"The Book of Kin will help convey the glad tidings to one's descendants, and help the soul of the beginning writer to once again embody itself upon the Earth."

"Well, Anastasia, you attach such importance to this book that I too have the desire to start writing one for my descendants. I have the intuitive feeling that in this idea of yours about the book is something most unusual and grand. Wow! That's quite a name: *The Book of Kin, The Kin's Book, the most holy book for the family.*

"But what should it be written on? Ordinary paper will soon yellow and disintegrate. And the binding on notebooks and albums tends to look rather primitive. After all, if the book is destined for one's descendants — if, as you say, it is of such great importance — then the paper and the binding should correspond too. What do you think? What should be used?"

"*That* kind, for example..." And she nodded in the direction of a book lying on my desk. I followed her gaze, and a moment later I was holding something quite extraordinary in my hands...

Some time ago a man named Sergei from Novosibirsk had sent me a copy of my *Anastasia.* The customary publisher's binding had been cut off, and the pages transferred to another — I was going to say *binding,* but that's not the right word for what these pages had been put into. A Siberian craftsman had created an extraordinary work of art. The whole cover, including the spine, had been made out of valuable species of wood — the edges were of beech with cedar inside the frame. All the details were decorated with finely carved ornaments, text and illustrations. One could hardly apply the ordinary term *cover* to all this. The term *casing* would probably be more appropriate. The front and back parts were fastened together on one side by the spine, on the other by a little lock. All the little parts were finely fitted together. When the book was closed, the pages were evenly positioned between the front and back parts of the casing, thus preventing the paper from buckling under conditions of either high or low humidity. The pages would not flutter even from a draught of air, in contrast to some other books which I put beside it for comparison. Many visitors who saw this work of art would hold it for a long time in their hands, looking it over carefully with joyful admiration.

Following Anastasia's gaze, I took the book with the wooden casing into my hands, felt its warmth and began to understand. Perhaps it was thanks to this extraordinary work that I really understood the tremendous significance of the Book of Kin Anastasia had been talking about.

She sat there meekly on the chair beside me, her hands modestly resting on her knees. But I got the feeling that she was wiser than all the priests and dynastic leaders right from ancient times, wiser than our modern analysts. And through her wisdom and purity of thought she is able to overcome all the negative manifestations in human society. Where did these capabilities of hers come from? What school or system of child-raising can endow Man with such abilities?

Wow! What an unusual, incredible step to think up — a Book of Kin! I couldn't stop myself from letting my mind get carried away and... Just look what a grand thing she's come up with!

Nobody has so far been able to counteract the flood of various kinds of suggestions which has been rushing at people in different countries minute by minute — first and foremost, at our children.

Suggestions! Our TV features a constant parade of action films supposedly for the purpose of public entertainment, but in actual fact demonstrating how splendidly Man can provide for his financial well-being through violence.

Suggestions! How great it must be to be a famous singer, to bask in the spotlight and the applause, to gad about to receptions in luxury limousines!

Suggestions! If it weren't for the power of suggestion, they would also need to show other, considerably longer segments from the life of these people. The most challenging everyday work routines, the never-ending intrigues instigated by entertainment rivals, the never-ending attacks by jealous wannabes, not to mention the paparazzi hoping to make money on the backs of celebrities under the so-called 'freedom of the press'.

One particularly monstrous suggestion comes in the form of aggressive and sophisticated advertising, which is ready to promote anything as long as you pay the money.

Suggestions! Never-ending news about all sorts of international do-good foundations coupled with wonder-boy politicos — and people are left with the impression that it is only thanks to our politicians that they can live all warm, fed and cozy in their homes. And then when the radiators go cold, people no longer bother asking themselves questions about how they can change their lives, how they can become independent of central heating, electricity and water-supply. Instead, they rush madly into the streets and shout *Gimme!* A suggestion of their own helplessness! Such false dogmas are being suggested to adults and children alike.

Children! How can we talk about raising children as long as we parents just stand on the sidelines? First we entrust the delivery of our children to strangers in an unfamiliar medical institution. Then we allow strangers to teach them in kindergarten and school. Then we allow them to be exposed to a plethora of explicit or disguised pornographic literature on our store shelves.

We allow strangers to recommend books and textbooks to our children to read. We allow strangers to produce TV programmes for them. Who? Who finds it profitable to hold the whole system of child-raising in their hands? Maybe that's not the important question. Maybe what's more important is our feeling of utter helplessness and insignificance? We feel we're totally incapable of putting a stop to such lawlessness. But this isn't true! Any parent can do it! If only he wants to. If only he thinks about it.

The Book of Kin! What a super idea! The end of lawless commercial suggestions! Such lawlessness may still flex its muscles and show off a little. But it won't be long before Man takes in his hands the Book of Kin, and finds there written — by the hand of his grandfather, grandmother, father and mother — a statement of Man's purpose in life.

We, today's parents, shall certainly be able to figure out what this purpose is. Most definitely! We are experienced, we've seen, heard and gone through a lot already. We only need to pause for just a wee bit, turn away from the flood of suggestions and think for ourselves, with our own heads. For certain, every parent must think about this. By himself! Only by himself. There's no point in looking for answers to questions on the meaning of life in books of wisdom from past centuries. No matter how celebrated or promoted these books are. And there's no point in seeking answers in the works of wise-men whose reputation is thousands of years old.

These wise-men were great preachers and messiahs. They endeavoured to preach and leave writings for future generations. But there is not one — not even one of these great works that we shall ever see. They have been most cleverly destroyed. This can be clearly understood if one but stops and thinks.

Just look and see what a difference it makes — how switching a single comma around in a brief sentence can change the whole meaning of a message. Remember the famous example: *Execute never, show mercy! / Execute, never show mercy!* And how many similar alterations have crept into the works of the ancient thinkers, either deliberately or inadvertently, at the hands of copyists, translators, publishers and historians?! And we are talking here not just about changes in punctuation, but the deletion of whole pages, whole chapters, and the writing of one's own interpretations.

The result is that we today are living in some kind of illusory world. Mankind is constantly at war. People keep destroying each other like hell and can't understand why wars do not stop. But how can they stop if mankind has not even once been able to determine who has been instigating these wars? It hasn't been able to because there has been no independent thought, and without independent thought it accepts suggestion as truth.

Who started the Second World War? Who fought with whom? Who won? The whole world community is convinced that the war was started by Hitler's Germany under Hitler.

Victory was achieved by the Soviet Union under Stalin. And these half-truths — or, rather, delusions — are accepted by the majority as absolute, unequivocal, historical facts.

And only a very few historical researchers occasionally mention Hitler's spiritual mentors — for example, the Russian lama Gudzhiev,[3] acting through Karl Haushofer.[4] Hitler had one other spiritual mentor — Dietrich Eckhart.[5] Historians know of contacts these spiritual mentors had with their superiors, part of a more elevated hierarchy. But at this point nobody any longer mentions names. Researchers say only that they have traced the connections to the Himalayas and Tibet, as well as to both open and secret occult societies existing at the time in Germany, and confirm Hitler's participation in them.

Germany witnessed the rise of organisations such as the *German Order*[6] and the *Thule Society*[7] — the latter's emblem was the swastika together with a wreath and sword.

[3]*Georgi Ivanovich Gudzhiev* (also spelt *Gurdjieff, Gurdzhiev*) (1872?–1949) — a Greek-Armenian mystic, later based in Paris. In 1922 he founded the Institute for the Harmonious Development of Man. He emphasised the principle of 'self-awareness', the need to awaken from the dream-like state that most of human existence seems to be. Gudzhiev authored a number of books, including the well-known *Beelzebub's tales to his grandson* (*Rasskazy Vel'zevula svoemu vnuku*).

[4]*Karl Ernst Haushofer* (1869–1946) — German geopolitician, believed to have influenced Hitler's expansionist policies. He was an avid student of Japanese culture and was instrumental in forging Germany's alliance with Japan following Hitler's rise to power in 1933. His link to Gurdjieff is a matter of some controversy.

[5]*Dietrich Eckhart* — German occultist, who was very close to Hitler.

[6]*German Order* (in German: *Deutsche Orden*) — a religious order founded for charitable purposes, known from the 12th century as the *Teutonic Order*, abolished on occasion by both Napoleon and Hitler (it still exists today in both Germany and Austria). The term *German Order* was also applied to the highest decoration awarded by the Nazi Party.

Someone was clearly and deliberately shaping their own unique, brand-new ideology in Germany, inculcating in its population a specific type of world-view. The upshot was large-scale war and masses of human casualties, followed by the Nuremburg trials where Hitler's cronies were tried. But those who appeared before the court were ordinary soldiers — even if they happened to be generals or field marshals, they were still soldiers, including Hitler himself. Foot-soldiers to the unseen priest who shaped the ideology. He — the chief strategist and organiser — was not even mentioned in the trial records. Who is he? Who are his closest secret associates and assistants? Is it all that important to know about them? It *is* important! Extremely important! After all, it is they who masterminded the war. And as long as they are allowed to remain in the shadows, they will start it again. With their growing experience, new wars will be even more sophisticated and on an even more massive scale.

What were these people really after, the masterminds behind the Second World War? Perhaps an examination of the following fact will bring us closer to solving the mystery.

For the Nazi ideologists in Germany at that time, there was an organisation known as *Annenerbe* which collected ancient books from all over the world. In the first place they were interested in Old Russian editions of the pre-Christian period. One can trace a rather bizarre chain — the Himalayas, Tibet, lamas, secret societies — all leading to a relentless hunt for the knowledge of our forebears from pagan Russia. We Russians saw no need to preserve these manuscripts, but someone else found them to be a vital necessity. Why? What secrets did

---

[7]*Thule Society* — a German occultist group in Munich, named from the Greek word meaning 'farthest [northern] land', founded in 1910 by Dietrich Eckhart. It is said to have sponsored the *Deutsche Arbeiterpartei* (German Labour Party), which Hitler later transformed into the Nazi Party.

this knowledge harbour within itself? Secrets which evidently had much more of an edge to them than anything known to the Tibetan monks.

But how to gain access to even one of these secrets? Just to one?! And if it turns out to be significant, then what kind of lost world might open up to people today if a few more — or, indeed, all — of them should be revealed? But where and in what millennia should we look for an answer?

Rome! Ancient Rome! Something extraordinary happened there four thousand years ago. More extraordinary than the exploits of the Roman legion. Oh, yes! That's it, an incredible discovery! The Roman senators were the highest élite group of that period. They were slave-owners, but all at once they began to give their slaves, who were skilled and desirous of growing food crops on the land... They began to give them *land*... for their lifetime use with the right of succession. Funds were allocated to a slave's family to build a house. A slave's family could not be transferred to another owner without their land. It — the land — became an inseparable part of the slave's family.

But what suddenly moved these slave-owners to such a humane and altruistic act? Was it purely from kind and noble motives, or did they receive something in return? What they received was ten percent of the harvest for their table. That is probably the smallest tax of the whole known period. This begs the question: why did the Roman élite do such a thing? After all, the slave-owner could have simply ordered his slaves to work in his fields by the sweat of their brow and take as much of the harvest as he wanted. But no! Why? Because back in pagan Rome they had still hung on to the Vedic knowledge. And the patricians and senators knew that the same product grown by a slave on land other than his own would differ sharply in its properties from that grown on his own ground and raised with love.

Back then they still knew that everything growing in the ground carries in itself a psychic energy. To be healthy, one must feed one's self with lovingly grown produce. This was mentioned in several ancient books in the Alexandria Library,[8] which was destroyed. What further knowledge, what wisdom was lost along with these books? Anastasia says that it is possible to resurrect this knowledge and all its attendant wisdom, beginning with their pristine origins, within one's self. Everyone has the ability to do it. I want to believe that statement, but I'm still not fully convinced. Where can we find proof that such a thing is possible? What facts can we draw upon from memory so that we can fully accept what she says?

Are we to remember everything we heard from our father and mother, or that we were taught in school, or read somewhere over our whole lifetime? But our recollections still do not contain any significant or absolute proof. What if I could remember everything I was told by Father Feodorit? But he didn't say all that much. He spent most of the time listening, and while he did give me some ancient books to read, there was no evidence in them. Then how? How can modern Man suddenly unfold within himself this treasured knowledge of his pristine origins? He can!!! No doubt there exist characteristic examples and proof in the recollection of every Man! In my own recollections I did come across one.

[8] *Alexandria Library* — see special footnote (from the original text) near the end of Chapter 6: "Imagery and trial".

A good and attentive grandmother

Grandmother! My grandmother was a witch. Not a fairy-tale witch, but a real, actual white witch. Oldsters, perhaps, will remember her incredible marvels. She lived in Ukraine in the village of Kuznichi in the Gorodnia district of Chernigov Region. She was called Efrosinya, and her last name was Verkhusha. On one occasion, when I was very young, I was present at one of her miracles.

Back then I hardly understood anything about them, but now it has all become crystal clear to me. O God, what simplicity there is in the most puzzling incredible phenomena! I have an idea at least half of the population today, especially the healers, would be able to freely duplicate her results. To provide a few more details, here is what happened.

All my early childhood I spent in the Ukrainian countryside, in a small white, straw-covered hut. I loved to watch my grandmother busying herself about the stove. Once after a scuffle with one of my classmates, someone taunted: "Your grandmother's a witch!" Other kids started to defend my grandmother, saying, for example: "My mummy says she's a good woman."

On a number of occasions I saw how my grandmother treated people's physical ills. I didn't attach any particular significance to it at the time — after all there were many healers in different villages back then. Some had better success treating one particular disease, some another. And nobody was called a witch. But my grandmother's abilities did not fall under the usual healing methods.

It turned out that my grandmother, who was only semi-literate, easily cured many animals. She did this by a method that seemed at first glance incredible. She would disappear for a day along with the sick animal, and by the time she returned it would have made a full recovery, or at least a partial one, in which case she would instruct its owner on how to continue the treatment.

When I heard my classmate insulting my grandmother by calling her a 'witch', even though children are generally afraid of witches, I did not begin acting any worse toward my kind grandmother. On the contrary, she — or rather, her actions — only awakened a greater fascination in me.

One day the collective-farm chairman's horse was brought to my grandmother. It was a purebred, recently bought for the chairman to travel about on his daily business. We local kids always admired this particular mare when the chairman happened to ride by. The mare held her head high, and her gait was friskier and more elegant than that of all the other horses in the area. But this time she was brought to Grandmother not harnessed to a wagon and not saddled. She was being led just by the bridle, looking very downcast and moving very slowly. This was a rare event for me — the chairman's horse right in our yard! I began following the proceedings with considerable interest.

Grandmother walked up to the mare and began stroking her, first from one side on her muzzle, and then around the ear, all the while quietly whispering soothing words. Then she unbridled the mare (taking the metallic bit out of her mouth). Carrying a bench out into the yard, she laid out bunches of herbs on the bench, then brought the mare over to them and began offering the animal various dried herbs in turn. With some of them the horse didn't pay any attention and turned away, while others she sniffed at and even took a small taste of them. The bunches that caught the mare's attention, Grandmother threw into a water-filled iron pot which was standing over a coal fire, and finally dropped her night-cap into the mixture.

I heard her tell the people who had brought the horse to come the day after next, in the morning. After the people had left, I realised that Grandmother was once again getting ready to disappear somewhere together with the mare, and

I started pleading with her to take me along. Grandmother, who had always granted all my requests, did not refuse this one either, though she did stipulate one condition: I was to go to bed earlier than usual that night. I obeyed.

Grandmother awoke me at dawn. The mare was standing in front of the house; she was covered with a small piece of canvas. After washing my face with the mixture from the iron pot, Grandmother gave me a small bundle containing something to eat, then took hold of the rope-lead (which she had fastened to the horse's bridle). Presently we set off along the border between the garden plots in the direction of the little forest that started just beyond. We walked very slowly along the edge of the forest. To be more specific, Grandmother walked alongside the mare and stopped each time the mare bent her head down to the grass to taste some kind of herb. Grandmother held the lead so loosely that it even slipped out of her hands whenever the mare, having spied something in the grass, jerked her head sharply to one side.

Occasionally Grandmother would still keep on leading the horse further, but after coming to a new place, she would once again give her free rein. We kept walking, either along the edge of the forest, or just a little ways in.

It was already past noon when we came to a mudhole in the middle of the field. We sat down by a haystack from the first haycutting for a little rest and a bite to eat. After snacking on milk and bread, I was tired from our long trek and felt like sleeping. On top of it all Grandmother took out of her bundle a small sheepskin coat, spread it out beside the haystack and encouraged me:

"Lie down and have a rest, little one. I guess you must be pretty tuckered out."

I lay down and began to fight off sleep, fearing that Grandmother might magically disappear along with the mare and without me, but sleep won out.

Upon awakening I saw Grandmother picking some sort of herbs right next to the mare's muzzle and sticking them in her bundle. Not long afterward we started heading for home, but a different way this time. As it began to get dark, I again felt as though I needed a rest, and once more Grandmother put me down on the sheepskin coat. When she woke me up it was still dark, and we continued once more on our homeward journey.

From time to time I could hear Grandmother saying something to the mare. While I don't recall the content of her words, I clearly remember her voice intonations — soothing, tender and cheerful. When we reached home Grandmother at once began to give the horse water, adding the mixture from the iron pot to the pail.

Later I saw her give the people who came for the horse the bunches of herbs she had picked during our walk and explain something to them.

The mare, who had by this time become a little friskier, was reluctant to leave our yard. She had already been harnessed again and kept turning her head to look at Grandmother, pulling on her lead.

For several days afterward I was angry at my grandmother for not showing me how she could magically disappear like a witch, but the whole time she had just kept on feeding the horse, picking herbs and tying them into bunches.

I might have soon forgotten about the walk and the witchery, but when I told the boy who had called her a witch that my grandmother didn't disappear anywhere, but simply fed sick animals, he — and he was just a bit older than me — cited a significant fact that neither I nor any of the village kids who were on my side could counteract:

"Why is it then that each time the chairman rides by your yard, the horse stops trotting, and goes by just at a walk — she doesn't even obey the whip?"

I don't remember how Grandmother explained this to me. It is only now that I understand the reason. I am confident that a lot of people today who have kind hearts and have an attentive relationship to Nature and animals could also treat creatures' ailments the way she did.

Now I realise that she allowed the horse to try bunches of various herbs simply to determine what specific herbs the ailing animal required. She also used this to decide the route she would take the next day, counting on finding these herbs along the way, and at the same time replenishing her own stock.

She needed to make this a whole day's trip, since each plant has a particular time when its consumption is especially beneficial. She held the lead loosely so as to allow the mare to determine for herself which herbs and how many she needed to take in. Animals can feel this in an inexplicable way. Since the mixture was prepared from herbs chosen by the mare herself, Grandmother's use of it for washing, as well as letting her night-cap soak in it, was probably to make the animal more predisposed to her.

See how simple everything turns out to be! Only it's still not clear to me how all this was known by my semi-literate grandmother. Oh, how we have complicated this simplicity! May that not be the reason for the large-scale epizoötic ('mad-cow-disease') that recently swept across Europe, and our modern scientific thought came up with nothing better than to destroy thousands of diseased animals!

I have cited just one example attesting to the fact that the achievements of our modern medicine are illusory. Indeed, I could cite a whole lot of similar examples of the illusory achievements of our contemporary society. But why talk of specific details when we can go right off to the main thing?

To live in a marvellous reality

What kind of society are we living in today, anyway? What are we striving for? What do we suppose we can build in the future? The overwhelming majority of the Russian population will answer without hesitation:

"We live in a democratic state and are striving to build a free democratic society, just like in the developed, civilised Western countries."

That is exactly what the majority of politicians and political strategists will say.

That is exactly what they say on TV and in newspaper columns.

That is exactly what the majority of people in our country think.

That majority opinion exactly confirms Anastasia's statement that a part of the people in our modern civilisation are asleep, while the rest, because of their programming, are mere bio-robots in the hands of a bunch of priests who imagine themselves to be the rulers of the world.

If one can just stop and withdraw one's self, even a little, from the world's feverish daily monotonous commotion and think independently, it should be possible to understand the following facts.

Democracy! Just what is democracy, anyway? What concept does the word itself denote? The majority will answer by quoting the well-known Great Encyclopedic Dictionary[9] or the Dictionary of the Russian Language,[10] both of which offer pretty much the same terse definition:

> Democracy is a form of political system or social order in a state, based on the recognition of the people as a whole as the source of authority. The basic principles of democracy are the authority of the majority, the equality of citizens...

And in highly developed countries people choose their parliaments and presidents by majority vote.

'Choose'? Utter nonsense! A complete illusion! There are no choices or elections! Not once, not even in a country which considers itself the most democratic and civilised on the globe, have the people themselves ever held power.

But the elections? They are a complete illusion! Remember what always happens before elections in any so-called democratic country. Teams of political strategists working for each candidate fight among themselves, spending huge sums of money and sophisticated methods of psychological influence on people through the mass media, TV and graphic promotional campaigns.

And the more highly developed the country, the more sophisticated the technological methods of suggestion employed.

It is clearly evident that the victory always goes to the team of political strategists that can exert the most influence and the greatest power of suggestion. It is under the influence of this suggestion that people go and vote. They think they are voting by their own will. In fact they are merely carrying out somebody else's will.

Thus it turns out that modern democracy *is an illusion of the masses. It is their faith in an unreal social order — an unreal, illusory world.*

---

[9]See footnote 9 in Chapter 9: "A need to think".

[10]Dictionary of the Russian Language (*Tolkovy Slovar' Russkogo Yazyka*), edited by S. I. Ozhegov and N. Yu. Shvedova, Moscow, 2002.

It all boils down to this: subordination to the majority does not exist in the natural world. All the groups of plants, animals and insects may be subject to instinct, the movement of the planets, the order established by Nature, or the leader of a herd. And in human groupings it is always the minority that is in control.

It is not the majority that has fomented revolutions and wars, but the majority participated in revolutions and wars at the consciously directed suggestion of a minority. That's the way it has been and that's the way it is now.

Democracy is the most dangerous illusion people have been exposed to *en masse*. It is dangerous because in the democratic world it is only too easy for any democratic country to end up being ruled by one person, or a small group of people. For that, all they need is a pile of money and a good team of psychologists and political strategists.

And we — today's parents, living under the influence of illusions, are still trying to raise our children. But in actual fact what we are doing is introducing — pushing, one might say — their consciousness into a world of illusion... We are in fact handing them over into somebody else's clutches... Only not to God. We are handing them over to some kind of opposite of God.

God's world is not illusory, it is real and beautiful. It has its own unsurpassed fragrances, colours, shapes and sounds. The gates to this world are always open, and we are always free to enter, if only we can shake off the illusions that have been fettering our consciousness.

I too shall write my own *Book of Kin* for my descendants — indeed, for myself. And among other things I shall most certainly write the following:

I, Vladimir Megré, lived in an age when mankind did not exist in the real world. Their flesh fed on the gifts of the real world, but their consciousness wandered in a world of illusion. This has been a very challenging period in people's lives. Right now I am attempting to bring my consciousness back to the real world of the Divine. This Divine world of Nature has suffered at the hands of people's consciousness. Suffered terribly. I realise this and am trying to correct the situation. I will do whatever I can, even if it is only creating a design for my domain. Perhaps even just a part of it. The main thing is to understand and have my children understand.

As before, Anastasia sat quietly by and listened while I vented my reasonings aloud. When I stopped, she got up, walked over to the window and observed:

"The stars are beginning to twinkle in the sky. It is time for me to go, Vladimir. You are right in many respects. But be careful not to let these new visions of reality make you want to control others. Get the better of such a temptation and do not join any organisations. Other people, too, are seeing this reality. Once they have organised, they will bring about a significant achievement on the Earth. You will understand your own destiny in life."

"I'm not aiming to join anything or control anybody, Anastasia. But what is this destiny of mine you speak about?"

"The time will come when you will feel this for yourself. Right now lie down on the bed, go to sleep and rest. You are excited. It is possible that an untrained heart will not be able to withstand such excitement."

"Yes, I know. But if I go to sleep, you will go away. You always do. Sometimes I have a strong desire for you to stay and not go away. I want you to be always beside me."

"I *am* always beside you. Whenever you think of me. You will soon begin to feel and understand this. Now wash yourself with water and go to sleep."

"I can't sleep. Lately I haven't been sleeping all that well. My thoughts have been keeping me awake."

"I shall help you, Vladimir. Would you like me to read some of the poetry your readers have sent in, and sing you a lullaby?"

"Go ahead and try, perhaps I really *shall* nod off to sleep."

After I washed and lay down in my bed which had already been made up, Anastasia sat down beside me and placed her hand on my forehead. Then she ran her fingers through my hair and softly sang a song written by one of my readers from Ukraine. Anastasia sang very softly, only it seemed that many people and the stars in the sky were listening to her song — listening to her pure voice and her words:

Take my hand this hour...
Tomorrow, you will see,
Is another day, but now
You can press your cheek to me.

Thus hour after hour
You may sleep in sweet relief,
For from your strands of hair
I'll gather up the grief.

And I shall spread a blanket fine,
Blue with stars all woven,
I shall stay a long, long time,
Just so you won't get frozen.
If only you'll receive me.

From the night I'll come and stand
All throughout the ages.
I've learnt to heal ills by my hand,
Which all pain assuages.
If only you'll believe me.

Down from a high incline
Past us stones will tumble.
I know ahead of time
Where you're going to stumble.

Into church and palace
You'll go, a hero bright.
All the pretty lasses
I shall keep from your sight.

In a world of black and white
I too'll live unimpeded,
So that swords and bows drawn tight
Will never more be needed.

If only you, if only you
If only you will love me.

I'll let loyal Sparrow fly up and team
With Crane in the heavens above you.[11]
I dare not come into your dream...
Too tenderly I love you.

Before immersing myself in a deep and calm sleep, I managed to think: *Of course, tomorrow* is *another day. It will be better. I shall describe the dawn of a brand new day. And many people will*

[11] A reference to the Russian proverb: *Luchshe sinitsa v ruke, chem zhuravl' na nebe* (lit. 'Better [to have] a sparrow (titmouse/chickadee) in one's hand than a crane in the sky'). Like its English counterpart, *A bird in the hand is worth two in the bush,* it suggests a cautious, conservative approach to life which the poet's heroine now finds herself ready to give up, releasing the sparrow so that she may join the crane in the sky.

start writing in their Books of Kin about how a splendid new beginning has been dawning on mankind. And these will be the greatest historical books for their descendants for thousands of years of time. And one of them will be mine. Tomorrow I shall start writing a new book, and now I shall be able to give it a more coherent-sounding design. And the new book will define a new historic turning-point for the people of the Earth — a turning to the marvellous reality of the Divine.

Until we meet again, dear readers, in this new and marvellous reality!

Vladimir Megré

To be continued...

Translator's Afterword

Suppose you've lived all your life in the same town at the base of a huge mountain. You've looked at that mountain day in and day out as you walked to and from school, ploughed your fields, shopped at the outdoor market, or cycled around the town on errands. You are familiar with every detail of its craggy surfaces, and on occasion have even climbed up part way to explore the foothills. But you have never been round to the other side.

Then one fine day you decide to take the night train to a town some distance away, about a quarter of the way around the mountain, where the local residents speak a completely different dialect from yours. Upon arriving the next morning, you set out to take a look at the mountain from this side. And there it is, looming just as large, just beyond this new town. Only at first it doesn't look like the same mountain at all, even though your angle has changed by a mere 90 degrees. What was familiar from a frontal view you now see in profile. Features you knew before in profile are now facing you head on.

Some of these features require a closer examination to identify. In fact, many of your fellow residents who made this trip before you and didn't bother to examine the scene in detail say the mountain here looks nothing at all like the one back home. Some of them refuse to believe it is the same mountain. A few even associate the unfamiliar appearance with something hostile and threatening.

Such impressions are further fuelled by the different way the locals describe the mountain in their own dialect — either with completely different words, or using the same words but with different connotations. Indeed, the terminological discrepancy is rather disconcerting at first. But little by little, the more you examine these features in detail and even try a bit of climbing exploration, the more you become convinced that you are dealing with the same mountain you have known all your life. And as you hear local residents speaking about it, you gradually acquire the ability to translate between their dialect and yours and realise they are talking about the same concepts you have known all along.

In sum, you find yourself simply amazed at what you are learning about a familiar landmark from a brand new perspective. That does not necessarily mean, however, that you have any plans to suddenly relocate your residence. But you are certainly able to make use of your new knowledge to enhance your appreciation and exploration of the mountain from your own home base.

This little story pretty much describes my experience in approaching Vladimir Megré's *Ringing Cedars Series.* Having been raised in the Protestant denomination known as Christian Science[1] (though I am sure people of many different faiths have had a similar experience), I was amazed, even 'blown away' by the new vistas of 'Mount Spirituality' that opened up to me from my initial reading of the Series. At first glance, like the mountain in the story above, some of the features,

[1]*Christian Science* — a Christian denomination founded in 1879 in New England by Mary Baker Eddy, designed to "reinstate primitive Christianity and its lost element of healing" (Eddy, *Manual of The Mother Church,* p. 17). Eddy's principal statement of her ideas is found in a 700-page volume entitled *Science and health with Key to the Scriptures* (Boston, 1911). As with Megré, one of Eddy's basic aims was to change the human perception of God's laws in action from one based on mysticism and the promise of future rewards to one based on reason and fact, demonstrable in our earthly experience here and now.

especially those given new names or whose names were interpreted differently, presented something of a recognition challenge. But the more I read, the more I realised I was not being presented with a new God or even a new religion, but simply with new views on the same God and spirituality I had known all along, only from a different angle. And these insights have indeed enhanced my appreciation and exploration of spiritual concepts from my own faith's home base.

One particularly striking example of being 'blown away' by a new view of familiar territory was my initial reading of Chapter 1 in the present volume ("Who raises our children?"), which seems to pick up right where Mary Baker Eddy's chapter on "Marriage" in *Science and health* (pp. 56–69) leaves off. Not only that, but a friend of our family's — a Catholic writer on theology — told me of a number of instances where intimate relations have been linked to a more spiritual outlook, including certain practices among Orthodox Jews and native peoples of North America.[2] She also referred me to the Book of Tobit (or Tobias) in the Apocrypha for an additional illustration. These examples, however, while fascinating, differ from the approach outlined in Chapter 1 in that their attention is still concentrated on the physical act of intimacy (albeit seen from a more spiritual standpoint), while the principal focus of Megré's discussion with the psychologist is *children*, the physical conditions playing but an incidental role.[3]

[2]For further exploration, see: Philip Sherrard, *Christianity and Eros* (London: SPCK Holy Trinity Church, 1976); Linda Sabbath, *The radiant heart* (Denville, NJ, USA: Dimension Books, 1977); Mary Shivanandan, *Natural sex* (New York: Rawson Wade, 1979).

[3]Compare Eddy's statement in *Science and health* (pp. 61–62): "If the propagation of a higher human species is requisite to reach this goal [of spiritual unity], then its material conditions can only be permitted for the purpose of generating."

Another group that has much in common with Anastasia's viewpoints on life are the Doukhobors — a sect that was persecuted in Tsarist Russia for their pacifism and opposition to the dictates of official church hierarchy. In 1899 they were helped to emigrate to Canada by the writer Leo Tolstoy, who recognised in them a living embodiment of his own simple, straightforward approach to a Christianity of the heart without ecclesiastical trappings.[4]

This past year I had occasion to present a conference paper entitled: "Links across space and time: the life and works of Leo Tolstoy, Mary Baker Eddy and Vladimir Megré", pointing out some of the many similarities not only in the ideas of these three spiritual thinkers, but also in their personal and professional lives. As specific examples, the paper compares similar statements from all three writers on the subjects of *life* and *prayer*. I have no doubt that the comparison could be extended to include some other spiritual thinkers too.

Indeed, to me one of the most remarkable features of Megré's whole account of Anastasia and her sayings is its sense of *inclusiveness*. Megré does not purport to take his readers into another universe, where all the worthy values they have held dear for so long must suddenly be regarded as worthless and forsakeable in favour of some new doctrine. He is not presenting them with a 'new mountain'. Rather, he is simply showing them the spiritual values they already have from a brand new point of view, thereby enhancing the significance of these values and helping his readers put them into practice more effectively.

As a translator, I was delighted to find that this sense of inclusiveness embraces not just people and their values, but the

[4]See, for example: Andrew Donskov, *Leo Tolstoy and the Canadian Doukhobors* (Ottawa: Centre for Research on Canadian-Russian Relations, 2005).

whole underlying foundation of *language* as well. Often seen as a divisive element in human society, in the *Ringing Cedars Series* (particularly the present book) language becomes a unifying force as fragments of its ancient roots are uncovered, enabling us to trace equivalent words in different languages back to their common origin.

At the beginning of Chapter 10, footnote 2 on the name *Medvedkovo* explains that *medved'*, the Russian word for the animal we call a 'bear', is comprised of the roots *med-* (honey) and *ved-* (know).[5] Surprisingly, both these roots have their counterparts in English: *mead* (an alcoholic drink made from fermented honey and water) and *wit* (an obsolete word meaning 'know', now more commonly used in the sense of 'quick understanding' or the ability to play intelligently with words and their meanings).[6] Historically, *knowledge* and *sight* were related concepts (we *see*, therefore we *know*), and hence words like *video* and *vision* can also be traced (through Latin *videre* = 'to see') back to this same root, as can the word *white* (something clearly seen). These examples show some of the many layers of meaning inherent in the original root.

But even more interesting, as my editor, Leonid Sharashkin, has pointed out to me, is the realisation of how these linguistic changes reflect the evolution of the underlying concepts in human consciousness: in both Russian and English the roots *ved-* and *wit-* have yielded in general usage to *zna-* and *know-*, respectively, indicating mankind's greater interest today in superficial, technological knowledge than in the

[5]On *vedat'* and its distinction from *znat'* please see footnote 8 in Chapter 5: "The history of mankind, as told by Anastasia".

[6]The word *wit* may be familiar to readers of the Authorised (King James) Version of the Bible in its variant *wot* — see, for example, Exodus 32: 1, where the people tell Aaron they "wot not what is become of" Moses. See also Acts 3: 17, Romans 11: 2.

multi-dimensional awareness and wisdom implied by the earlier terms. In fact, with some of their derivatives in both languages, e.g., *ved'ma = witch,* the original positive reference (in this case, to someone capable of harnessing the extended abilities of the human mind) has given way in popular perception to a more negative connotation (of one who uses such abilities for devious or evil purposes).

Like many Russian roots, *ved-* comes directly from Sanskrit (along with Latin, one of the two proto-tongues from which the whole Indo-European family of languages is derived).[7] And this highlights another aspect of inclusiveness evident in the Series — namely, certain indications that language transcends mere human invention,[8] hence its great potential for unifying instead of dividing the peoples of the Earth. On a visit to Russia in the 1960s, renowned Sanskritologist Durga Prasad Shastri discovered remarkable similarities between present-day Russian and the Sanskrit spoken in India some twenty-five centuries earlier. In fact, his knowledge of ancient Sanskrit enabled him to understand spoken Russian well enough that he could get by without an interpreter.[9]

And this is one more illustration of how Vladimir Megré, through relating Anastasia's sayings on mankind and its

[7]Another interesting insight from Sanskrit is the origin of the name *Anastasia.* In Sanskrit the first letter *a-* is a negating particle (as in *asymmetrical* in English), while the root *nast-* signifies 'deterioration' (compare English *nasty*) — hence *anasta* = 'without deterioration'. This also underlies the use of *anastasia* in Greek to signify 'resurrection'. (I am grateful to my editor for pointing out this etymology.)

[8]See, for example, "A book of pristine origins" in Chapter 2: "Conversation with my son".

[9]See: D. P. Shastri, *Links between Russian and Sanskrit. Meerut District Conference of the Indo-Soviet Cultural Society* (Ghaziabad, 1964). Again, I thank my editor for bringing this reference to my attention.

history, brings together people of not only different religions and cultures but also of different chronological periods, to recognise and embrace their common heritage as children not of different genetic backgrounds, but rather of the one universal God.

Perhaps the author's future volumes will not only show us still new views of our familiar 'mountain', but transform our whole perception of a 'mountain' into a dimension we cannot yet fathom. Think of how a mountain seen from space may resemble, let's say, a cedar nut! Then imagine how what we see as a 'mountain' of spirituality might be perceived through spiritual vision itself! The possibilities are endless.

Ottawa, Canada
December 2006 John Woodsworth

THE RINGING CEDARS SERIES AT A GLANCE

Anastasia *(ISBN 978-0-9801812-0-3)*, Book 1 of the Ringing Cedars Series, tells the story of entrepreneur Vladimir Megré's trade trip to the Siberian taiga in 1995, where he witnessed incredible spiritual phenomena connected with sacred 'ringing cedar' trees. He spent three days with a woman named Anastasia who shared with him her unique outlook on subjects as diverse as gardening, child-rearing, healing, Nature, sexuality, religion and more. This wilderness experience transformed Vladimir so deeply that he abandoned his commercial plans and, penniless, went to Moscow to fulfil Anastasia's request and write a book about the spiritual insights she so generously shared with him. True to her promise this life-changing book, once written, has become an international bestseller and has touched hearts of millions of people world-wide.

The Ringing Cedars of Russia *(ISBN 978-0-9801812-1-0)*, Book 2 of the Series, in addition to providing a fascinating behind-the-scenes look at the story of how *Anastasia* came to be published, offers a deeper exploration of the universal concepts so dramatically revealed in Book 1. It takes the reader on an adventure through the vast expanses of space, time and spirit — from the Paradise-like glade in the Siberian taiga to the rough urban depths of Russia's capital city, from the ancient mysteries of our forebears to a vision of humanity's radiant future.

The Space of Love *(ISBN 978-0-9801812-2-7)*, Book 3 of the Series, describes the author's second visit to Anastasia. Rich with new revelations on natural child-rearing and alternative education, on the spiritual significance of breast-feeding and the meaning of ancient megaliths, it shows how each person's thoughts can influence the destiny of the entire Earth and describes practical ways of putting Anastasia's vision of happiness into practice. Megré shares his new outlook on education and children's real creative potential after a visit to a school where pupils build their own campus and cover the ten-year Russian school programme in just two years. Complete with an account of an armed intrusion into Anastasia's habitat, the book highlights the limitless power of Love and non-violence.

Co-creation *(ISBN 978-0-9801812-3-4)*, Book 4 and centrepiece of the Series, paints a dramatic living image of the creation of the Universe and humanity's place in this creation, making this primordial mystery relevant to our everyday living today. Deeply metaphysical yet at the same time down-to-Earth practical, this poetic heart-felt volume helps us uncover answers to the most significant questions about the essence and meaning of the Universe and the nature and purpose of our existence. It also shows how and why the knowledge of these answers, innate in every human being, has become obscured and forgotten, and points the way toward reclaiming this wisdom and — in partnership with Nature — manifesting the energy of Love through our lives.

Who Are We? *(ISBN 978-0-9801812-4-1)*, Book 5 of the Series, describes the author's search for real-life 'proofs' of Anastasia's vision presented in the previous volumes. Finding these proofs and taking stock of ongoing global environmental destruction, Vladimir Megré describes further practical steps for putting Anastasia's vision into practice. Full of beautiful realistic images of a new way of living in co-operation with the Earth and each other, this book also highlights the role of children in making us aware of the precariousness of the present situation and in leading the global transition toward a happy, violence-free society.

The Book of Kin *(ISBN 978-0-9801812-5-8)*, Book 6 of the Series, describes another visit by the author to Anastasia's glade in the Siberian taiga and his conversations with his growing son, which cause him to take a new look at education, science, history, family and Nature. Through parables and revelatory dialogues and stories Anastasia then leads Vladimir Megré and the reader on a shocking re-discovery of the pages of humanity's history that have been distorted or kept secret for thousands of years. This knowledge sheds light on the causes of war, oppression and violence in the modern world and guides us in preserving the wisdom of our ancestors and passing it over to future generations.

The Energy of Life *(ISBN 978-0-9801812-6-5)*, Book 7 of the Series, re-asserts the power of human thought and the influence of our thinking on our lives and the destiny of the entire planet and the Universe. It also brings forth a practical understanding of ways to consciously control and build up the power of our creative thought. The book sheds still further light on the forgotten pages of humanity's history, on religion, on the roots of inter-racial and inter-religious conflict, on ideal nutrition, and shows how a new way of thinking and a lifestyle in true harmony with Nature can lead to happiness and solve the personal and societal problems of crime, corruption, misery, conflict, war and violence.

The New Civilisation *(ISBN 978-0-9801812-7-2)*, Book 8, Part 1 of the Series, describes yet another visit by Vladimir Megré to Anastasia and their son, and offers new insights into practical co-operation with Nature, showing in ever greater detail how Anastasia's lifestyle applies to our lives. Describing how the visions presented in previous volumes have already taken beautiful form in real life and produced massive changes in Russia and beyond, the author discerns the birth of a new civilisation. The book also paints a vivid image of America's radiant future, in which the conflict between the powerful and the helpless, the rich and the poor, the city and the country, can be transcended and thereby lead to transformations in both the individual and society.

Rites of Love *(ISBN 978-0-9801812-8-9)*, Book 8, Part 2, contrasts today's mainstream attitudes to sex, family, childbirth and education with our forebears' lifestyle, which reflected their deep spiritual understanding of the significance of conception, pregnancy, homebirth and upbringing of the young in an atmosphere of love. In powerful poetic prose Megré describes their ancient way of life, grounded in love and non-violence, and shows the practicability of this same approach today. Through the life-story of one family, he portrays the radiant world of the ancient Russian Vedic civilisation, the drama of its destruction and its re-birth millennia later — in our present time.